Pearl Foster was born in London and
and to complete a degree in Econ
education was followed by ten years
deaths. She has pursued a lifelong i
particular a branch of the Lara and
barbarities of the Portuguese inquisition and fled to England.

Pearl is married, has two children, is happily retired and will be pleased to hear from anyone tracing similar lines.

The author can be contacted at lara.furtado@yahoo.com.

PEARL FOSTER

JEWS IN GEORGIAN SOCIETY
The Laras of London

SilverWood

Published in 2017 by SilverWood Books

SilverWood Books Ltd
14 Small Street, Bristol, BS1 1DE, United Kingdom
www.silverwoodbooks.co.uk

Copyright © Pearl Foster 2017
Images pp 7–12, p29, p39, p88, p90, p102, p108, p118 © Pearl Foster |
p35, p41, p191 © The National Archives | p154 © British History Online |
p166 © Birmingham Museum and Art Gallery | p180 © Wellcome Library |
p208 © Westmeath County Library and Leo Daly

The right of Pearl Foster to be identified as the author
of this work has been asserted in accordance with the Copyright,
Designs and Patents Act 1988 Sections 77 and 78.

All rights reserved. No part of this publication may be reproduced,
stored in a retrieval system, or transmitted in any form or by any means,
electronic, mechanical, photocopying, recording or otherwise,
without prior permission of the copyright holder.

ISBN 978-1-78132-673-2

British Library Cataloguing in Publication Data
A CIP catalogue record for this book is available from

London Borough of Redbridge	
30108032977824	
Askews & Holts	
920 LAR	£11.99
5610606	**REDGAN**

Contents

Genealogical Trees	7
With Special Thanks To…	13
Preface	15
Introduction	21
Abraham Lara and Rebecca Bell	27
Judith and Esther Curry	65
Jacob Lara and the Buzaglos	79
Esther Cardozo, Sisters and Sara Carcas	91
Moses Lara and the Da Costas	115
Rachel Mendes	143
Benjamin Lara and the Walters	151
Sarah Rey King	199
Epilogue	229
Notes	231
Abbreviations	247
Bibliography	249

THE NUNES DE LARA FAMILY
(Daniel and Rachel)

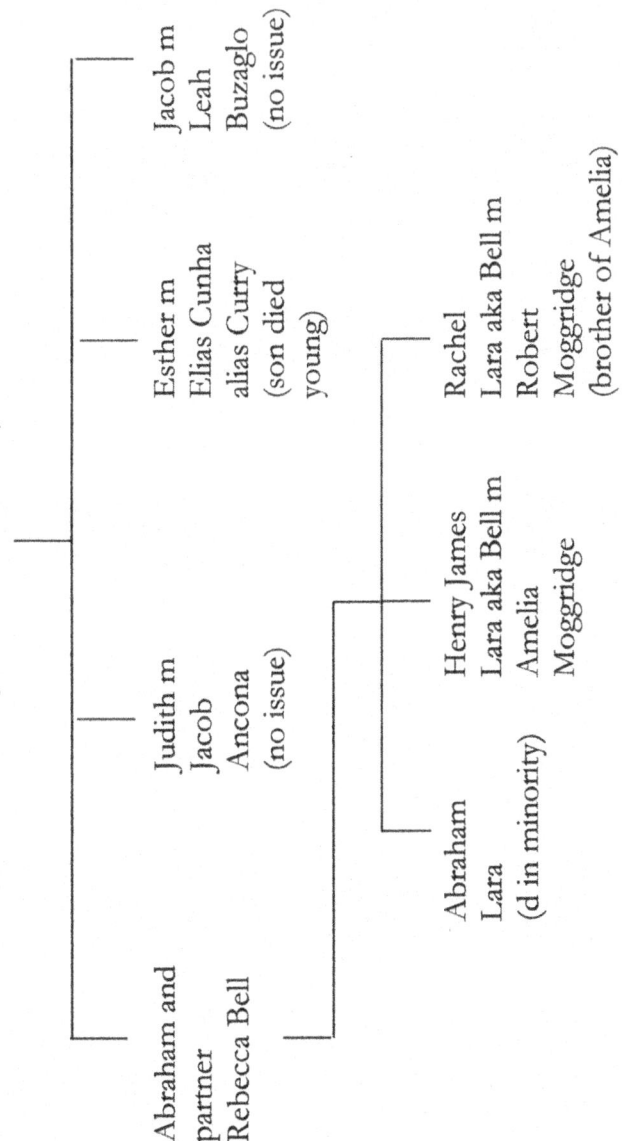

- Abraham and partner Rebecca Bell
  - Abraham Lara (d in minority)
  - Henry James Lara aka Bell m Amelia Moggridge
  - Rachel Lara aka Bell m Robert Moggridge (brother of Amelia)
- Judith m Jacob Ancona (no issue)
- Esther m Elias Cunha alias Curry (son died young)
- Jacob m Leah Buzaglo (no issue)

THE BELL FAMILY
(Henry James Lara aka Bell and Amelia)

| Amelia Henrietta m Henry Miller | Henry Lara m Mary Ann Dale | Eliza Lara Bell m William Erwood | Emily m Thomas Leagas | George m Hannah Sharp |

(followed by two Alfreds who did not survive childhood)

THE MOGGRIDGE FAMILY
(Robert and Rachel)

Lucy m	John m	Robert m	Mary Ann m
Charles	Julia Elizabeth	Eliza	Nathanial
Bithrey	Allen	Golden	Bowring
	(no issue, two		
	stepchildren)		

(and Edward Lara, Robert and William who did not survive childhood)

THE LARA FAMILY
(Benjamin and Rebecca)

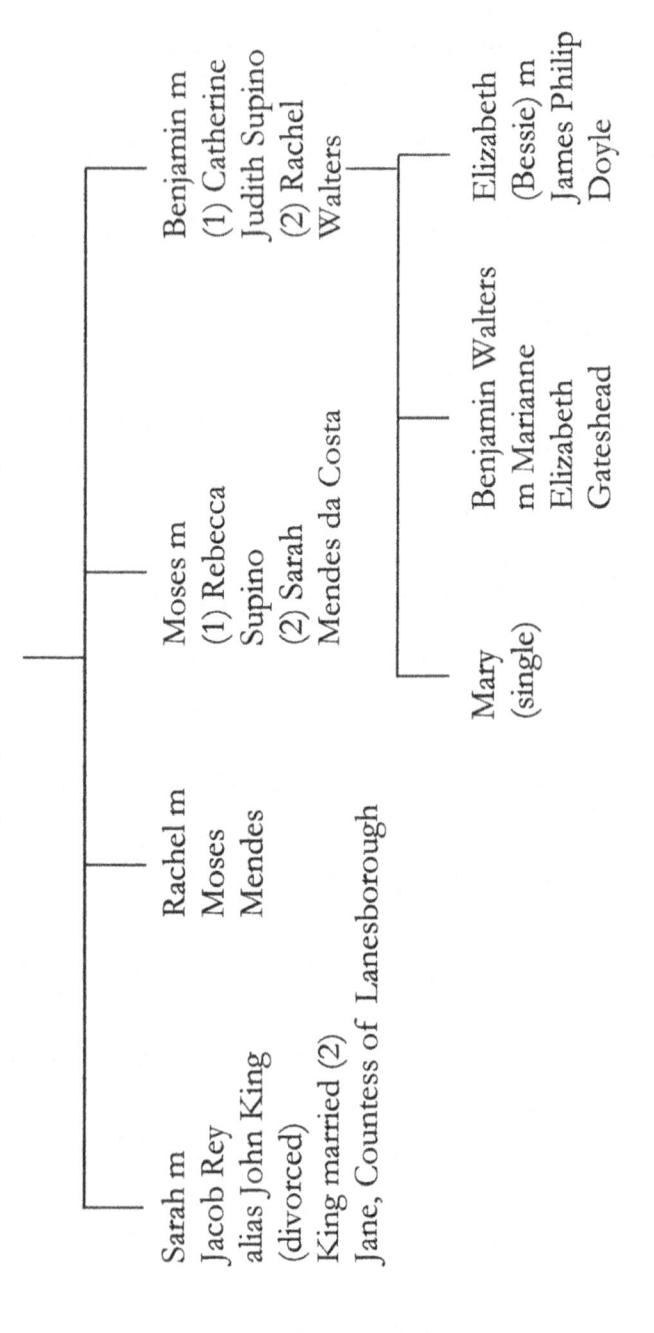

```
         ┌─────────────────────────┬─────────────────────────┐
       Sarah m                  Rachel m                   Moses m
       Jacob Rey                Moses                      (1) Rebecca
       alias John King          Mendes                     Supino
       (divorced)                                          (2) Sarah
       King married (2)                                    Mendes da Costa
       Jane, Countess of Lanesborough
                                                           ┌──────────────────────┬─────────────────────┐
                                                        Mary              Benjamin Walters         Benjamin m
                                                       (single)           m Marianne               (1) Catherine
                                                                          Elizabeth                Judith Supino
                                                                          Gateshead                (2) Rachel
                                                                                                   Walters

                                                                                                   Elizabeth
                                                                                                   (Bessie) m
                                                                                                   James Philip
                                                                                                   Doyle
```

THE KING FAMILY
(Sarah and John)

- Charlotte King alias Rosa Matilda alias Charlotte Dacre m Nicholas Byrne
  - William Pitt Byrne
  - Charles Byrne
  - Maria Byrne
- Sophia King m Charles Fortnum
  Fortnum m (2) Letitia Basden née Stephens
- Benjamin Charles King

THE LARA FAMILY
(Isaac and Sarah)

(liaison with Jewish lady)

Sarah Lara m
Aaron Carcas

Isaac/Joshua
Carcas and siblings

Rebecca

Esther m
Aaron Nunez
Cardozo

Rachel

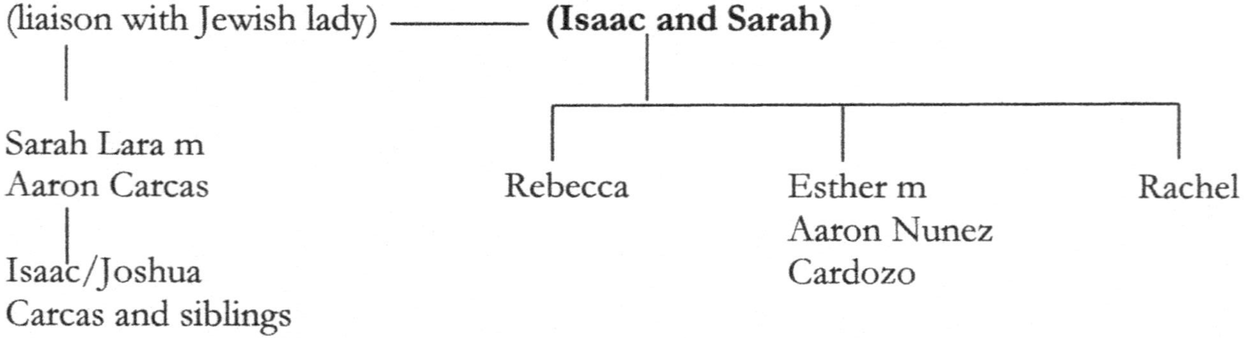

With Special Thanks To...

The British Library for the eureka moment when I found Abraham. The National Archives for their extensive collection, including wills, letters, court cases, prisoners' lists and surgeons' log books. Miriam Rodrigues-Pereira, Honorary Archivist of the Spanish and Portuguese Jews Congregation of London and her co-workers for the huge task of transcription of the registers. Many thanks for access to the early manuscripts of Bevis Marks. I could not have managed without them. The London Metropolitan Archives and the collaboration which put the Land tax assessments and fire insurance records online. Thanks to The Wellcome Institute which really lives up to the sound of its name.

I am grateful too for the digitisation of various newspapers and all the internet-based resources which have developed in recent years. I wish they had been available years ago!

My cousins for their unstinting interest and encouragement with this project. My mother and grandmother who first interested me in our family history and above all, Tony.

Preface

When I was a child my grandmother often showed me her family photographs, including one of Henrico de Lara. It was taken from an oval etching passed down through several generations of the family. My great-grandfather had made some copies in the 1890s, and had given them to his children. I was fascinated by Henrico, especially as his story was at the heart of our family legend.

My great-grandfather, in his nineties and then blind, dictated to his young granddaughter, my aunt Doris, the story of his life. He included a short preface about his ancestors. He said that his great-grandfather was Henrico de Lara, from Andalusia, who had a 'goodly estate'. Owing to 'revolutionary' activities he was outlawed and came to England as a refugee. Here he married a Miss Bell and adopted her surname, with the prefix De Lara. They had a son called Henry Lara Bell and two daughters. This son, Henry, knew seven languages and was a wonderful penman, though his sons were brought up without any schooling.

There was one more element to this. It was not written down, yet my grandmother recalled it clearly herself from the tales her father had told her – some of Henrico's fortune was in diamonds.

This is the man who got me hooked on genealogy. I vowed to trace my family history and find out about Henrico. In my innocence I never realised the task would be so hard and frustrating. I had just one tangible piece of evidence to prove his existence: the copy of the etching. I needed to find him and answer some questions.

Picture a Georgian gentleman in formal dress, complete with

bagwig. The twinkle in his eyes and matching enigmatic smile suggest he's a man who's going somewhere. He is not one of the masses of London's poor. The photo shows he had a round face and chubby cheeks too. He looks well fed. Anyone would think his father was a noted supplier of cakes and pastries. Oh dear, I've given that one away!

Could the Victoria and Albert Museum help out? One of their archivists said the coat and revers dated from the 1780s and was formal dress for a middle-class person and informal for an aristocrat. Crucially it had to be someone with the means to commission a portrait of himself and this wasn't cheap. So now a clearer picture is starting to emerge.

Henrico was said to have a son called Henry and two daughters. Henry was baptised in 1789 as Henry James Bell, the son of Henry and Rebecca Bell. The choice of his mother's surname suggests she may have arranged this, or perhaps the couple were not married. Sister Rachel was born around 1792. The third sister remains a mystery.

Henry James was married in the name of Bell, though there are many instances where he called himself Henry James Lara. His wife was Amelia Moggridge and his sister, Rachel Lara, was the one witness at their marriage. It is from Henry's son George that I am descended. Rachel married Robert Moggridge, her brother-in-law, now calling herself Rachel Bell. Both Henry and Amelia Bell were their witnesses. This couple also had several children, the eldest of whom, Edward, was given the middle name Lara.

Our names are our identity tags. They link us to family, friends and colleagues. People are rightly fussy about their names – misspell an address, (that's OK, provided nothing is lost in the post) anything else misspelt (try to find a mailshot or flyer which isn't), but misspell someone's name and you will almost certainly be corrected. 'Henrico' didn't sit right as a name. This made me speculate that it had been distorted, not necessarily intentionally. The English populace was largely uneducated so it could have easily been misrecorded, given the complication of a foreign accent. Exhaustive searches proved negative.

Much later we found 'our' family of Jewish refugees, called Nunes de Lara or simply 'Lara'. In Portugal, their homeland, some were known as Henriques or Henriques de Lara. Was this the reason for the confusion some centuries later in the name Henrico de Lara?

Are legends more fable than fact? John Hurt in *Who Do You Think You Are?* was most disappointed to find that his family's legend of descent from the Marquis of Sligo from his Irish ancestry was completely fabricated. Was mine to be like that?

Was it the diamonds as much as the picture that enticed me? They definitely formed part of the lure into a life-long search for Henrico. I wasn't the only one on the trail. My grandmother's brother and cousin employed an investigator to search for him and his fortune, only to be told it was taken by the Franco Regime. The investigator had access to family papers (subsequently lost in a house move), but he probably did little actual research. He had no computers or indexes to help, and no background of genealogy. If anything was filed in chancery as he said, it would be there, and if it was there I would have found it.

My husband and I shared the trials, tribulations and pleasures of this research. We've had the good fortune to handle original registers – a slow process – and one which can often be done virtually instantaneously now with current technology. Not that I would have had it any other way. After forty-five years of searching – on and off as time/family and work constraints, finances, wavering doubt and multiple frustrations dictated research – I finally had that 'Eureka' moment.

I'd previously discovered Henry Lara, the son, in the lowly position of Watchman of the Peace. His signature, beautifully scrolled amidst the 'x' of all the other uneducated Watchmen, was given in the Magistrate Sessions as part of the arrest procedures. This testified to his skill at handwriting.[1] Later when Robert Peel, the Home Secretary, instigated the Metropolitan Police Force in 1829 he was just too old to join, so he had even lost this job. He subsequently became a gun-maker. Not very successfully, as he ended up in a debtors' prison for failing to pay his bills. Given special dispensation by the board as an upright (but clearly impoverished) citizen, he was released soon after.[2] This alone showed me there was *no* money in our family by then.

Henry was in dire straits long before having to work as a watchman, and his later imprisonment. He simply could not find suitable work, work which would pay enough for his family to decently live on and which was more in tune with his education.

There were no employment agencies in those days. Either you followed in the family occupation, had the benefit of a good apprenticeship, personal recommendation or favour, or you were on your own. Henry had none of these advantages. He had no network. So what could he do? In apparent desperation he wrote a job application letter.

Who did he write to? My search led me to our wonderful institution the British Library. The letter was indexed as 'Letter from H J Lara to the Earl of Liverpool'. Henry often used the middle name James, so H J Lara rang all the right bells. But why would he write to an earl?

The earl's family name was Robert Jenkinson. His father, the first earl, had bought the Eastwood Park estate, where he built the family seat. Nowadays Eastwood Park is used for a range of functions, including wedding ceremonies. I used to attend there as a registrar for marriages. Jenkinson was well regarded (he was prime minister) in 1819 when Henry wrote his letter.

We were not returning to London for another six months. I would never have waited such a time had I an inkling of what was to unfold!

The lengthy letter was pasted onto thick sheets and bound with other correspondence into a large leather tome. The most striking initial impression, setting it apart from the others, was the craftsmanship of the handwriting, along with Henry's recognisable signature.

The memorial (as such letters were frequently called) included the words: 'My name is Henry James Lara, son to the late Abm Lara, who did in the year 1784 present a Scheme to defray the National

Disbursements into the hands of the Right Hon William Pitt which consisted of 50 or 60 different taxes...'[3]

So his deceased father was actually called Abraham Lara and not Henrico. No wonder he had been impossible to find! Much more information followed about both Henry and his father. No mention of the diamonds – but who cared! It was the start of a new beginning.

I decided shortly afterwards to write up Abraham's story so it would not be lost for future generations, and place a copy with the British Library as a tribute to how it all developed. Then I found his cousins had equally, if not more compelling tales to tell. So this book is not just about Abraham, it's also about the exploits of some of his siblings and cousins whose dramatic lives impacted on many of the London populace, not just those in the Jewish sector.

Subsequent research was unlike any I had experienced before. Family holidays abroad centred around Portugal, Gibraltar and Spain where we could study the local records. At home, the Sephardic records for Bevis Marks Synagogue are transcribed and absolutely indispensable. The National Archives houses taxation records (a jungle), correspondence with prime ministers (never-ending), court cases and chancery records (often heavy, grubby parchment rolls). Many Bevis Marks records are now kept at the London Metropolitan Archives and can be inspected with permission from the archivist. Early minute books were often written in Portuguese – a minor difficulty. A few years ago we spent a week intensively researching in the National Archives at Lisbon. This gave me the desire to learn sufficient 'old style' Portuguese to enable me to understand many early Catholic Church records and decipher some of the inquisitions which families often had to endure, generation after generation.

Years ago I'd read of Clara Henriques de Lara 'who escaped to England, bringing not only her six children but also the seven children of her uncle, José Nunes de Lara.'[4] I thought at the time, wouldn't it be wonderful if I had such colourful ancestry in my family. Little did I know! Abraham was born in London. It was his parents, Daniel and Rachel, who were amongst the party of refugees.

Stories can be flexible – just like my family legend – with a mixture of truth, omissions and facts 'tweaked' to fit in with perceptions. This book is the result of the author's life-long interest in genealogy and determination to find out the truth behind a complex family legend. What fun!

Introduction

Bevis Marks is the oldest synagogue in Britain. It opened in 1701. As Jews were prohibited from building in a public road the site chosen was in a tiny back street of St Mary Axe, London. Close by today is the familiar landmark known as the Gherkin and within a short walking distance is Petticoat Lane, the site of one of the most famous markets in the East End.

The congregation of Bevis Marks had always welcomed Sephardic Jews from Spain and Portugal. Many of these had made the often perilous journey in search of freedom to live within the precepts of the religion of their forefathers, and to escape the terrors of the Inquisition. Any conversos (styled as New Christians in their interrogations) who were found to follow their ancestors' beliefs were declared guilty as 'Judaizers'. This was a heresy since they had been baptised Catholics. Consequently they lived with the knowledge that their children would in time be subjected to the same process. The numbers of Jews in London rose exponentially in the eighteenth century from around 1,000 to 25,000. Most of the original settlers were Sephardic Jews, though the vast majority of those arriving in later years were Ashkenazi Jews from Eastern Europe.

At times the huge influx of Sephardic Jews put great financial pressure on the congregation of Bevis Marks. The Inquisition charged for board and lodging, and wealthier detainees generally had all their assets confiscated. So, many people became virtually penniless and needed help to pay the ship's passage. Once safe in England there was a pressing and immediate need for food and lodgings. Then the new arrivals had to be assimilated, with proper religious instruction. Much of the core knowledge and Jewish customs had been lost or altered over the generations. They had to learn to speak English as soon as possible, to find employment, and to integrate into the community.

The arrival of one particularly large group may well have provoked mixed emotions. The epitaph on the tomb of Clara Henriques de Lara (the widow of Gaspar Mendes Furtado) records fourteen of the family who escaped to England. Yet there were others in the party. Not just the fourteen. The Lara siblings were accompanied by their widowed mother Maria Henriques, her brother, and Clara's sister-in-law. Also with them was Clara's brother, already married to his cousin Rachel Lara. This Catholic marriage was not recognised at Bevis Marks so they were remarried according to Jewish rites. A prior necessity for Daniel Nunes de Lara would have been circumcision, though few records survive for this and his is not amongst them. Ketubahs (marriage contracts) legally require fathers' names to be included, yet this was not the case for this couple. Why not? Their fathers (Bras Nunes de Lara and José Nunes de Lara) were nominal Catholics, having been baptised, married and buried within the auspices of the Catholic religion. Anyone whose father was not a Jew was officially regarded as fatherless, as was the case here.

Names had to change. Birth names – by and large those of Catholic saints – were discarded and new ones chosen in the Jewish tradition. Popular choices were Abraham, Isaac and Jacob for the men. The women were given names such as Sarah, Esther and Rachel. Last names also needed to be adjusted. On the Iberian continent women had retained their last names on marriage, whilst their children might be given a mix from each of the last names of their parents. This is not the tradition in England, so all José and Maria's children adopted the surname Nunes de Lara which for everyday use became just 'Lara'.

Initially vulnerable, it would be in everyone's interests for all newcomers to assimilate as soon as possible. Most of them lived out their lives within the district surrounding the synagogue (Duke Street,

Bury Street, Bevis Marks and James Court), whilst those achieving a measure of wealth moved away a little; some to Goodman's Fields, a desirable location with landscaped public gardens boasting trees, flowers and shrubberies. It was here that the first indoor swimming pool opened in 1742. From life in isolated towns and villages in the Serra da Estrela (the highest mountain range in Portugal) to the largest city in the world. Even those of the group who had lived in Lisbon for a while would have been unprepared for such a dramatic change of environment.

Those who subsequently married and had a family brought them up within the religion. All the refugees were, at the end of their lives, buried in the New Cemetery of the Congregation. Some left wills and made substantial bequests to the synagogue that had supported them in their quest for freedom. Their journey ended well.

But times were changing. Whilst social and economic reform moved apace, the Mahamad (the ruling elders) at Bevis Marks did not. Their intransigence led many to desert their religion, either becoming Christian, or just failing to attend the synagogue where they felt, with some justification, that the rules had become too harsh and inappropriate for life in modern London.

For London was changing fast. This was that period of history known as the Georgian era, named after the four Georges, the Hanoverian kings of Britain. When the Laras arrived in 1735, George II had been on the throne for some eight years. During his time there started a true shift of power from the monarchy to parliament, with Robert Walpole, the longest serving prime minister, leading the Whig party. Politics became a topic for discussion – the Laras became part of this, writing to the prime ministers of the time: the Earl of Liverpool, and William Pitt the Younger. Aaron Lara (the eldest of the Lara siblings) introduced his sister-in-law Rebecca to his friend, Benjamin D'Israeli. They married and had one daughter, Sarah, who was to marry her cousin Aaron, the foresaid Aaron's second son. D'Israeli remarried after his wife's death, and her stepbrother Isaac (also moving in the same circles as the Laras) was the father of another prime minister, Benjamin Disraeli.

The new, prestigious Royal Exchange allotted twelve places to Jews. Aaron Lara became a successful merchant, and in time was admitted to the corporation. He, along with his brother Benjamin and two of the Mendes Furtados later became denizens. This option was taken up by many of the more prosperous Jews, as it allowed them most of the rights of a citizen and to 'lose' their alien status, assigned to anyone who was born outside England or Wales. The alternative, naturalisation, required an Act of Parliament, and so was difficult, time-consuming and expensive. Denization worked well, but even so the son of a denizen could not attend university or inherit land. This meant they could not study to become, for instance, qualified surgeons and they were barred from some professions like lawyers or members of parliament. However, Jews were to be found at all levels of society, ranging from itinerant street sellers to diamond merchants and moneylenders. They were permitted to be Freemasons, so many of the next generation of Laras took advantage of this opportunity. A member of this family was in the same lodge as Isaac D'Israeli and another was in the forefront of fundraising for the new headquarters.

Newspapers flourished, alongside handbills with up-to-the-moment news to be read and gossiped over in the coffee houses. There was a growing desire amongst the populace for culture (at least amongst those who could afford it), such as the theatre, music, arts, pleasure gardens, and architecture. The Royal Academy of Arts was founded by George III in 1768. The literate could enjoy a range of books and show off their personal collections, one tangible measure of the wealth they had accrued. The first Encyclopaedia Britannica was published in 1768. In the early 1800s Charlotte Dacre, granddaughter of Benjamin Lara, published a Gothic novel, shocking the literati. Having enjoyed the arts since infancy (Handel's music had been premiered in 1743), the brothers Charles and John Furtado became players in the musical scene. Wedgwood brought his china to sell in London to help furnish the homes of the wealthy, who also started adorning their walls with wallpaper. Georgian architecture moved apace, with its own fashionable look, and Abraham Lara employed the Adams Brothers for his London dwelling. Industrialisation started in earnest and affected every part of life. Beyond these isles merchant shipping trade prospered (aided by the East India Company), bringing new luxury items such as sugar, tea, textiles and tobacco. As the Empire grew, the knock-on effect was extraordinary. Many thought the slave trade had little to do with them but lots of their material comforts were due either directly or indirectly to it. 1759 was known as 'annus mirabilis' – the miraculous year, when Britain became a world superpower and had a string of victories in the Seven Years' War. By the time George III came to the throne Britain had the largest naval fleet in the world.

But not everything was rosy. Cartoons of the time show Jews were still subjects of derision. One was of Charles Furtado, a musician simply following his talent and craft, who was lampooned for no other reason than spite and malice. Also when the Jews did get into problems (as the Laras certainly did) they were the first to hit the news headlines. This only served to strengthen anti-Semitic feelings. The sometimes illogical and unreasonable persecution of minority groups did not extend solely to the Jews. The Gordon Riots, essentially an uprising against the Roman Catholics, would have left other minority groups feeling vulnerable. History is full of instances where one tolerant generation is followed by a reversal in attitude. In the Georgian era Jews were fair game, but discrimination did not descend into persecution.

The Laras were in the vanguard of changes in London. A lot happened in their lifetime. Many tales exist about them. Here is an open door into the true stories of the lives of some of the first generations of the Lara family: the children of Daniel and Rachel, Isaac and Sarah and Benjamin and Rebecca. Please come on in…

Abraham Lara and Rebecca Bell

> In this world nothing can be said to
> be certain, except death and taxes
>
> *Benjamin Franklin*

That their son Abraham was born alive and well must have been regarded as somewhat miraculous by his parents. Daniel and Rachel Lara had already lost four sons and three daughters in the thirteen or so years since their marriage under the auspices of Bevis Marks Synagogue.[1] They subsequently had three other children: Jacob, Judith and Esther. Both parents were Portuguese and had come to England as refugees, part of a much wider family grouping. They were from very large families, so may have expected to have a number of children themselves. A significant factor in their long wait for a healthy baby could be that they were first cousins, now living in the strange, bustling environment of London. This could not be more different from their homeland, with towns and hamlets scattered like a broken string of pearls along the high mountainous range of the Serra da Estrela.

Daniel, Rachel and the three youngest children were listed in 'Genealogia Hebraica', which was an attempt to record some of the more prominent Jewish families from the Iberian Peninsula. But what about their eldest son Abraham? He was conspicuous by his absence! His place in the Jewish community in London in the eighteenth century seems to have escaped everyone, for good reason.

There is no record of his circumcision surviving, but as he was known as 'Junior' throughout his life, this indicates he was younger than his cousin Abraham who was born in June 1746. They would both, in all probability, have been named after the patriarch of the family, uncle Abraham Monsanto. Abraham's birth year must have been in or after 1748, since twins were born and buried the previous year.

It can be said with little room for doubt that he did not get married. His siblings' marriages are recorded in the registers for Bevis Marks. His was not there, and extensive searches reveal no sign of a marriage. Yet he did have children: two boys and two girls. So why didn't he marry their mother? It was not until over fifty years later, in the very early days of the reign of Queen Victoria, that civil marriages became legal. Here we have Abraham Lara, a Jew, and Rebecca Bell, who was not, unable to formalise their relationship. So they had little choice but to live together to all intents and purposes as man and wife.

Indirect confirmation of this arrangement came when their first son (named after his father) died as a juvenile in 1800. His burial entry at the cemetery of the Spanish and Portuguese Jews records him as the son of Abraham and grandson of Daniel Nunes Lara.[2] The fact there is no row or grave number in the entry for him is relevant. The boy was buried 'behind the boards'. This type of burial is reserved for those whose credentials are suspect yet a Jewish burial is desired by the family. He was not permitted the full burial rites when he was interred as his parents did not have a Sephardic marriage, and he was not circumcised.

He was fifteen when he died, having been christened at St Leonard, Shoreditch Parish Church in 1785, as Abraham, the son of Abraham and Rebecca Lara.[3] How sad for Abraham and Rebecca to lose their eldest son on the cusp of manhood and for his siblings to lose their eldest brother.

His father, Abraham, did not leave a will, nor was an administration taken out for him. The only other official record for him is his own burial entry. Here he is recorded as Abraham de Daniel Nunes Lara, buried 15 May 1816. This specific wording confirms Abraham was the son of Daniel Nunes de Lara.[4] But for the burial registers for himself and his son, Abraham did not leave the normal footprints of life. Rather odd really, as his cousins were at the forefront of Jewish life in Georgian London.

One other tangible piece of evidence is his portraiture. That alone is unusual as there are many in museums, stately homes and general collections for whom the provenance has been lost. The one for Abraham has been wrapped in mystery for generations. He was reputed to have been called Henrico de Lara. The likeness is of a jolly fellow, with round face and plump cheeks indicating a taste for treats (hardly surprising when his parents and brother were pastry cooks). What prompted him to commission this etching? And why was his real name so different from the one passed down through the generations? Questions to be addressed.

Abraham Nunes de Lara (originally believed to have been called Henrico de Lara)

There is a well-known portrait of Mozart taken in the 1780s which depicts him in a remarkably similar wig, one which falls to a deep 'widow's peak' at the forehead, close cropped and brushed back with two tight curls on the side. It is tied at the nape of the neck with a black ribbon. The hair at the back could be styled in a variety of ways, such as a queue, or be placed (as appears to be the case for these two gentlemen) in a black silk bag, hence known as a bagwig. The two side curls were known as *ailes de pigeon* (pigeon's wings). According to an archivist at the Victoria and Albert Museum the coat and revers of the likeness of Abraham date from the 1780s and was formal dress for a middle-class person and informal for an aristocrat. Crucially it had to be someone with the means to purchase portraiture, which wasn't cheap.

Diamonds are forever

Diamonds? Yes, let's look for the diamonds. It is reputed that Abraham was wealthy and that part of his fortune was held in diamonds. Did the refugees bring diamonds with them? Unlikely, as they had no chance to amass these. Many of the party had been through inquisitions and their assets were systematically seized.

A few years ago the major British newspapers linked up with funding agencies to digitise their past editions. Some, like *The Times*, have been achieved with a considerable amount of success, if one can forget the painful hours looking up 'hits' on Lara which inevitably prove false. The more obvious are words such as declaration but then there are others very poorly digitised such as Lord, Place and Lark, which are real time-wasters. One excellent find though was in 1791, in *The Star*[5]:

Lara v Bird
The Plaintiff Mr Abraham Lara who was by profession a jeweller brought this action against Mr Bird who is a young gentleman of fashion.

The action was brought on two Bills of Exchange, the one for

£400 and the other for £100. These Bills had been given to the Plaintiff by the Defendant for some diamonds and money which was lent to Mr Bird sixteen years ago when he was a student at Trinity College, Cambridge.

When this cause was fully heard it appeared that the Defendant was a minor at the time he drew these Bills and that he had made no promise to pay since that period. In consequence of this, the Jury found a verdict for the Defendant.

Abraham's diamonds glittered and sparkled on the screen. This had to be him. Perhaps he had access to diamonds in his trade? That seems possible.

The London diamond trade

London became the main centre of the trade in rough diamonds following the resettlement of the Jews in England in the mid seventeenth century. By the mid 1730s when the Laras came on the scene it had been long established and a small number of influential and wealthy families were running the business. Many of these were firms in the Jewish-Portuguese community of London. The rich diamond merchants imported diamonds, initially from India, and traded them for commodities and jewels such as corals, rubies, pearls and silver.

They sold these on in the city to prominent middle men, a compelling venture for Abraham's Uncle Aaron, who had been an experienced merchant in Portugal. As one of the few Jewish members allowed to work in the Royal Exchange he was able to broker deals with the importers for diamonds and other products. Wholesale merchants and traders like him then sent the diamonds to Amsterdam or Antwerp to be cut and polished, or sold on to the local jewellers in the City – 'people of lesser means who bought finished stones or polished them themselves and manufactured all kinds of jewellery'.[6] It is clear Aaron Lara lived in a different league from many of his kinsmen, and definitely to his nephew Abraham, who was a craftsman.

The jeweller

Abraham was said at the trial to be a jeweller and was styled as Abraham Lara Junior. Jewellers were at the bottom of gem trading – the third tier – buying stones to finish or polish and sell to the general population. Though he was only a few years younger than his more affluent, well-known cousin, as the newspaper article shows he would generally be known by the title Abraham Lara Junior, to distinguish between the two.

Money-lending

Did Abraham – who was in business as a jeweller – also trade part-time as a moneylender? Under the law only Jews were allowed to lend. They were often derided for that, but as this was one of the few professions open to them, they filled the gap. Abraham would be well aware that some of his cousins and more distant relatives traded in this way. The lure of apparently 'easy money' could have been a factor to encourage him to dabble in it too. This involved advancing loans to those who expected to inherit/receive money at some future time but were temporarily in need of funds. It could be a fairly risky occupation as dealers needed sufficient funds to advance to make it worthwhile, an ability to be able to judge people's character and training/expertise to put in place legally binding contracts. Another of Abraham's cousins, Rebecca, was married to Benjamin D'Israeli (his grandson would be the future Lord Beaconsfield, Queen Victoria's favourite prime minister). D'Israeli tried this money-lending for a while, and found it was not for him. Sarah, another of Abraham's cousin's, was married to John King, who was well known as a moneylender, but that's another story!

The sting

Abraham was about to make a wrong call, perhaps taken in by the thought of an easy profit. It is quite probable he was chosen since his cousins (moneylenders and brokers) had proper training, knew how to set up legal contracts, and were too astute to be taken in so readily.

He was approached by an intermediary for a young man called Mr Bird (a student at Cambridge) who wanted to borrow money and diamonds. This representative would have searched out the 'best' person on his client's behalf. It would not have been unusual for a middle man to conduct the proceedings as the gentry did not always want to be seen personally arranging loans. Abraham Lara fitted the bill. Firstly he was a Jew. Then he was a jeweller so had access to diamonds. The *coup de grâce* was his youth and inexperience as a moneylender.

Bird's representative was obviously persuasive as Lara accepted his assurance that Bird would in the future be able to repay the debt, and he agreed to the deal. When approached a second time he must have been just as convincing, as Abraham advanced more funds including money, articles and diamonds. In exchange for this sale he was given two promissory bank notes (Bills of Exchange). They were worth £610 and due to be redeemed in 1776. In today's worth (using 2013 to calculate with a link to the Retail Price Index), we are talking of some £71,680. Not a huge sum, but this is the least it was likely to be. Other measures such as wages, for example, vastly inflate this figure. Presumably the value of these bonds included a certain amount of interest, especially as it was agreed the loan would not be repaid for another six years. So in the year 1775 Abraham had high hopes that his involvement with Bird would be lucrative or else he would not have entered into the arrangement.

Where are you, Mr Bird?

It was six years before Mr Lara took his promissory notes to the bank to find they were useless – the bank would simply not accept them. There was nothing he could do until he could discover Bird's whereabouts after Cambridge. Some years later he found out where Mrs Bird (the mother) lived and went to the house. His companion was Mr Buzaglo, brother of his sister-in-law Leah. Buzaglo accompanied Lara as a precaution for both support and as a witness. At the house Lara and Bird talked, and Bird made it clear there would be no money forthcoming. Bird would not talk in the presence of Buzaglo, and Lara made another poor judgement in meeting without a witness present at all times.

The court case

However good a newspaper summary, it cannot be as informative as the actual proceedings. A further article in *The Times*[7] mentioned the action was held at Westminster Hall before Judge Kenyon, the Lord Chief Justice. This Hall is the enormous magnificent space within the Palace of Westminster that survived the disastrous fire and is now encompassed by the Victorian edifice recognised throughout the world today, known as the Houses of Parliament. This was a civil case, hence judged under King's Bench, one of the most complex to search.

These particular records need to be ordered three days in advance from the National Archives, as they are stored off-site in the salt mines in Cheshire.

They are arranged into the four terms of the academic year, namely: Michaelmas, Easter, Whitsun and Trinity. Within these they are indexed by defendants, rather than plaintiffs, not the order one would expect.

The entry indicated that the case was to be held on 3 December 1790, Michaelmas term in the thirty-first year of the reign of George III, and was between Abraham Lara and William Bird Esquire.[8] This was the first time Mr Bird's name of William was mentioned, as the newspaper articles omitted this information. His full name was vital in ultimately leading to the documents themselves.

The trial records

These are huge, cumbersome and too heavy for one person to handle. The outer wrapping for the bundle which contained Abraham's case wasn't good, which did not bode well for the contents. Only too true. Inside were numerous bound sets of parchments in very poor condition.

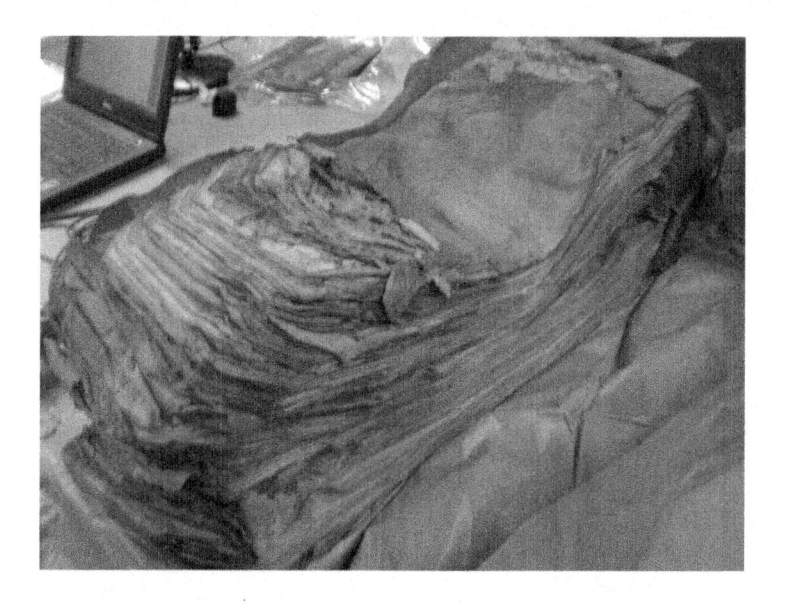

Court case records for Abraham Lara v
William Bird, The National Archives

Lara's was somewhere in the middle. Irregular parts were still intact after bacterial damage from inadequate storage over the years, which had occurred prior to their removal to their current storage facility. In it his description as Abraham Lara Junior, a Jew and a jeweller, was clear enough to read.

What to do next? It was common to have debtors committed to ensure they did not flee – the payment of a small fee would ensure this was done – then take the debtor to court to plead your case for recompense. Mr Bird said he knew as much about the law as Abraham. Of course he did – a great deal more. After university he worked at Lincoln's Inn, so he had both a sound education and experience of legal issues. The court case notes report Mr Lara had Mr Bird taken to the Knight Marshal of the Marshalsea. Because of its position in Southwark near the Thames, the Marshalsea was also used to incarcerate pirates and smugglers. Though the smallest of the debtors' prisons, it was a notorious place in which to be sent.

It would have been bearable only for the fortunate few who could afford the fees and use the facilities there, perhaps being allowed out during the day to continue working. Imprisonment for debt was common and over half of the prisoners in the eighteenth century were there for this reason.

A drama made for television

This saga had begun several years earlier. In the meantime Lara had committed much time, effort and expense to another venture – preparing taxation plans for the prime minister – so must have felt the real need to recover some of his earlier losses. To aid his case he employed one of the brilliant and successful barristers of the time, Thomas Erskine, later King's Counsel and Lord Chancellor. The judge for the case was Lord Kenyon and it was held at the Court of Common Pleas. Both Erskine and Kenyon were depicted in the TV series *Garrow's Law*.

The ribbon seller

Let's go back a bit now. How did this saga begin? William Bird was partway through a three-year academic course at Trinity College which ran from 7 June 1773, and was in dire need of funds to support the lifestyle to which he aspired. Charles Bird, his father, sold ribbons, and lived in Wood Street, Cheapside. This was not the most salubrious of areas and he was not of the background, employment or substance to provide the funding at the level his son required. William realised there would be no inheritance forthcoming when his father died. It is at death when loans were often repaid (the borrower being a major beneficiary). There is no evidence of any will or administration, so he had to continue to survive on his own wit and merits. William took out the loan and received cash and diamonds to spend as he wanted, clearly having neither the expected means nor intent of repaying the loan.

Sadly Lara's hopes for a successful conclusion were shattered. In the case he was styled as Abraham Lara Junior, and although his occupation was stated to be a jeweller, he was also confirmed to be a Jew and seen as a moneylender. Neither of these 'tags' would have made him seem as respectable as the university-educated, well-positioned William Bird.

A dedicated follower of fashion

Though Bird was described as a 'gentleman of fashion' the court did not equate this with someone who aspired to a flamboyant lifestyle, expensive clothing and activities beyond his financial means. The odds were against Lara from the start.

Charles Dickens had a much clearer grasp of the reality of these self-styled gentlemen of fashion. In 1812, four years before Abraham died, Dickens was born in Portsea, Portsmouth. This was the naval port where another of Abraham's cousins, Benjamin, lived and worked. In one of his novels, *Little Dorrit*, Dickens exposed the gentlemen of fashion who would happily sponge off anyone willing to 'give' them money. His character, Henry Gowan, was one such who married 'Pet', much in the hope of gaining independent funding through her devoted and concerned parents. That book also portrays William Dorrit, who was consigned to the Marshalsea prison (with his children) for debt, a fate which befell his own father, John Dickens.

Sixteen years to wait for your money?

The loan would have been made in about 1775. It was due to be settled after six years. Why had it dragged on for so long? Did Bird hide his whereabouts so well that Lara was unable to locate him for another ten years, or had he been remiss in searching? Would the conditions of the loan have expired after such a time? And crucially, would he still be able to legally reclaim his money?

Findings in the court case indicate that the bills were made out to Drummonds and Company, Bankers, at their headquarters in 49 Charing Cross, London. The bank is now part of the Royal Bank of Scotland. Abraham appeared to have altered the bills' due date to a later year. Possibly he was aware the time lapse would prove problematic, and also his private conversation may have drawn his attention to another potential pitfall, so he falsified the date to appear that this wasn't the case.

About a boy

Bird knew exactly what to do. He obtained evidence of his birth date, and proved he was underage when he took out the loan. He was indeed not yet twenty-one, whilst Abraham was (though only a few years) older than him.

Under the law of England infants were only *bound for necessaries*. They might make an express promise to pay when they came of age, but this was absolutely necessary to bind them. Bird said he had never promised to repay the money and he got away with it.

Much of his stock would have gone to this trickster. Had Abraham been given his money back he would in all probability have had sufficient to live out his life in some comfort, and probably have some to pass on to his heirs as well.

The end result was that Lara ended up even poorer once he had paid his solicitor, Erskine. He was also probably disappointed and disillusioned with the English judicial system, his adversary having been let off on a point of law.

In this world nothing can be said to be certain, except death and taxes

Benjamin Franklin might as well have been referring to this Abraham when he reputedly said this. We know for certain Abraham lived and died since his body was buried. On the second count his involvement with taxes for the nation is well documented by the parties concerned, in the form of private letters.

So here he is, a man aspiring to the wealth and comfort afforded to his cousins, yet his advancement had not only been stalled – it had been reversed. This may have been as a result of a lack of business acumen, poor judgement in not meeting the client himself or checking his credentials, rather than taking the matter on face value, and his desire to pursue 'easy money'. How could he attempt to reverse this loss? By means of a grand scheme!

It's your time now, number five

Abraham died in 1816. A few years afterwards his son, Henry Lara, wrote to the Earl of Liverpool. This letter is now in the British Library, as part of that family's papers. As a reminder, the circumstances surrounding this discovery are given in the preface.

British Library, Euston Road, London

In the letter he gave his father's name, and said that Abraham had prepared a scheme to bring in new taxes for the Right Honourable William Pitt, Prime Minister of Great Britain. This was presented to Pitt's private secretary Dr Pretyman over thirty years ago, back in 1784.[9]

Robert Banks Jenkinson, the second Earl of Liverpool, was a high profile man. He was prime minister and First Lord of the Treasury, coming to power as a young man upon the assassination of the incumbent prime minister, Spencer Perceval. He had been the fifth person approached by George, the Prince Regent, as the first four chosen candidates were unable to form ministries. Liverpool served in this capacity throughout many crucial years during his premiership. The final campaigns for the Napoleonic wars were fought during his office. He also stood on the international stage for the abolition of the slave trade, helping to gain acceptance from Europe for this. Owing to his position and perceived honesty Henry considered him an appropriate person to write to.

Let's talk about taxation...

Abraham Lara's scheme was prepared for a previous incumbent of the office, William Pitt the Younger. Though Pitt had taken office in December 1783, his party was beset with problems. A few months later (in March 1784) King George III dissolved parliament, following which Pitt gained an overwhelming victory at the polls. With the support of the majority of the House of Commons Pitt was able to embark on a process of making Britain great. His priority was to reduce the national debt, now at astronomical levels following the wars with the French. He was often lampooned about this in the satirical cartoons of the day and there was even a mention of his obsession with this in the film *The Madness of King George*.

Everyone knew this was at the heart of his policies. So lots of people wrote in with taxation ideas. Lara was one of them. The 1784 Scheme had to be found. Where to look? The National Archives of course!

Red tape

In true bureaucratic fashion the Treasury kept meticulous care of letters. The department separated them into Letters IN and Letters OUT. The absence of either a letter or a response shows Abraham did not write in a letter about his ideas for taxation to raise revenue.

There was, however, more detail in the 1819 letter to Prime Minister Jenkinson. Henry James Lara confirmed that he and his father had jointly presented a memorial to Mr Vansittart on 20 October 1812, which included a further suggestion on taxes upon organs, pianos and harps. This had been refused. Jenkinson knew Nicholas Vansittart well, as he was the Chancellor of the Exchequer in 1812 at the start of his leadership, and remained so until well after 1819.

The letter was not initially found, but this was because Henry mistakenly gave the date as 20 October 1812 when it was actually 20 January 1812. The marginal note against the outgoing letter index said: 'A Lara Junr Esq, Memorial Refused'. It was sent on 30 January, eight days after receipt on 22 January.[10]

The letter itself was in date order within a huge pile of incoming letters for 1812. This memorial explained the circumstances of how the earlier scheme had been presented, thus clarifying why it had not been located in the Treasury documentation. It also said that he had compiled the scheme with the aid of his best friend, Isaac Mendes Furtado, information which had been repeated in the later letter from his son.

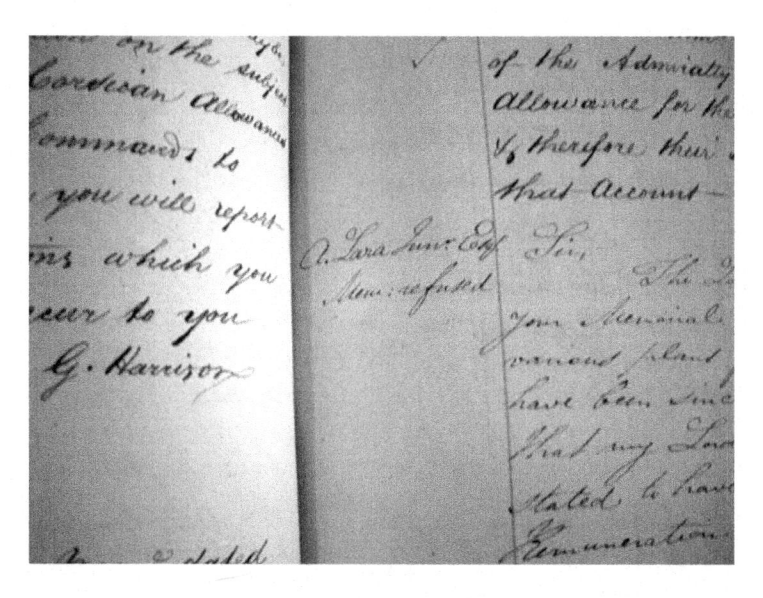

Outgoing letter book entry, Treasury Department,
The National Archives

My best friend

Who was Isaac Mendes Furtado? Abraham described Isaac as his 'best friend'. What was their actual relationship?

Not best friends as we use the expression today. Obviously

friendly enough as this was a major venture on which they had to work together, but in eighteenth-century England the term was used differently. In wills it often refers to someone who is a relative, but not close enough to be called a cousin or nephew. This was not the case here. The six Mendes Furtado children of Gaspar and Clara were close relatives. Abraham's father was Clara's brother, so they were indeed cousins. His mother was Clara's cousin, so by this relationship they were second cousins. Why didn't Abraham call him cousin? He was twenty years younger than Isaac, so perhaps felt 'best friend' was the clearest way to describe their relationship.

Fashionable Moorfields

Together they concocted a truly ambitious scheme. They would have spent a lot of time on it, either at the home of one or the other (as they both lived in Moorfields) or more likely at one of the coffee houses which Furtado frequented for trading. Isaac was a well-known notary at the time and this would have been his usual place for business.

Around this time Moorfields was a good place to live (provided you weren't incarcerated in the old Bethlem Hospital that is). Some one hundred years before, in the wake of the Great Fire of London, it had become a crowded, tented place with people living in miserable conditions. There was an upper and a middle Moorfields. This was later followed by lower Moorfields (within which was Finsbury Square, built between 1777 and 1791). The square boasted being on a par with the beauty and size of the best squares in London's West End. It was this area that attracted doctors and surgeons who were the high earners of the time.

Abraham was still living in Moorfields on 15 September 1784, when the first manned balloon flight in England was made by Signor Vincent Lunardi. Abraham and Rebecca were likely to have been amongst the excited crowds who went to witness this spectacle.

Isaac Mendes Furtado would surely also have gone with his young family, as he lived nearby in South Side, Finsbury Place, Moorfields. Later he went to Stoke Newington, whereas Abraham Lara moved in a downward spiral.

All the best laid plans...

So what was this scheme about? It was a proposal for several specific taxes, as mentioned by Henry Lara in the 1819 letter to the Earl of Liverpool, which was called 'A Scheme to Defray the National Disbursements'. This was a series of inventive ideas on a grand scale, one which reputedly turned into an outstanding nationwide money-raising venture. In fact so successful was it, Abraham suggests that millions of pounds were raised. It would not be right to speculate whether the plans implemented came from this particular scheme, or were an amalgam with others. No paperwork relating to this was kept or, if it was, it has yet to be found. However he clearly considered it a concept on a gigantic scale and repercussions of this affect us all today.

An idea to help the nation – and hopefully provide a decent personal pension!

As long ago as 1733 Hogarth showed a remarkable insight into the future. The seventh of his paintings in *The Rake's Progress* depicted Tom Rakewell as an inmate of The Fleet (the debtors' prison), experimenting with ideas to raise cash. In the scene was another prisoner who had written a treatise on how to pay 'ye debts of ye nation'.

Years later, in 1784, the gossip of the day was of the prime minister and First Lord of the Treasury, William Pitt, who was trying hard to address the parlous state of the nation. The national debt had risen to levels never seen before and he took it on board to use his power and position to not only check its growth, but substantially reduce it in size. All sorts of new taxes were being proposed. Letters from members of the public either objecting to specific proposed taxes, or suggesting new ones, were sent in.

Few individuals have the ability and wherewithal to devise a money-making scheme and see it through from start to finish. Most need some form of help with certain aspects of the task. So they need to bring in at least one more person with the personal skills, contacts, financial backing, or other vital contributions to help oil the wheels that move a venture along.

Abraham must have been well aware he did not have the connections needed to bring this to the attention of those who might find it invaluable to the nation. But he knew a man who did! His 'best friend' Isaac Mendes Furtado.

Isaac was an official notary with friends in high places, almost certainly clients of his! He managed to obtain an introduction by the Right Honourable Earl Camden (this was his title from 1786 and the one by which Abraham and Isaac referred to him). Camden was an experienced politician who in his lifetime served in the cabinet for fifteen years and under five different prime ministers. He approached the Right Honourable Mr Pitt on their behalf, who, seemingly impressed, in turn passed them on to his personal and private secretary, the Reverend Dr Pretyman. The Reverend Pretyman was Pitt's mentor and tutor at Pembroke College, Cambridge, by now his trusted and respected aide who dealt with such matters.

Off to Downing Street

What a sensible approach: seeking a meeting rather than just sending in correspondence. So to his private offices they went for an appointment. This was at Downing Street, in the house proffered to Sir Robert Walpole by King George II as a personal gift. He accepted on condition it would not be his to dispose of as he wished, but one which was the residence of every subsequent First Lord of the Treasury. Traditionally regarded as the first prime minister, Walpole lived in Downing Street from 1735. But not at number ten, the house with the famous black door. Back in May 1784 when Pitt was appointed to office it was called number five, and only later changed to ten. But what an impressive place to meet! As Pitt came to power in May that year and was anxious to bring in new laws at the earliest opportunity, the meeting was likely to be soon after. Reverend Pretyman lived a short walk away in Great George Street, according to the rate books.

They would all have been aware of the need to approach such

schemes with a mix of compassion and ruthlessness, since taxes were then, as now, generally disliked. One of those most hated was the window tax, hence the number of buildings in London particularly which became bricked in: no light, no tax.

Dr Pretyman must have been impressed as he was a highly astute man and with the burden of his job could not have afforded to waste time on poorly put-together schemes. According to Abraham he saw them five or six times; a huge commitment of both time and effort for all concerned.

Some taxation proposals

In the letter for 1812, Abraham went into more detail about the plan to discharge the great public debt, which he said was presented by him and his cousin, which he asserted 'that no other individual ever before or since presented'. The following give an indication of how wide-ranging the ideas were:

On additional postage on letters
On legacies
On tonnage upon shipping
On unclaimed dividends in the Bank
On houses kept for pleasure
On bricks and tiles
On physic and doctors of physic
On pawnbrokers
On probates of wills
On assessed taxes
On leases on lands
On promotions places @c
On settlements and portions on marriages
On attorneys at law
On counsellors
On passengers to foreign ports
On owners of British ships
On proctors

On barges and lighters
On instate estates
On salesmen selling live cattle
On £100 privilege tax
On dignities

No doubt he felt obliged to go into this detail, since by now Pitt was dead. Pitt was some years younger than Lara, so his early demise would have been unexpected and quite a setback for proving this claim. George Pretyman – who was about the same age as Lara – had been appointed Bishop of Lincoln in 1787 on Pitt's recommendation, in spite of the king's misgivings about one so young occupying this position. Though he died some years after Lara (in 1827), Pretyman continued to concentrate on Church affairs rather than those of government.

Money, money, money

Back in 1784 the prospect of reward for diligent, thoughtful planning on a grand scale with unbelievably high stakes (where even a slight fraction of a percentage would make one rich beyond belief) must surely have excited Abraham and Isaac. However, just as before when Abraham was outwitted by William Bird, he (and his partners) failed to take into account the vital need to have the discussions independently documented. Where was his proof that his scheme, passed on with the very best intentions to the highest in the land, would be attributed to them and honoured? In innocence, they assumed that they would benefit substantially from these ideas as they were dealing at the high end of government.

The government's point of view…?

Either there was a deliberate decision not to reward them, or there was a misunderstanding on their part and the intention was never more than to take advantage of the intelligent reasoned hard work of some of this nation's citizens. For it was the Treasury's coffers which were filled. Was there ever an intent to pass on a 'fee' for ideas from some of their citizens?

The petitioners' point of view…?

They were not spending this time and effort in framing a scheme just for the benefit of the nation. They had themselves to consider too. A letter written by Isaac Mendes Furtado referred to this, saying that no reward had yet been paid. This was dated 22 November 1795 and in it he referred to Lara, himself and a man called Penny as being the proponents of this work.[11]

The three of them expected to be paid (or recompensed was how they put it) when the schemes were introduced, and left their meetings with Dr Pretyman believing this would be the case only later to find they were totally overlooked. Abraham 'was honoured by an approval of his plan by obtaining an assurance that all due attention should be paid to your petitioner and although he with pleasure did see many of the taxes he proposed adopted and which produced many millions sterling annually your petitioner was unfortunately totally forgotten although the sole projector of so valuable a plan.'

The letter from Furtado to Prime Minister William Pitt's office is independent confirmation of Lara's assertion that many of their proposed taxes were instigated, and that these had raised huge sums for the Exchequer. How Lara worked out the amounts raised is unknown; however, he did not believe in downplaying the amount of monies he believed had been raised in direct consequence of it:

'That your petitioner has been at a vast expence (sic) trouble and loss of time in the invention of the many taxes contained in his plan and surely at least upwards of £200,000,000 Sterling received and brought in the space of 26 years and much more to come into His Majesty's Treasury may with propriety allow some little deduction to gratify the projector.'

When he left the employ of William Pitt the Younger, it appears that Pretyman's papers about these meetings were not passed to the Treasury Office. Thus when Lara wrote in enquiring about recompense, the brief reply simply said no trace of them could be found. Without proof that the schemes came from them, they had no comeback at all.

He had high apple pie in the sky hopes

No diamonds and little money left. No payment at all for Abraham's scheme. Yet he was a dreamer – a quality he appears to have passed on to his son, Henry Lara, who was to submit his own projects to the Earl of Liverpool. Abraham had hoped all would yet be well as he obviously had the intellect to work out money-making projects, but every time he was let down. Indeed, some years ago – after he had lent money to Bird, but before the taxation scheme – there came about another even more forlorn hope that he might inherit some money. Just as for the taxation scheme, he continued to pursue this dream throughout his life.

Enter Uncle Isaac from Gibraltar

In Abraham's words from his memorial:

> Your petitioner's uncle by name Isaac Lara resident at Gibraltar 47 years has rendered great services as well as your petitioner to government. He was appointed Consul at Barbary 14 years recovered many valuable prizes taken by the Dey of Algiers he lost all he had in the world by the siege of Gibraltar – Governor Eliott assured him he should be rewarded as also Lord Howe but (alas) died broken-hearted in the 89th year of his age and your petitioner remains his only heir to claim such services as your petitioner can prove by his several letters, all these matters your petitioner trusts will draw your Lordship's notice and attention to his claim.

This quote indicates Abraham believed he was heir and beneficiary to the estate of his Uncle Isaac, who had been a very rich merchant in Gibraltar prior to the siege. This had lasted from 1779 to 1783.

The Siege of Gibraltar

Why did Abraham believe he would be Isaac's heir if his fortune was restored, when his uncle had three daughters? As it happens this wasn't to be an issue as no recompense was paid to him. But on the point of inheritance, one of his daughters is known to have died prior to the 1812 letter, and as Abraham says he is 'his only heir' it may be that the others had too.

Uncle Isaac and his family had been bundled out of Gibraltar. They were one of the last families to leave after the governor insisted they should go. He stayed to get assurances from Governor Eliott personally that his case would be presented to government for some redress. Isaac Lara had to pay for the passage on the naval ship to England for himself and his three unmarried daughters, which shows he still had some funds at his disposal. As with the other refugees, after the hostilities were over he wrote to the government pleading for assistance to return to Gibraltar. He wanted to try to build up his business again, and got nowhere. During their stay in London the probability is that they lived and were mainly supported by his nephew Abraham. So many Gibraltarians had arrived needing help, that where they had family still living in Britain, they were naturally expected to help out.

Isaac's exact relationship with Abraham and the other Laras of London could only be confirmed by the Gibraltarian census, Portuguese Church records and those of the infamous Inquisition. The age given in the census indicated he was born around 1714. The only Lara who was born around that time and had survived childhood was João (John) the second son of José Nunes de Lara and Maria Henriques.[12] He was one of several siblings who came to London. His mother, Maria Henriques, along with others in the group, had left Covilhã and on reaching Lisbon met up with Isaac who was living there with one of his sisters. Isaac chose to leave with them, his sister did not.

Isaac may have chosen Abraham as his heir apparent, should he get any of his fortune back, in gratitude for his kindness to the family during the trying circumstances whilst they were in London. He would have felt able to make this promise for two reasons. The first was he needed Abraham to continue to champion his case whilst he was in Gibraltar. Secondly one of his children married a highly successful merchant, which took away from him the need to support his daughters. As she was then unlikely to have a family of her own, there remained the outside possibility that if she was widowed, then she might 'remember' her cousin in her will. This did not happen. Her husband outlived her.

Tutoring

Isaac, in his role as Vice-Consul, was an accomplished letter writer and in the course of his foreign trade and travel would have learned several languages. English of course was one, as well as his native Portuguese, and others such as Spanish, Arabic, Italian, and German were likely. To while away the time and actively help the man who was assisting them it is possible he took pleasure in conversing with Abraham and passing on some of the skills he had acquired. Abraham, along with his brother Jacob and two sisters, would have attended the school run by Bevis Marks Synagogue as their parents were unlikely to have afforded tutors. This was a grand opportunity to have a basic education enhanced, skills which he later passed on to his own children. Over a hundred years later, Abraham's great-grandson (Henry James Bell) recorded that his grandfather (Henry Lara, son of Abraham) knew several languages and was a beautiful 'penman'. Notaries and affluent business people employed unusual signature scrolls. Isaac did and it was exactly this elaborate style employed by a later son of Abraham (Henry).[13] If Abraham had this basic schooling supplemented by his uncle, this explains why his sons were well educated, when they had an illiterate mother.

Abraham appears to have told his son Henry stories of Gibraltar, which were in turn recounted to his own children. George (the youngest surviving son) may well have only heard a small part of this inference to their European background. But it would have been Gibraltar, not Portugal, which figured in the conversations. Geographically Gibraltar is at the southern tip of Spain. The opening words of *A History of the Siege of Gibraltar*[14] show its significance: 'Gibraltar is situated in Andalucía, the most southern province of Spain.' This was probably the reason for subsequent generations to believe the family originated from Andalucía.

Gibraltar was the pulsing heart of the British navy in the Mediterranean, with trade routes spreading far and wide, protecting and extending the government's influence. Spain to this day lays claim on Gibraltar, enforcing this even now with the likes of petty disruptive border controls, whilst the inhabitants resist and remain steadily rock-fast British.

Government assistance was only forthcoming to one family from Gibraltar, but not to Isaac's. Eventually he and his daughters did make their way home in an attempt to rekindle some part of their past lives. Isaac never did have any recompense. When he died Isaac had too little to pass on any inheritance to Abraham, not even enough to consider it worth leaving a will.

Abraham did all he could to help his uncle with his claim but to no avail. His letter of January 1812 written just six months before his own death shows how, even to the end, he tried to establish a claim for the benefit of his children. His surviving son Henry kept his papers as proof of his father's involvement in the tax scheme and of his great uncle's circumstances. He may even himself, for a while, have continued to hope some redress might be forthcoming.

The grateful aunt

One of Abraham's elderly aunts became ill and unable to cope on her own when she was in her eighties, a ripe old age even by today's standards. Her name was Judith de Solas, and she was one of his mother's sisters. Judith had always lived in the Bevis Marks area, close to Rachel, so would have met her family more than the other nieces and nephews. Most of her other relatives – brother Benjamin, his children and those of her other brother Aaron – were very well off indeed but as oft happens it was those with least to give who gave the most. She left her house, sold her furniture and moved in with Abraham's sister Esther and her husband Elias Curry. She had been left fifty pounds by both her late brother Aaron and Abraham Mendes Furtado (her late cousin Abigail's eldest son, who was brother to Isaac). But that was some years ago and was probably spent by now. This aunt lived with the Currys for more than three years before she died. She had no real reason to leave a will, since she had pitifully little, but she wanted to express her gratitude to the three family members who had done so much for her. These were Esther, Jacob and Abraham. Abraham in particular was praised. Tellingly she called him Abraham Lara Junior as she wanted to separate him from her other nephew Abraham Lara. Here is more proof – if it were ever needed – that the Abraham Lara Junior of the diamond court case was her nephew.

Aunt Judith's special mention of him makes it sound as though he was the prime motivator and instrumental for her care and well-being.

The witness

Her will was such an amazingly important find in yet another way. It was written in December 1788 a few years before Judith died, showing she had been dependent on them for a long time. One of the witnesses was Rebecca Bell, who assigned her mark. The only other references to Rebecca were on her sons' baptism records. The eldest son, also called Abraham, had died in 1800, and his birth entry was recorded as the son of Abraham and Rebecca Lara. The second was for Henry James, recorded as the son of Abraham and Rebecca Bell.[15]

The 'x' on the will shows she was illiterate, and confirms that she was not married to Abraham, even though by then their eldest son Abraham was three. Nothing else is known about her, but the mere fact she was asked to be one of the witnesses to the will is a good indicator that she knew Abraham's aunt well and was accepted as part of the family even though she was not a Jewess. More than this, to have as a witness someone who was not as educated as herself can only reflect well on his aunt's nature.

Lara or Bell?

Miss Bell was reputably of Scottish origin. She may have died before 1810 when Henry married Amelia Moggridge in Whitechapel as she did not appear as a witness. Both Henry James and Rachel were married within Abraham's lifetime, and during the next few years a number of his grandchildren were born.

There is nothing to say whether Abraham was present or not in the church. The only witness for Henry's marriage was his sister Rachel who signed as Rachel Lara. A couple of years later she married Amelia's brother Robert. The register entry shows she now called herself Rachel Bell, and that both Henry and Amelia Bell were their witnesses.

Little wonder Henry James was unsure how to address himself. Lara or Bell? He had been brought up using the Lara surname, yet he was not Jewish and his parents had not married. So he chose both. For any official dealings with the Church of England, such as marriage and baptism registrations, he was always Henry James Bell. When it came to occupations the opposite was true.

His eldest daughter, Henrietta Miller, was the informant at his death in October 1855. She gave his age as sixty-seven – only five months out – calling her father Henry Bell and again giving his occupation as watchmaker. His wife, Amelia, when registering the death of her mother, Lydia Moggridge in 1841, gave her own name as Amelia Lara.

Censuses (surveys of population numbers) have been carried out by civilised societies for years. The first national census for England and Wales for which records widely exist was held in 1841. Enumerators were appointed to walk specific routes and required to find out for each household the names, relationship of each individual to the head of house, ages (often rounded up/down), occupation and whether or not each person was born in the county in which they now resided. This was conducted on 7 June 1841. It was easy enough to find Henry and Amelia since they had been living at 6 Godfreys Place, Austin Street for some time. The head of house was given as Henry Miller, with his wife Henrietta and family, father-in-law Henry Lara and mother-in-law Amelia Lara along with Henrietta's brother George Lara. By the time of the 1851 census Henry and Amelia were still living with their daughter, son-in-law and grandchildren. The census showed London's population was 2,363,405 and growing strongly. A large part of this growth was due to the continuing influx from the surrounding countryside and from abroad. This time Henry Miller called his in-laws Henry and Amelia LaraBell.[16] Henry's birthplace was given as Finsbury (a district rarely recorded in these early censuses); accurate since he was born in Moorfields. Though his children had the surname 'Bell' many of them (daughters as well as sons) were baptised with 'Lara' as a middle name. His son William Lara Bell used both names as his surname; consequently initiating a family line called Lara Bell.

Henry James's sister Rachel had no such problems since she followed the custom of adopting her new husband's name on marriage, so she became Mrs Rachel Moggridge. Her first child, a son, was named Edward Lara Moggridge – a combination of his paternal grandfather's first name and maternal grandfather's last name. Sadly this boy did not survive, and the name was not given to any of her other children. Rachel herself died in 1837, her age at death indicating she was born in 1792.[17]

The King's shilling

As a part-time soldier in the Loyal Whitechapel Volunteers he was known as Henry James Lara. Henry enlisted under Lieutenant Colonel William Hardy, and War Office pay lists show he joined Thomas Evitt's company in January 1807. He was not yet eighteen. He was paid a shilling for each day's exercise in the volunteers. This usually amounted to just eighteen days a year, but increased when the threats were deemed higher. In 1808 when Napoleon invaded Iberia, declaring his brother Joseph King of Spain, and in 1809 when the Napoleonic wars resumed after a brief period of peace, Henry was called for duty on twenty-eight days. He was listed yearly until 1814, when these records cease. It is quite possible he remained there after this time, because it was not until mid-1815 that the allies finally defeated Napoleon for good at Waterloo. Perhaps he had been in another company earlier, since Henry recorded that he had served for fourteen years in all. Or did he exaggerate somewhat![18] There is nothing else to point to an inaccuracy here since everything else he wrote in the letter to Liverpool has been proved. Thousands of soldiers returned from the war needed jobs and homes. This meant there were large numbers of unemployed in the towns. At the same time more factories were using machinery instead of men, adding to the unemployment and social unrest. This would surely have been contributory to Henry's inability to find work.

By 1819 Henry was, he says: 'reduced to the greatest poverty. I have four small children under nine years of age and I really cannot gain a living for them'. It is for this reason he petitioned Jenkinson for a small situation in the customs house, or the excise office – to no avail. But Henry had also said he was willing to take on any job 'if ever so menial'. What did he end up doing? A job which has long been considered as suitable for frail, old men – not a strong and healthy man of just thirty years!

Hog Lane to Worship Street

He started as a watchman for the Coleman Street ward, working throughout the night for ten hours in winter and seven in summer. He remained in this capacity from at least 1822 to 1830, proved by pay records and court appearances.[19] Henry was attached to the Worship Street police station, Finsbury, living at 12 Edward Place, Old Street Road. Incidentally Worship Street was given this name around 1745, because the first new houses there were redeveloped using building materials from old church at St Mary, Islington. Much more pleasant than the previous name of Hog Lane.

Watchmen

The watchmen would report to the constable on duty to make arrangements. With the allocation of lanterns, candle and armed with a staff, they worked in pairs. One would remain in the watch-house for an hour, whilst the other patrolled the streets in the ward, calling out the hours. The base salary for this work was low, so it was difficult to attract able recruits. Faded copies of the original pay sheets show they all received eleven shillings a week in July 1826, rising to fourteen shillings a week by the end of

January 1830. For those people who remember pre-decimal currency, the former equates to seventy pence in today's money, not taking into account inflation. Though not highly paid work, it was certainly more than labourers would receive. Somehow Henry also found time to work part-time as a watchmaker.

Some men were brave enough to confront offenders and make arrests. Rewards were paid for these and for aiding victims, an excellent inducement.[20] Henry was strong, fit and proactive in his job. As a result of his actions he had to attend the Old Bailey to testify on a number of occasions. Three of his detainees were subsequently transported to Australia, whilst others received short prison sentences.

Peelers

Sir Robert Peel, the Home Secretary, introduced an Act of Parliament creating the Metropolitan Police for London. He wanted to standardise the civil policing, organising it more effectively instead of the hotchpotch of watchmen, Bow Street Runners and others. By September 1829 the first police (known as Peelers), were on duty in London. Their headquarters, then as now, was known as Scotland Yard, named after the street at the rear entrance to the building.

One of the requirements was recruits should be under thirty-five and by then Henry was considered too old to join, so had to leave his position in February 1830.

From detainer to detainee

So now he was once more out of work. In April 1832 he testified on behalf of a friend at the Old Bailey, giving his occupation as a gun-maker. He used the name Henry Lara. There had been many small workshops near the Tower of London, contracting to supply guns to the Board of Ordnance and trading companies such as the East India Company. The work was industrialised around the start of the nineteenth century. Consequently the numbers of small companies declined and by around this time just over half of the gun trade workers in the area came from the east end. Austin Street, where he lived, was a notorious slum area at this time and bordered one side of the new St Leonard church at Shoreditch – designed by George Dance the Elder it was completed a few years earlier in 1736.

When his business failed, in May 1842, he was incarcerated as a debtor in Whitecross Prison[21] Until early in the century debtors had been sent to Newgate Prison and Whitecross was built specifically as a Debtors Prison for London and Middlesex to ease the overcrowding and disease amongst inmates. An etching of the time shows the formidable buildings – several stories high, surrounded by a yard and an outer wall.

Cripplegate coffeehouse

A Parliamentary Paper for the House of Commons – just months after Henry's incarceration – reported it was cleansed and limewashed, in good order with a surgeon in daily attendance. There was a large room provided for inmates so they could, if they wished, choose to work at their trades and keep all the earnings they received. Food, such as bread, tea and coffee, could be brought in and up to a pint of wine a day, though no gambling with dice or cards was allowed. Perhaps it was for this reason that the prison's nickname of Cripplegate coffeehouse was penned![22]

It was possible for insolvent debtors to spend the rest of their lives in prison, so this would be something Henry would be desperate to avoid. *The Gazette* (the main source of all bankruptcy records) indicates he was taken to the Court for Relief of Insolvent Debtors in Portugal Street, Lincoln's Inn Fields, on Thursday, 14 July 1842 at 9.00am. His description was 'Henry Lara, lately lodging at No 7 Godfrey's Place, Austin Street, Hackney Road, Middlesex. Dealer in and repairer of guns, swords and pistols, and general dealer'.[23] Government records then confirm that fortunately for him and his family his debts were forgiven and he was discharged forthwith.[24]

George and Alfred

Henry and Amelia had eight children in all, though the last two did not survive childhood. The date of birth of their third son, George, was written as 23 September 1823 in the Bell family Bible, yet his baptism was not listed at St Leonard, Shoreditch then, or any time soon after. His baptism entry was eventually discovered. This was in 1836 when he was thirteen, and on the same day as his younger brother Alfred, who was by then seven. An earlier Alfred had died aged fourteen months. There were 382 christenings on that day alone, showing how the church served a huge local populace. Their entries were not consecutive: Alfred's was 2146, whereas George's was 2178.[25] Alfred died two years later. The burial was at the St Leonard Church on 14 October 1838, recorded as Alfred Lara Bell, aged eight years.

Though the sad episode which follows occurred after the rule of the Georgian Kings, the event was significant enough to justify its inclusion here. A national system of registration of births, marriages and deaths was introduced shortly after Queen Victoria became monarch. Alfred's registration was the first for this family. He was recorded as Alfred Lara, who died in West London, far away from his home in Austin Street. His body was of course brought back for local burial. Why did he die so far from home? The death certificate told the sad truth. Alfred had died at St Bartholomew's Hospital, West London. The cause of death was 'accidentally shot by a small cannon being fired off in play'. The certificate was signed by William Payne, the Coroner, who registered the death.[26]

The Inquest

Few inquest records survive, but this one did and is stored at the Corporation of London library. It was eventually found in a collection of old documents, so tightly folded together and appearing not to have been disturbed for over 150 years, it seemed they would fall apart at the sharp edges. The proceedings were handwritten, and as people spoke quickly the clerk would have found it a struggle to keep up. Some of his writing is barely more than a squiggle and the paperwork was stored under the misread name of 'Lard'.[27]

Little Alfred had gone off on a mission for his father on the Sunday afternoon just before 3 o'clock with two friends, James Harris and Charles Clarke. They stopped at the back of St Leonard churchyard – very close to his house – the only nearby open space. They watched another older friend, Thomas Baker fire a small cannon which he had placed on a wooden block on the ground. Baker was about thirty yards away and inside the churchyard. One of the pieces of wire he had loaded hit Alfred in the eye. It oozed with blood and would have been incredibly painful. People came running when they heard the screams, including Henry, who first took his son to the local surgeon, and then on his advice to the hospital. Nothing could be done for him. Alfred died in agony the following day.

The constable of the Coleman Street ward, along with members of a jury he had assembled, was presented to the inquest the day after Alfred died. Henry had to give his account of the events and was generous enough to speak up for Thomas Baker 'I am sure there was no malice in the boy'. Baker had previously taken his father's cannon, so it was now locked up. But he found the key and managed to sneak it out all the same. The jury came to the conclusion that 'the said Alfred Lara in manner aforesaid accidentally, casually and by misfortune came to his death and not otherwise'. William Payne, the coroner, and all the jurors signed and sealed against their names.

From this tragic family note, we return several years earlier to Henry's father, Abraham Lara, who had been experiencing problems of his own, but not before a final note on his two children.

Henry passed away in 1855, and his widow Amelia lived until she was eighty-four. She might well have lived in some poverty during this time, without the meagre support her husband could provide, had it not been for family support. Her younger spinster sister, Lydia Moggridge, predeceased her and bequeathed to Amelia all the dividends and interests of her investments for Amelia's natural lifetime. When she died the securities were to be sold. A number of relations then inherited, including Amelia's daughter Henrietta, son William Lara Bell, and three of their children. Other bequests went to her nephews, John and Robert, sons of Robert Moggridge and Rachel, née Lara/Bell.

A rock

Retirement was not an option for the masses. Most people worked until they died. Abraham was definitely still working four years before his death, because in 1812 he said 'your petitioner has been in business upwards of 45 years with credit and reputation'. His own father, Daniel, had died in October 1767, so this suggests he started full-time work around 1766. As a child he would have attended the school attached to Bevis Marks, and possibly been assisted in a short apprenticeship, perhaps to a jeweller. He also said he had 'many severe losses' in his working life, which suggests his business acumen was tested more than has been shown here.

The letter included the statement that 'his character bearing the nicest scrutiny has brought up a numerous family'. He had but four children. This was hardly a large family in those days, so what did he mean by this? For a start, as the eldest son he would have borne the most responsibility in providing for his widowed mother and younger siblings. But these alone do not constitute 'a numerous family'. He may also have had his aunt in her diminished circumstances in mind when choosing those words. Then there was his sister Esther who would have needed both caring brotherly help and financial support in some unusual circumstances. And finally of course there were Uncle Isaac and Abraham's three cousins who were little short of destitute on their arrival to London and largely reliant on him for four years.

An unfortunate man

Londoners, if not others, will have heard of Brick Lane: infamous for nineteenth-century rioting, and again later on come to that! It was so named after the brick and tile manufacturing trade which had grown up there using local products. Brick Lane is in the East End (now a highly sought-after area) but in 1799 was far from salubrious. This was where Abraham found himself in his later years, a world away from his far more pleasant earlier surroundings in Moorfields, Finsbury.

His reduced circumstances forced him to live amongst the poor and unskilled immigrants attracted here: originally the Huguenots (who by now had mostly moved up and out), but then the impoverished Irish and the Ashkenazi Jews from Eastern Europe. Nowadays the Brick Lane street sign has its name repeated underneath in Bengali, so although this area is fast becoming a desirable (and therefore expensive) place to live, it still houses a huge concentration of immigrant families.

The Sephardic congregation to whom he belonged were generally more prosperous and so unlikely to be found there. This was a very low point in Abraham's life. The land tax assessments – for which he was liable – placed him in Osborn Place, off Brick Lane. Osborn Place was the part which connected Whitechapel High Street to the southern stretch of the lengthy Brick Lane. A trade directory at this time shows our man in a similar trade to his early years, advertising his services as a watchmaker, but clearly not a trade dependant on the high value stones he had used in previous years.[28]

He was here at Brick Lane for at least four years. By 1812 Abraham had moved to a slightly better area: off Kingsland Road, near St Leonard Shoreditch Parish. It was from 26 Crescent, Kingsland Road (stating he was late of Moorfields) that Abraham Lara Junior wrote his letter to the Treasury on 20 January 1812. The address is near where he had lived with Rebecca when they had started their family.

1816 was known by many names, one of which was 'The Year without a Summer'. Fog, cold and rain heralded in the year, and the weather showed no signs of improvement later on. In June there was snow. Harvests throughout Europe failed. Consequently, there were famines and hunger strikes. This was the year Abraham died. His burial took place at the new cemetery of the Spanish and Portuguese Jews' Congregation situated in Mile End Road. The register entry gives his full name as Abraham Nunes Lara, son of Daniel, buried on 15 May 1816. Though full names were rarely used in life, they were invariably recorded at momentous events such as this. Would his son Henry have been allowed to make the arrangements? As he was not a Jew, no. It is more likely to have been one of his cousins

(Abraham Senior, Phineas or Moses). Abraham would have wanted to have been buried there, in the same cemetery as his parents and son.[29]

It sounds as though it weighed heavily upon Abraham that in spite of all his endeavours he was reduced to such low circumstances and saw no brighter prospects for his children. This vision of an 'unfortunate man' – the term used by Henry James to describe his father – is far removed from the confident happy portrait of his youth. At the start, the question was posed as to when and why did Abraham have this etching of himself made?

Dressing to impress

These questions can now be addressed. In the year 1784 he would have wanted to impress Dr Pretyman and give himself the confidence boost to meet with the 'ruling classes' within their elegant surroundings. Most people would want to dress smartly and appropriately for an appointment at the office of the prime minister. Abraham, looking forward to a bright, prosperous and successful life, would surely have wanted to record the moment this was all about to happen. This suggests the etching was produced soon after he bought the outfit, probably in mid 1784.

He, along with his son Henry, may have continued hoping – against all the odds – that the government would pay for some of the ideas that Abraham had been encouraged to pass on and consult with Prime Minister Pitt's First Secretary. But recompense for his resourcefulness in devising a scheme (and as such helping to frame some methods to help address the national debt), did not come. The findings of the court action against Bird in an attempt to retrieve his loans was also unsuccessful. He did inherit from Uncle Isaac.

What's in a name?

The other consideration was his supposed name, that of Henrico de Lara. It turns out that was not so far away from his real name, if you drop the 'Abraham' part of it. Henrico de Lara, as a surname, is very close to his actual surname of Nunes de Lara. The grandfather of Abraham, his siblings and all the cousins mentioned in these pages, was called José Nunes de Lara. He died in Portugal. This fact has already been revealed by Jewish historians. But it was not previously known that the wife of José was Maria Henriques, nor that she came to London with some of her children. With heavy Portuguese pronunciation, and the final syllable of the word 'Henriques' accentuated, her name would have sounded just like Henrico. Perhaps this was the reason the name Henrico de Lara was handed down through the generations. His only surviving son was named Henry, a typical English name, yet with hints of his ancestry.

The end of the beginning

Abraham's life experiences with its hopes, trials and pleasures were, like for most people, intertwined with those of his relatives. Incredibly there are fascinating stories to tell about many of them. This is the end of the journey for Abraham – and now it seems appropriate to take a look at the life of his sister, Esther.

Judith and Esther Curry

> Infamy, infamy, they've all got it in for me
> *Kenneth Williams, Carry on Cleo*

Abraham's two sisters were called Judith and Esther. Along with their brother Jacob they were the four children of Rachel and Daniel Nunes de Lara.

Their father, Daniel, died intestate in 1767 with insufficient assets for his widow to feel the need to take out an administration for him. All of his children were underage at the time. The following year their uncle Aaron died. He was their mother's brother. Aaron Lara was wealthy and, as the following extract of his will shows, he kindly included some provision for his niece:

> Give and bequeath unto my niece Sarah Lara, daughter of Mr Daniel Nunes de Lara, the sum of One Hundred Pounds to be paid and payable to her on her attaining the age of twenty-one years or marriage which shall first happen, the principal to be invested and the interest paid to her as it shall become due.

Only one niece was mentioned and he called her Sarah. Where does she fit in? Clearly Judith and Esther nearly didn't get a dowry from their uncle Aaron, but things worked out well in the end. Of course there had been a mistake. When it was discovered, a correction was made within a codicil to his will. In effect Aaron Lara changed the name of Sarah to Judith and also made the same provision – one hundred pounds on marriage or at age twenty-one – for her younger sister Esther.[1]

In families it is often the women who keep in touch with other family members. Aaron's young wife Rachel had died a few years earlier, so with his unexpected sad loss and the continued need to care for his own family, it is not surprising he misremembered names of some of his nieces.

Unlike business documents, where 'Errors and Omissions Excepted' (E&OE) may be employed as a disclaimer against legal liability, there is no such redress for a will. The executors would have a problem in providing Judith with the inheritance intended for her (proof that Sarah was really Judith might be problematic, time-consuming and costly against the estate). And there would be absolutely nothing for a sister who was not mentioned.

Someone told him that his niece's name was Judith, and that his sister Rachel had another daughter called Esther. Presumably that informant was either his daughter Sarah (who was to be one of the executors) or his widowed sister Rachel. Aaron must have been aware of his own grave ill health, and made haste to correct this since the codicil was written, signed and sealed just eighteen days later. Two months later he died.

When were they born?

It is speculated that Abraham, the eldest, was born around 1748, so Judith was probably born a year or two later and Esther in the early 1750s. A burial entry for Esther gives her age at death in 1813 as sixty-two. If – and it's a big if – it really is an entry for this Esther, then that links up conveniently with a birth year of 1751. If this is her burial, that is…

The short life of Judith Nunes Lara

Why might Aaron have thought Judith was called Sarah? It was a perfectly natural mistake, since eldest daughters were invariably named Sarah after the oldest female relative in the Lara family. But their mother Rachel appeared to have a closer relationship with her sister Judith so this might have been the reason for a different name. Another possibility is that one of her numerous babies who did not survive had been called Sarah and she might not want to use this name a second time.

Both sisters married in the same year: 1771. First was Judith. Her husband was Jacob Ancona, son of Judah and Sarah Ancona.[2] They married three months before her cousin Aaron (named after his father), whose wife was to be Rachel d'Israeli (the future half-aunt of Benjamin Disraeli, one of our most well-known prime ministers). Judith died seven years later.[3] There is no evidence of the couple having children. Three years after that, in 1791, her widower married a second time to Sarah, daughter of David Haim Supino and Rachel Pereira de Paiba. Farewell, Judith.

The complex life of Esther Nunes Lara

Had Esther not married, or simply married and had an 'ordinary' life, then her story would be even shorter than that for her sister. But it is not. She did marry, and it is due to her husband that over 260 years after her birth we know something of their lives.

Esther married Elias Cunha on 21 August 1771. Even by the time of their marriage he was accustomed to using the alias Curry. The spelling for these early registers is often phonetic, and it was recorded as Corre, a close approximation.[4]

The dowries of Judith and Esther sound comparatively small (considering the £1500 dowries Aaron gave each of his own three daughters). However even a small amount would have been gratefully received as it meant the family were spared from having to go 'cap in hand' to the congregation to apply for a special grant. In fact, one hundred pounds then was not insubstantial at all. A House of Commons library research report using various price indexes suggests that £100 in 1768 would be equivalent to an income of £8974 by 1999.[5] Their mother Rachel definitely received the dividends towards their maintenance and education until the time they married, as confirmed in one of the numerous chancery documents arising from the trust fund established as a result of Aaron's will.[6]

Esther's husband was born in Portugal, as were her own parents. The Sephardic congregation of Bevis Marks Synagogue provided for Elias until he was old enough to make his way in the world. His father was presumed dead. The evidence for this lies in the absence of his name in the ketubah (marriage contract) for Esther and Elias. It was standard practice to include the family name unless the father had never been a member of the congregation. Thus Esther was recorded as a daughter of Daniel Nunes de Lara, whilst Elias's father's name was omitted. There are however a few references to be found of a Moses Curry, and a mention of his mother, so it is probable that Elias came over with them as a boy, rather than taking the unusual step of a youngster journeying on his own.

An early reference to Elias was when he became a godfather to Isaac Soares, six years before he married Esther.[7]

Esther and Elias had a son the year after their marriage, whom they named Isaac. Both alternative last names of Cunha and Curry were recorded. His name Elias had on occasions been spelt as Eliau; this time in the Bevis Marks index Elias's name was mistranscribed as Elijah. Eight days later, 3 June 1772, their son was circumcised, with Isaac Gomes Serra as godfather and Esther's mother Rachel Nunes Lara as godmother.[8] Isaac died less than a month later and was buried according to Jewish traditions.[9] They had no other babies.

On the way up

Only those persons who were comfortably off and confident in their future would choose to become denizens of Great Britain. It was not a cheap option, though one considered essential if you had assets you freely wanted to pass on to your heirs. This was Elias's choice, so he must have considered himself to be on the path to a settled and successful life at this time. The Court Rolls of King George III, which can be seen at the National Archives, provide the following basic details:

Elias Curry of Bevis Marks, London, Merchant, Alien born was denized 3 May 1774[10]

This entry confirms he was living at Bevis Marks. This can be confusing as it is the name of the street, as well as of the synagogue.

Land tax assessments for London confirm he was paying taxes under the name of Elias Currie. There are entries for every year from 1781–1787 at Bevis Marks, Aldgate, City of London Ward.[11] It was not the custom in this ward to name the streets, but once in 1784 the address was recorded in full as Camomile Street. This street was next to St Mary Axe, Berry/Bury Court and Bevis Marks. Given that his name occurred in the book in the same sequence throughout this period and that the rent remained in the order of £1 19s, all the indications are he was probably living in Camomile Street for some years.

In nearby Bevis Marks Rachel, Esther's mother, lived until her death in 1785. Also there were her aunt Judith and brother Jacob Lara. Nowadays these are in spitting distance of a well-known London feature nicknamed the Gherkin.

Infamy, infamy, they've all got it in for me...

Barely a year later, in 1785, there was a terrible scandal surrounding Elias. The circumstances of this were quoted in *Sketches of Anglo-Jewish History*.[12] This article was written in the mid 1800s. It is a one-sided, pro-Jew diatribe, derisive against anyone who flouted the authority of the Mahamad (the ruling body of the synagogue) in the least degree, so best read in that context. Here are some quotes from the treatise which relate to Elias Curry:

It starts off with 'the case of Elias Curry...the person who adopted this pseudonym.' Every person who fled from persecution to the safe shores of England, on becoming a member of the congregation dropped their Roman Catholic baptised name and adopted a Jewish name. Enter Elias Cunha. It seems he soon preferred to use an alternative last name, Curry. So too did his brother Moses. This change may well have flouted the strict rules of the Sephardi and the way this introduction to the 'case' of Elias Curry is worded gives a clue to the tone of the article.

In his cups

Like many others at the time Elias attended the synagogue 'tolerably regularly'. Later rumours spread that Elias had turned to drink, indulging in 'fiery liquors' and whilst 'in his cups' had boasted that he was now a baptised Christian. The assertion he had been 'converted to Christianity over a bowl of punch, and the rum which it contained no doubt exercised a lively influence in changing his theological opinions' sounds about right. A drink-befuddled mind is not a thinking mind.

The archaic expression 'in his cups' refers to a drunkard. The same expression is used in the book *Twelve Years a Slave* referring to Edwin Epps, who was a plantation and slave owner.[13]

Members of the faith are allowed to drink, but moderation is key. They would not tolerate overindulgence with the disgraceful behaviour which often accompanies it. Elias's drunken behaviour would be considered abhorrent and a disgrace, but it seems no one confronted him about it or tried to find out the reasons behind his changed behaviour. Instead a member of the congregation who had heard reports of his drunken boasts 'took considerable pains to ascertain the truth of the reports; he searched the baptismal register of various churches.'

Take your pick – churches are ten a penny

At this time there were a considerable number of parish churches in the locality. The search would have been no mean feat. The informant expended a lot of time and effort on this and was clearly determined to find out the truth. Even today with the wealth of indexes often freely available to peruse, this entry is not so simple to find. The investigator had to go as far afield as the parish church of West Ham before he was successful.

This is at Stratford, known as All Saints. The original church was built in the twelfth century. Although largely rural Stratford was one of the most populated places in Essex and by the eighteenth century the parish was extensive. Unsurprisingly the later build is a vast edifice. Stratford was known as the Gateway to London, because of its position; now even more so with the regeneration of the Olympic site in its midst. These days, in spite of falling congregations, the mission is clear: to give hope and inspiration to the parish. The Church records are no longer kept in situ. Unlike the inquisitive member of the Bevis Marks, one has to go all the way to Chelmsford where the Essex Record Office is based.

The entry in the Baptism Register for All Saints Church, like all the others, was short and precise.[14] It said: *Baptised 6 April 1785 Elias Curry an Adult Jew.*

The incumbent vicar signed at the end of each page as W Cropley. His full name, is Reverend William Cropley, is listed in the guide to the parish church as being the vicar of that church from 1775–1804. The eighteenth-century sleuth spoke to Reverend Green who confirmed he had performed the baptism. There is no record of him at the church or in the registers so he must have been a curate, probably the person responsible for day-to-day activities such as baptisms. Rev Green is reported to have said, 'Before the latter could be recognised as Christian, he considered it was necessary to perform again the ceremony which had not been attended with due solemnity.'

There is nothing to show that he had any such reservations at the time, or made any attempt to follow this up, but this comment does indicate he was aware Elias Curry may not have taken the ceremony seriously.

What's to be done?

When the wardens of the Portuguese congregation were informed of the situation, they decided to dismiss Elias Curry from the community. We are told this occurred 'early in 1785'. It is further stated that in April of that year (in other words, following his baptism) 'Elias Curry wrote an insolent letter to the Mahamad, in which with affected contempt for that body, whom he designated by the novel designation of "little court" or "tribunal of great injustice wherein Prince Satan presides as First Lord", he took leave of those to whom he was beholden for many benefits.' Oops. The elders wouldn't have liked that one little bit – and they had a long memory...

We further hear: 'For once ingratitude and want of principle met with condign punishment. Elias Curry did not prosper in his new creed. He became poor; he became unhappy; he became conscience-stricken. In 1791 the burden of remorse became more than he could bear, and his heart longed to return to his old faith and early associations. He wrote a most penitent letter to the authorities of his community entreating their forgiveness, and craving to be received back into the synagogue. He was not satisfied with the refusal he received; he prayed again to be admitted as a proselyte, which he thought would be facilitated by his being a foreigner, and he offered in vain to make any atonement, to undergo any penance. A year after this, the elders, who would not open their arms to Elias Curry in life, granted him six feet of ground in death. At first, indeed, they refused; but the entreaties of a relative, the tears of his mother, had their effect. Three witnesses declared that the sinner had made a solemn recantation on his deathbed, and that he departed this life a sincere Jew. The wardens consulted the beth din, and eventually the wretched man was interred in a corner of the cemetery.'

Around about 1785, Elias was clearly in desperate need of emotional support, and probably financial assistance, yet none appears to have been forthcoming from his fellow Jews. He took his desperate solace in drink, and made rash decisions when he was not in full control of himself. What about the man who was looking for him? He was no doubt a zealous, pious person. This could be justification enough for him to want to find out for certain about the rumours which had come to his attention. Was he tasked with this undertaking on the auspices of the ruling body?

Rules are rules

This article shows how strict the Mahamad were if anyone flouted their authority. It was this rigidness which forced the departure of others from their community, including relations and friends of the Lara family: Isaac Mendes Furtado, the Bernals, and Isaac D'Israeli to name a few. The synagogue had their rules, so were entitled to ensure everyone adhered to them. They clearly did not believe the path of humanity and forgiveness brings its own rewards.

Elias came to a very sad end! He did not know at his deathbed that he would be allowed to be buried in accordance with his true beliefs. That he was – grudgingly and not even in the main cemetery – would no doubt have afforded some comfort to his family, but the change of heart came too late for him.

Out of sight…

The registers for Bevis Marks show he was buried in 1792 'behind the board'. His name was recorded solely of Eliau Cunha, rather than the name he had used for several years.[15] Another slight? The unusual term of 'behind the boards' is applied to a specific area of the cemetery, away from the main Carreira (regular rows). It was set aside for burials of recognised Jews, who for religious or moral reasons were not permitted in the Carreira.

In the introductory section to this register under the heading 'Burials: Behind the Boards and Under Other Restriction'[16] is a note concerning Elias Curry, which is included in full below:

'The first burial recorded in the Novo registers in the periods between 1792 and 1820 was that of Eliau Cunha, alias Curry, in August 1792. He had been baptised in 1785 but later repented. His fervent appeal to the Mahamad in 1791 for forgiveness and readmission to the community fell on deaf ears. However, shortly before his death his brother-in-law, Jacob (de Daniel) Nunes Lara, petitioned the Mahamad on his behalf. The Mahamad relented and agreed, subject to the permission of the beth din, to allow the burial.'

It is good to know his brother-in-law, Jacob, supported this request so strongly. A petition from him would carry more weight than one from her elder brother Abraham, since Jacob had remained within the congregation. Was he one of the three witnesses at his deathbed? Elias was clearly surrounded by loving, compassionate family at his demise.

It should be noted that the Church of England was then no gentler in their approach, with people – even babies, who had died before being baptised – often not allowed to be buried in hallowed ground and so interred outside the churchyard.

Now here's the conundrum

Let us return a few years. The above account definitely states Elias had become poor after 1785, the year of his Christian baptism. We have already seen he lived at and around Bevis Marks until at least 1787. Yet then he appears to have moved to a more expensive property, judging by the amount of tax he had to pay as tenant. It is understandable he would want to move away from the neighbourhood of the synagogue after such a major falling out with the congregation. It was only in 1784 that he had become denized, so had his prospects – so recently considered good – gone sour suddenly? If so, was it mainly due to the drink and new companionships he had mistakenly taken as friends, or had he made some poor business decisions? If his fortunes had changed rapidly, then how did he afford the move, the rents, and the rates? Was he supported by family?

For 1787 there were two entries in the tax assessments for him; one at Bevis Marks and the other in Moorfields. This was not unusual. One explanation for this may be when tenants moved they were often beholden to both areas. From this year onwards at his new lodgings his name was spelt as Elias Curry. This was also the spelling he used when he addressed himself to the Mahamad in 1785 and 1791. He was educated so this has to be the correct spelling of his name. The new home for Elias and Esther was in the Fourth Precinct of the Coleman Street Ward, within the City of London.

The assessments there continue without break for the period 1787 until 1793.[17] The rent was always round about £31, considerably more than at their previous address, with taxes of well over £5 being payable. No specific address was given, but the 1792 assessment clearly shows the property was close by Bethlem Royal Hospital. This is in Moorfields, which tells us he had moved close to Esther's other brother, Abraham.

Home is where the heart is

Abraham, Jacob and their surviving sister Esther had an aunt called Judith Mendes da Solas. In her will she stated she had moved to Moorfields. It seems this was shortly before December 1788. Judith was aunt to all the Lara cousins, and sister to this particular family's mother, Rachel Nunes de Lara. In her old age and time of greatest need of assistance, when she could no longer cope on her own, to whom did she turn?

She had many nieces and nephews who were affluent and could easily have afforded to help support her. Judith was most certainly closer to Rachel and her family as they had all lived in and around Bevis Marks, when the more affluent relatives had moved onwards and upwards. Two of the others (Joshua and Aaron, sons of her brother Aaron Lara) had already died so it would be a dead loss to consider aid from them.

So this is what happened. She sold all her property and furniture, left the house in Bevis Marks where she had been living for very many years and moved in with her niece Esther and her husband Elias Curry. It is a measure of her gratitude for this hospitality from Esther, as well as from her brothers Abraham and Jacob, that we have an insight into the kind and caring side of this little family grouping. It was they, and not the others, who came to her aid.

Was it Abraham who helped towards the rent for this property? It is only speculation, but if the reports of Elias's inability to earn a good living are correct, this is one possible solution. Another is that another relative – Moses Curry perhaps – helped out.

Aunt Judith lived with her niece for around four years and died just a couple of months before Elias. She left a small will in which she left her few possessions jointly to her sister Sarah and her niece

Esther. This had been written some years earlier, and as it happened her sister Sarah's death had preceded her. This meant that whatever Judith had, however little, it all came to Esther.[18]

What does a poor widow do?

Elias Curry died in August 1792. Esther had few options: she either had to have a new husband to support her, or one of her brothers had to take on this responsibility if she was not to be totally impoverished. By now Abraham's fortunes had changed, and neither brother was in a position to greatly help her out. She remarried. Esther married Moses, the presumed brother of Elias. They married according to the rites of the Jewish faith and the entry in the marriage contracts states: *Moses Curry (alias Moses Mendes Cunha) and Ester de Eliau Cunha*.[19]

She didn't have to move either. The tax assessments, though not a true census and open to interpretation, give the occupier of that same property from the year 1793 as Moses Curry. The level of assessment was still about the same as before and there is no doubt he was now the tenant of this same property in Coleman Street Ward.[20]

Moses' name is flagged up continuously until 1803 when the occupier is given as Late Moses Curry. This indicates Moses had either moved, or died.[21]

Actually he moved. The efficient transcription of the Bevis Marks Burial Registers reveals that Moses (Mendes) Cunha or Curry did not die until 1815.[22]

So it looks as though Esther was settled. All we need to know now is when did she die? Actually it turns out that just finding (or not) her burial will not end speculation as to her life after marriage to Moses. There's a twist.

The registers show that Moses married a second time. This was again at Bevis Marks and less than two years after his marriage to Esther. There are very few references to anyone called Cunha or Curry, and no one else other than his late brother Elias had both names, so it is pretty certain it was her second husband to whom this marriage relates.[23]

Where's the evidence?

This suggests that Esther died between her marriage date in March 1793 and his second marriage in January 1795. Perhaps she died in childbirth, thus enabling Moses to take another wife? If she was interred at the burial ground for Bevis Marks then her name has been missed out from the index. This possibility has to be considered, albeit most unlikely. Another one is that she might have been buried elsewhere – possibly even a Christian burial? A search has revealed just one possible entry.

There is a burial in the Parish of St Saviour, Southwark, for Esther Curry. She lived at Lambeth (and it was not the workhouse as this would have been mentioned) and the burial took place on 16 September 1813. This is two years before the death of Moses. There are no other burials with the family name Curry in that area. It stands as an individual entry. Her age at death – sixty-two years – indicates the Esther Curry buried here was born in 1751. Now that's a coincidence: exactly when we surmise our Esther would have been born.

So if it was her, why was she in Lambeth, or more intriguingly, how did her second husband Moses manage to remarry when she was still alive?

But, consider another option. Perhaps the marriage did not work out to their satisfaction. One, or both of them, could have wanted to separate. If it was *his* choice, they could.

Jews were exempt from the English laws for divorce which required an Act of Parliament if either of the parties wished to remarry. So how did members of the Jewish faith deal with this issue? They had their own laws which enabled a man to divorce if he was so determined. To do this he would first need to obtain a 'Get', which is a Hebrew word for a divorce document. The husband would then need to present it to his wife to effect their divorce. The text of the Get essentially decrees that 'You are hereby permitted to all men' – in other words she is no longer a married woman.

Was Esther divorced by Moses? If so the burial for 1813 may yet be hers. If not, her burial prior to 1795 has still to be found.

Jacob Lara and the Buzaglos

> I am the God of thy father, the God of Abraham,
> the God of Isaac, and the God of Jacob
> *Exodus Chapter 3, v6*

Jacob Nunes de Lara lived in Jamaica and was denized as a British citizen on 27 February 1750.[1] Another man by the same name was born in the early 1750s in London, the city where he lived out his life. To find two people called Jacob Lara would not be a huge surprise, but two by the complex name of Jacob Nunes de Lara? That combination is unexpected and unusual. So it's a good reminder that family historians shouldn't presume that they have found the 'right' person simply because they have found a reference to the name they are seeking. Supporting evidence is vital.

The red herring

How and when the elder Jacob came to be in Jamaica, and his family origins, remains a mystery. He would have been at least in his mid twenties by 1750, so there is a good chance he moved there from Portugal and was a relation of the Nunes de Lara siblings who decided to come to England (and generally dropped the 'Nunes de' part of their surname for all but official synagogue records). Fortunately the physical distance between the two Jacobs and the twenty years or so age gap helps keep the two identities separate.

Our London-based Jacob was the younger brother of Abraham, Judith and Esther – and the son of Daniel and Rachel Nunes de Lara. The first reference we have for him was his marriage in 1778 according to the rite of the Bevis Marks Synagogue when he would have been in his late twenties. His bride was Leah, daughter of Jacob Buzaglo.[2] How apt. Leah was the name of the first wife of the Biblical Jacob.[3]

Her parents' marriage was also in those registers, indicating her father Jacob was the son of Moses Buzaglo and mother Elisabeth (recorded as Elisebah) was the daughter of Jacob Salom Morenu.[4] Jacob and Leah did not have children. She was some years older than him which might explain it.

Bah humbug

Genealogia Hebraica includes a selection of the more important families of Portugal.[5] It appears to have a rather haphazard choice of entries and – at least for those connected with the Lara family – is inaccurate, or at the very least incomplete. There is a mention of Jacob and Elizabeth Buzaglo with their three children: Ester, Lea and Rachel (sic). These appear likely to have been born some time after the marriage with at least one earlier baby not surviving. The eldest, Esther, married Moses Masias in 1764 and went on to have a large family.[6] Rachel, the youngest sister, married a year after Leah to Samuel de Moses Cohen.[7] This couple also had a family.

According to this book Jacob and Elizabeth had a family of three girls. Incorrect! There were two brothers also. The eldest (Elias/Elijah) was a translator/interpreter and he was the man who assisted Abraham Lara, his brother-in-law, in an attempt to resolve a major financial problem. This was recorded in the story about Abraham and his diamonds. The second son was called Aaron.

Jacob Lara, his sisters Judith and Esther, along with their parents Daniel and Rachel are also in the aforementioned book. But there is no mention of his brother Abraham. Nor are the other

Laras from Portugal or Spain mentioned at all, so quite possibly this particular entry is there by virtue of Jacob's link with the Buzaglo family. And what a family they were!

The amazing clan of Buzaglo

The lengthy article by Cecil Roth entitled 'The Amazing Clan of Buzaglo' is fascinating, well-researched, and well worth a read.[8] This is a complex tale of the Buzaglos, of whom Leah's father, Jacob, is the stay-at-home merchant brother.

Of direct relevance to this tale was Leah Moreau, maternal aunt and namesake of Leah Buzaglo. Her marriage was also to one of the Buzaglos: Leah's paternal uncle Joseph Buzaglo. Roth says of him, 'If in the annals of the eighteenth century there was any career more fantastic than his it has escaped the notice of the present writer.'

That's a sweeping statement. What did Joseph do to warrant this? He and wife Leah had one son, called Solomon, who was born around 1733. He was set to be a wealthy adult, as he had many large legacies which would be paid to him when he reached twenty-one. Solomon's mother, Leah, died when he was a baby. His father is reputed to have remarried twice; both times abroad. So far nothing much out of the ordinary! But then the 'fun' bit starts… Joseph was abroad for most of Solomon's childhood, much of this time not by choice! For some (unknown) reason he was sentenced by the French to work on the galleys for ten years. Coming out of this alive would have been a major achievement. You'd think he would stay clear of France after this, especially as leaving the country was a condition of his release. But no, he continued to travel and conduct business there, ending up in the Bastille on a charge of spying for England. Eventually he was released, after which he became an intermediary/interpreter to the Danish government, for whom he went to Morocco. More problems! There he was imprisoned and sentenced to death by burning (along with his brother Abraham who was his assistant). Thankfully both were later pardoned through the efforts of an intermediary. In the meantime his neglected son Solomon was in London, most unhappy, and he ran away from home to be a soldier in a Dutch regiment. He was underage so not yet able to receive his inheritances. He hated the climate in Guiana, a Dutch colony in the West Indies, and wrote back asking for funds to pay off his discharge so he could return home. These never materialised and it was years before his father came home and discovered this. Distraught at the news, he straight away went looking for Solomon so he could bring him back to England. However, he died in 1761 before he found him. It is reputed his son died soon afterwards. Solomon's inheritances could not be paid out until his death could be proven, nor the substantial wealth that Joseph had accumulated over the years. Both deaths took many years to prove. In the meantime the money was held in a trust in chancery. Now came the dogfight. The money was up for grabs. Relatives fought for precedence and one of Joseph's brothers came up with a plan which he hoped might improve his own family's fortunes.

Who might be eligible? Along with the maternal line, the Morenus, there were all Joseph Buzaglo's brothers. One of these was Jacob, father of Leah and Jacob Lara's father-in-law. Joseph and Jacob Buzaglo had married sisters: Elisabeth and Leah Morenu. Under the Rules of Intestacy, both Jacob Buzaglo and his wife Elizabeth (née Morenu) would be eligible to inherit as they were uncle and aunt to Solomon in their own right. Elisabeth died four years after her nephew Solomon[9], but as she was still alive during his lifetime, her share could still be claimed by her husband, and after he died – if nothing had been paid out by then – their claims passed to their sons and daughters, including Leah Lara.

Another of Joseph's other brothers was the widower Shalom, a Kabbalist who had come to England from Morocco after experiencing torture by fire at the hands of the Sultan. He had four children by his first marriage and decided to marry Joseph's widow (and third wife) Esther Bentubo. At the same time he arranged the marriage of his only daughter Rosa Esther to her uncle Abraham, the fourth brother.[10] No doubt he felt these two marriages would enhance the prospects of the inheritance staying with the Buzaglos, and more particularly with his own family. Brother number five was Isaac, who was living in Jerusalem.

…surpass in utility, beauty and goodness anything hitherto invented in all Europe

Unlike his brother Joseph, Abraham returned to England after their death sentences in Morocco were reprieved. About a year later he married his niece (Rosa Esther), and settled down as an inventor – quite a change from his previous advertised occupation as a tanner, specialising in Moroccan shoes. It may have been the cold weather he experienced on return (particularly compared with Africa) which caused him to be inspired to invent and develop a coal-burning heater, for which he obtained letters patent in 1765.[11] He marketed it as suitable for every type of community, ranging from churches, public offices, large shops, greenhouses, to private homes. He even said it was suitable for children's nurseries, as the equipment was considered accident-proof. According to his advertisements there would be no need for repairs in a hundred years, no dust, a far lower consumption of coal than other stoves, surpassing anything ever invented in all Europe. It all sounds too good to be true.

But he wasn't finished yet. He also promoted its use for health remedies, especially for those prone to gout. Could he have noticed the relief in suffering gained for those sufferers living in hotter climes and made the connection?

Denization

Jacob Buzaglo, Leah's father, applied for British denization, which was granted on 30 April 1772.[12] This suggests his finances were healthy at this time. He was described as Jacob Buzaglo the Younger, which indicates an elder Jacob (an uncle?) was alive at that time. Of the seven being denized that day, a second was Abraham Mendes Furtado, a close relative of Jacob Nunes de Lara. Abraham had come to England as a child with his mother Clara

Mendes Furtado, and several other family members, including her cousin Rachel Lara. Shortly after, Rachel married Daniel Nunes de Lara and Jacob was their younger son. Others in this wider family had been denized together the previous year. These were Abraham's brother Isaac Mendes Furtado, Leah's uncle Abraham Buzaglo and Jacob's uncle Benjamin Lara. All three Mendes Furtado brothers (Abraham, Isaac and Jacob) had witnessed the will of Abraham Buzaglo back in 1763. It is clear there was a close relationship between these families.

Just two years later in 1774, business went far from well for Jacob Buzaglo and he was forced to file for bankruptcy. So it seems the family could now benefit from financial assistance. Did they still nurture the hope the Buzaglos and Morenus would inherit from Solomon Buzaglo? By the time Jacob and Leah married, one imagines they were all sufficiently realistic about the poor prospects of this. Because no such thing happened. There is talk the money was lost in speculation (with the South Sea Company) or else in the costs arising from the prolonged litigation: the lawsuit opened in 1767 and dragged on until as late as 1791.

So yes, Leah had some eccentric near-relatives. Jacob Lara had his fair share of spirited cousins and brother, but by any comparison his own life was pretty pedantic.

He was mentioned in the minutes of Bevis Marks (stored at the London Metropolitan Archives). This was because he had needed to go to the Court of Elders in an attempt to force repayment of a loan he made to Isaac Gomes de Costa. This man was later to marry Esther, the daughter of Leah's cousin Jacob. The loan was overdue, so Lara went to the Court of Elders to press his second demand. At this hearing, on 27 January 1778, de Costa was given ten to fifteen days longer to repay the sum due of four pounds and four shillings. Full payment would satisfy the terms of the licence in keeping with the Jewish laws of the land. Both these reports were written in Portuguese.[13]

On another occasion he also called on Daniel Henriques Valentine, who he said borrowed four guineas from him about a year ago, and an extra half-guinea was also due as profit on some transaction. Valentine acknowledged the debt and said a Mr J Lurria a relative of his wife) would be security. He promised to pay one guinea a month. Lara agreed on the condition Mr Lurria made that promise in the presence of Mr Saa, and this was done. Though neither of these loans was substantial, it is an indication that Jacob did have some 'spare' cash available.

The next reference to him was again found at the London Metropolitan Archives, for a land tax assessment in 1791.[14] Jacob lived at Bevis Marks, in the parish of Catherine Cree, in Aldgate Ward Four. He paid £2 12s 0d for rates for a property at Bevis Marks (the street). After the collaboration between the LMA and Ancestry to digitise these records, the land tax records for much of the City of London have now become available online from mid 2012, making it easier to find Jacob in other years. These records showed he lived at Bevis Marks from 1790 until 1799. We know why he lived there, and what his profession was, by virtue of a mention in Holden's London Directory for 1799. His full address was given as 19 Bevis Marks and he was stated to be a pastry cook.

Following in his father's footsteps

This choice of occupation was unsurprising for two reasons. His father, Daniel, had been a renowned pastry cook. A house/bakery situated in Bevis Marks was perfect for serving the Sephardic congregation at Bevis Marks Synagogue, and also for the Ashkenazi worshippers at the nearby Great Synagogue.

Then his mother took over her husband's business on his death and her address was 19 Bevis Marks.[15] Jacob was probably working with her all that time, and more than likely even living at the same premises. There were after all only about eight properties in this small street. The Laras would have been working and dealing from this one house. They would not have had a separate shop. So with this type of work, he was never going to get rich, but had regular work!

His aunt Judith also lived in this small street. Could she have shared a property with her sister? Might this also have been where her nephew Jacob and wife Leah lived?

Leah may well have assisted her husband in his work, just as his mother before him had for his father. If so, they would have been very busy people in a physically hot and tiring environment. Leisure time from an extended working day would be limited. When Aunt Judith became frail and finally could not manage without extra help, they would hardly have been in a position to look after her properly. What was she to do? Which relatives would look after her? In the stories of Jacob's siblings, Abraham and Esther, we have already heard that their aunt Judith had more contact with them and Jacob than her other nieces and nephews, and it was agreed she would move to Moorfields to stay with Esther. Jacob and Abraham would have been instrumental in making arrangements for this.

Shortly after, towards the end of 1788, she wrote her will.[16] Now the purpose of a will is to ensure assets are distributed according to the testator's personal wishes. From time to time (especially if the will is handwritten) it is also used as a vehicle to express personal comments, sometimes designed to shock and explain why a direct ancestor may have been unexpectedly omitted or have tiny inheritances. Such was the will of Elias Buzaglo in 1805 (the brother of Leah) who passed everything to his wife, Ann, and mentions son Isaac: 'who expressly gets nothing'. Oops. What did he do to so antagonise his father?

A poor woman's will

Aunt Judith was different. She had very little indeed. In fact she had nothing to justify writing a will at all, and the cost of proving it could possibly have been a burden on the recipients. Yet she wrote one. Why? Part of the reason was to clarify her burial arrangements, but for this a will would not really have been necessary. It seems she just wanted to record how much she appreciated the generosity she received at her time of need, and Jacob was one of those persons singled out for a thankful mention.

A rich man's will

Jacob's uncle Benjamin died the year before his aunt Judith. Other than major legacies for his own children, and small ones for his other surviving sisters, the only other relation to benefit from his will was Jacob. He was cited as 'Nephew Jacob son of deceased sister Rachel Lara'.[17] Benjamin was an active elder of the congregation. Of all the nieces and nephews, Jacob was the person who appears to have attended most regularly, and via his work met and knew many of the congregation. It could have been out of respect for him that this token amount was included. There is also the possibility Benjamin was his godfather, though there is no extant record to indicate whether this might be the case.

More help needed

There is also a third possibility as to why Benjamin singled out Jacob. A few months before Benjamin wrote his will, there was another death in the family. Jacob's brother-in-law, Elias Curry, died in 1792 and was buried in August of that year. He had been baptised a Christian, but sincerely wanted to be readmitted to the Sephardic community – but they were unforgiving. Jacob Lara was a member of the congregation, sufficiently well known to those who enforced the Ascamot (their traditional bylaws) and petitioned the Mahamad on Elias's behalf. This time the pleas hit home. They eventually relented, and agreed to a burial 'behind the boards' (for an explanation see Esther and Elias). Could Benjamin have been so impressed by Jacob's actions that he decided to leave him ten pounds? Sadly this is all speculation, as he gave no reason for his decision.

A Jewish burial

Jacob and Leah had no children, or if so they did not figure in any Bevis Marks records. Jacob himself died in 1800, being buried on 24 August of that year. His name was recorded as Jacob Haim Nunes Lara.[18] This is the only time when the name 'Haim' which means 'life' has been included in records mentioning him. His nephew Abraham, son of his brother, also died earlier that year, but Jacob's burial would have been more widely attended.

Part of the new burial ground, Mile End Road

There is a magnificent little book in the Berkshire Record Office, essentially a diary, kept by a Mr William Savory.[19]

Incredibly someone had read through the book and taken the trouble to catalogue anything of interest, and referenced them in the card index. And this definitely was of interest, for his brother-in-law was a funeral director who attended some Jewish burials. Mr Savory records a burial in Mile End Road in October 1786. The burial records for Bevis Marks show there was only one burial on the stated date, which was for the Ventura family.[20] This was the family into which Jacob's cousin Hannah Lara, daughter of Phineas, had married.

Here is part of Savory's writing on the subject:

> We went to a Jew's burying. There was a hearse as is customary to convey the corpse, two mourning coaches and upwards of 21 Hackney carriages followed. A corpse is never carried on the shoulders as is customary with us but when they got to the

burying ground the corpse is taken out of the hearse and so many as can assist convey the corpse into the meeting house upon their arms. [...] The lead of the coffin is unhasped (as they seldom use nails or screws) and then the relations garment is rented by cutting the coat with a knife; afterwards a few prayers are spoken in Hebrew, the lead of the coffin is hasped again and conveyed to the grave.

I was astonished to see so many relations and friends of deceased persons weeping and praying over the grave for the good of the departed soul. Tombstones are laid horizontal. Most of the inscriptions are in Hebrew. [...] A common custom is to put lime in the graves and when the body is put in throw in some water to burn the body. Sometimes there are holes at the bottom of the coffin for the heat of the lime to get at the body and sometimes the body is put in the ground and the coffin broken to pieces and thrown in afterwards. They generally inter the body in the earth as soon as it has resigned its breath if it is before sunset.

Since mourning clothes were cut as part of the ceremony, they could not easily be used again. Hence money was often bequeathed to relatives to purchase this type of clothing.

Woe is me...

His widow lived for several more years, remaining in their home at Bury Street off Bevis Marks. Possibly she continued the family business as a pastry cook, either on her own or with assistance.

Leah's name is given in the land tax assessments as 'Wo' or 'Widow Lara'. Her first entry was for 1801, the year after Jacob died, with the last being for 1814 after which no entries for her were located.[21] If she had been working, possibly that was the time she gave this up, for there is no record of her for the last six years of her life. She was buried on 17 October 1820 in the same cemetery as her late husband, the Novo Cemetery at Mile End Road.[22]

With all probability, they expected to remain there in perpetuity. Some hope![23] The remains from the earliest burial in the new cemetery up to the mid nineteenth century were exhumed in the 1960s for a re-dedicated burial at Coxtie Green burial ground, Dytchleys, Essex.

There remains only a small but well-tended part of the original burial ground, containing burials within the last one hundred years, which has been protected and is open for visitors.

Part of the Jewish Sephardi Cemetery, Coxtie Green

Many of the monumental inscriptions there contain names long associated with the original émigrés to this country. This, along with the little annexe to Jewish history in the Mile End Road, are well worth a respectful visit.

Esther Cardozo, Sisters and Sara Carcas

(in death, everyone is equal)

Hello Abraham, we're your cousins, we've come to stay

It was not until he was well in his thirties that Abraham met one group of his cousins. That's because they weren't born in London, not even in England for that matter. They had lived all their lives in Gibraltar and were only here because of 'circumstances'. Their father, Isaac Lara, had come as a refugee to London with his family when he was a young man. The others stayed, he left. Now he was returning over forty years later, once more a refugee, but this time with his daughters.

Were Abraham, his brother, sister and his London-based cousins aware they had relatives living abroad? It is difficult to know how much contact Isaac retained with his siblings and if they talked about him to their own children. Perhaps his nieces and nephews would never have known of this family had it not been for the extraordinary events surrounding the siege of Gibraltar.

Isaac Lara had originally come to London in the mid 1730s with members of his family including his brothers Aaron and Benjamin and sister Rachel. Apart from Isaac the others settled permanently in London. A few years later, in 1739, he decided to seek his fortune elsewhere and left for Gibraltar, where he stayed for a couple of years. Whilst there he was 'talent spotted' and recruited for work in the Barbary Coast (the name used to refer to the regions of Morocco, Algeria, Tunisia and Libya). This involved spending much time there, as well as in Gibraltar.

Several years later he married Sarah, a Gibraltarian – one of just over half the population who were born there. They had a family of three girls and all five were listed in the 1777 census of Gibraltar, in the section set aside for Jewish families.[1] By then the Jews comprised almost a quarter of the whole population. The information Isaac provided suggests that his wife Sarah was born in 1725, with daughters Rebecca, Esther and Rachel in 1750, 1756 and 1758 respectively. Censuses give a handy general idea of ages, but since we don't know whether or not a person has just had a birthday, the birth year extrapolated from the ages could easily be a year awry either way. However it is known he spent much of 1752–1755 in Arzila (Morocco) which ties up neatly with the gap in ages between the two elder girls.

The naming of names

It was standard Jewish family tradition to name children after senior relatives. If those relatives had Catholic names these would not be appropriate. Isaac's mother was called Maria, so he would have to look elsewhere for a name for his first daughter. No extant records from that time exist in Gibraltar.

His next two were called Esther and Rachel. Of all the siblings who moved to London, Isaac was closest in age to his sisters Rachel and Esther. This may have given them more in common with each other, particularly as he was twelve years younger than his elder brother and his younger brother was some years younger than him; a big gap for a young adult. Could they have got on really well together and did he name two of his daughters after them? It's speculation, but a possibility, especially as it was from Rachel's children that assistance was given during the Gibraltarians' stay in London.

The end of their world

One can only imagine the three sisters had an idyllic childhood, flourishing in the cosmopolitan atmosphere and way of life befitting a wealthy family in this territory. But then their world turned upside down. Isaac and his family were caught up in the terrifying and life-changing events of the combined Spanish and French onslaught on Gibraltar. The 'Great Siege of Gibraltar' started on 24 June 1779. Two years later, by 1781, conditions were extremely harrowing there. The bombardment had gained strength, there was a lot of damage to buildings and food supply was running low as convoys were unable to get through. By then citizens were required (rather than merely volunteering as many had) to help with the protection of the colony. A notice was posted commanding 'All Roman Catholics and Jews were required to work from seven o'clock in the forenoon.'[2] This demand for assistance, under the cover of darkness, appears to include women too. The Jews had already been forced to leave their homes, even where they were undamaged, moving to premises they could find in higher ground, with tents provided for those in need. An evening curfew was enforced. At a time of war, there would have been ever-present fears pervading the community. These included the terror of everyday life under attack, the problems of inadequate food and the thought that if the Spanish were victorious they, as Jews, would be taken before the Inquisition.

After the Jews were told to leave their homes, the governor ordered that their houses and businesses be destroyed. Anything of value was plundered, largely by the troops.[3] Following this action, the Jewish residents were required to leave Gibraltar. Where would they go? There were a variety of options, and some, like the Laras, chose to travel to England under the protection of the navy. For this they had to submit the names of all family members involved.[4] Many of those leaving were now destitute as a result of the naval bombardment and activities within their tiny land, a place which until then had been a haven for so many diverse persons. Their mother, Sarah, had recently died, so it was just the three unmarried daughters who came with their father – one hopes more relieved to be away from war than scared at the prospect of what might lie ahead of them. They landed at Portsmouth, having to pay their transportation costs to the navy.[5] The Laras were some of the last to leave (delayed whilst Isaac tried his best to secure compensation for his losses), arriving after the first wave of travellers. From Portsmouth they travelled to London and it was three long years before they were able to return to their homeland. None of them could have had known then that they would be away for such a period of time. The siege lasted for three years and seven months, and was the longest one endured by the British Armed Forces.

London life

So what was it like in London in those years? King George III was on the throne and the country was in the middle of both the American Revolutionary War and the Great Siege. The Laras would have been most concerned about keeping an anxious eye on the events that directly concerned them.

The differences in everyday life probably made the most impact. They were now in a crowded bustling capital city, of vast proportions compared with Gibraltar whose total population was only 3210 plus troops in the garrison when the 1777 census was taken. Three years later that number was swollen by a tripling of the troop numbers, but was still a relatively trifling amount. There, apart from the border with Spain, they had been encompassed by the beautiful blue Mediterranean Sea with the constant comings and goings of seafaring ships – central to their lives – along with the exotic nature and languages of their neighbours. Here, the vibrant Thames with its dockyards surely would have paled into comparative insignificance.

Gibraltar was not a particularly healthy place to live because of the heat and suffocating winds from Africa, but they would have had a varied Mediterranean diet. Like many new arrivals from hotter climes, the change in climate must have been another unsettling factor to contend with. The year after their arrival was a notably wet one, especially during the summer months, though a hot dry summer in 1783 compensated in part for the continual rain of the early months of the year. This was spoiled by the eruption of the Laki volcano in Iceland and the sulphurous haze which spread, causing thousands of deaths in Britain, an event far more devastating than the Eyjafjallajökull volcano eruption of 2010.

Who will help?

In all probability they attended the Bevis Marks Synagogue, perhaps marvelling at its size and the likeness to the edifice erected on their home soil. Would the congregation support them during their enforced stay in London? Everyone was offered assistance in writing letters to the government and endorsing their pleas for aid. Isaac did not need this; he was more than capable of penning his own petition. Financial support may not have been easily forthcoming to this family, as many of the others were in dire straits which would have strained the goodwill and resources of even the most generous members of the congregation. Also most had no relatives in England. Isaac did. At the time they came over there were still four of Isaac's siblings alive in London: Sarah, Judith, Rachel and Benjamin.

The first three were all widows with few assets, so unable to assist much. Benjamin was wealthy, but unlikely to have been willing to assist his brother. He was a very religious man, a stalwart of the synagogue, and may not have welcomed the arrival of someone whose personal problems would have caused the Laras turmoil in the past. However there would have been plenty of time for the girls to meet their aging relatives, if this is what everyone wanted.

There were also a number of Isaac's nephews and nieces around; the girls' cousins. Whether or not he wanted this, Isaac's fate would have been in their hands right from the start. It is clear from various letters written by Abraham (Rachel's eldest son) that he was the man who filled this breach. Abraham was still single, so perhaps he offered his services as the person most able to accommodate them all. Others had far greater resources but some had young families – for whatever reason, it was all left to him. At that time his finances appear to have been still relatively sound.

Educated guests

To keep himself occupied and to try to avoid being too great a burden on his nephew, there is little doubt that Isaac, a highly resourceful man, would have done as much as he could to repay the hospitality. He may even have assisted Abraham in some aspects of his business. He certainly passed on some of his skills at languages and letter writing.

Going back

The Great Siege was not to end until 2 February 1783. The family's greatest wish would have been to return as soon as possible after that time, but for this some sort of compensation for their losses had to be given by the British government. This was resolutely resisted, so their return had to be postponed until they had some other financial assistance to help them on their way. Consequently they were not able to arrive back in Gibraltar until 18 July 1784.[6] Some form of funding from the family would have been instrumental in allowing them to eventually return.

A suitable match

Possibly all Isaac's daughters married on their return to Gibraltar, but the absence of records for this period does not help here. None of them married during their stay in London, as the marriage contracts would have been with the Bevis Marks Synagogue. Marriage in England would have been problematic, as by now all three were above the usual marriageable age and also they would not have the benefit of a family dowry.

But it was not just the women whose lives had been put on hold during the last four years of the war. The same applied to the men so when people returned home everyone was bound to want life to return to 'normal' as far as this was possible. Finding a suitable marriage partner would be part of this. Esther was found a very good match. Few men in Gibraltar would be able to afford a good dowry for their daughters, so this was less of a problem here than in other parts of the world. Her father, Isaac, had been a well-known member of the community and this would have been in their favour. Also, he had been an (unofficial) consul, the same position as a man named Aaron Nunes Cardozo which gave them much in common.

Esther married Aaron. Aaron's life is well documented, as he became a major player in the politics and life not only of that tiny island, but also a very important contributor to the security and safety of England and a friend of Admiral Lord Nelson.[7]

The Gibraltar archives

The National Archives for Gibraltar are in the governor's building, so one has to run the gauntlet of the guards to enter. The shelving of the rooms they occupy are piled high with documents, overflowing to the floor. Research there is not a quick or easy matter! Fortunately a number of the Jewish records there have been researched by a very cooperative local genealogist. A private tour of the beautiful synagogue by one of the members of the Mahamad was also a fantastic opportunity. Its design was modelled on that of Bevis Marks in London as the founder had been a member of the congregation there. This was a smaller version, though the similarity was striking. It transpired an ancestor of Mr Belio, one of the synagogue's guardians, left a will, for which Isaac Lara was one of the witnesses. This is framed and hangs on his office wall. He had the synagogue records too and was able to confirm that none existed for the time when Isaac and his daughters were there.[8]

Ask a busy man…

Cardozo was a prosperous merchant, whose business was importing supplies for the garrison and the Royal Navy from North Africa (Morocco and Algiers). Later he acted as consul for the beys of Tunis and Algiers, similar work to that of his father-in-law, Isaac Lara, when he was a much younger man.[9] As a consul he was in a good position to act as prize agent for many of the vessels the RN had captured and returned to Gibraltar. From 1791 he was asked by His Excellency Sir Robert Boyd to take on the administration of the police in Gibraltar and also to become the representative of the Hebrew inhabitants of the island. He took on these demanding responsibilities for many years until in 1804 his poor health led him to resign from the latter position. This did not go down well at all! He would not change his mind until he was finally approached by Thomas Trygge, Lieutenant-Governor, asking him to reconsider, and through his urging he continued in this position for another ten years.[10] Only a very capable, intelligent and tirelessly busy man could have attempted half of what he packed into his life, yet in everything Aaron Cardozo excelled. It is both a sign of the times and a measure of his importance that Aaron Cardozo has a webpage on Wikipedia devoted to him, with links to source material, some of which are mentioned here.

My friend Sir Horatio Nelson

Nelson is depicted by biographers as a strong and unyielding leader of men, exactly the type of person needed in times of war to inspire and motivate. These traits were not those which would allow a man to form personal friendships easily considering the complications this might involve. So who would he feel was worthy of his friendship and would also feel the same? Enter Aaron Cardozo.

The friendship and rapport between the two men is well documented.[11] They were close in age, with Nelson being the elder by only four years. Nelson often had to stop over at Gibraltar during which time he met up with Cardozo. He would have stayed in government quarters, as the type of property Jews were permitted would have made homestays for prestigious visitors impossible. Aaron (and possibly Esther) met and entertained him on more than one occasion, when his ships came to Gibraltar for provisioning. Nelson was well aware of their predicament and it is reported he vowed to address the position of Cardozo directly if he returned alive from the forthcoming Battle of Trafalgar.

It was his friend Cardozo who donated so much of his personal fortune to provisioning the fleet for their wars, ongoing since the Great Siege of Gibraltar – and notably for the Battle of the Nile in 1798. British coffers were stretched, and the aid provided was lamentably short whilst at the same time the government commanded him to seek out and destroy Napoleon's fleet, an unrealistic task without the necessary funds. Had it not been for Cardozo's largess Nelson's chances of success would have been limited. As it was he was able to take his fleet to Egypt then wage a surprise night attack on the French fleet and so annihilate it. This removed the threat of the French from the seas for some years to come. Had this aid not been forthcoming, then this and other victories might well have eluded him.

To hear of his death at Trafalgar must surely have been doubly distressful to Cardozo, losing both a friend and an ally. Most of London were said to attend Nelson's funeral cortège in London in 1805 and it would be indeed surprising if Abraham, his children and the wider Lara family were not amongst the crowd.

Bountiful generosity

The regard in which Cardozo was held by others too was shown in a shining testimonial by His Royal Highness Field Marshal the Duke of Kent. He said Cardozo was 'always distinguished as the most active and zealous individual on the rock, to promote the service of government without considering the sacrifice of private fortune; that his liberality has always been proverbial there, through every class of society.'[11]

This statement reflects not only on his diligence but also opens a window into how he spent vast amounts of his wealth. Not only was much of his fortune donated to the coffers of the British government to aid provisioning of their wars, but to others too.

Cardozo's friends and fellow Jews in Gibraltar were not forgotten. Their lives were greatly enhanced through his charitable donations, plus his tireless work as president of the community and appointments such as administrator of branches of the town police, and advisor on local matters to successive governors. It appears the majority of Jews and Moors were very poor immigrants, without the education and wherewithal to much improve their lifestyle, and his significant direct involvement would have made a huge difference to them.

But then to cap it all he supported the Spanish in their wars against the French – those who had single-mindedly persecuted so many Jews and non-persona not so many years ago.

In other ventures Cardozo, when requested, actually risked his life in the service of the garrison and the fleet. He did not pass the onerous assignments to others where he felt he alone would be able to accomplish the task. It has been said by some his generosity, though freely given, was in the hope of benefitting sometime in the future. This may be true, but few individuals would have been prepared to throw largess in such huge waves in the mere hope of some nebulous future benefit.

Some noted personalities in England and America especially have used their great wealth in schemes to help the disadvantaged and impoverished as well as their nation. Aaron Cardozo was one of the more flamboyantly generous of these.

The rich and their servants

Today many people have part-time help with work around the house, particularly whilst they are at work. It was customary for the wealthy, in previous eras, to have full-time servants to take complete care of the household chores. The housekeeper and cook would be the main contacts between the indoor staff for the lady of the house, and through them she would ensure the orderly running of the day-to-day requirements. TV programmes such as *Upstairs, Downstairs* and *Downton Abbey* have given millions of viewers an idealised insight into their lives. These come to mind when considering Cardozo's property in Gibraltar. It occupies a very large plot at what was once the very centre of the row of houses overlooking the sea. It was in fact built especially for Isaac's daughter and her husband as their home and a suitable place to entertain all the dignitaries who came to Gibraltar.

An ornament to the Almeida

House number D.10.H.6 – an unusual number, and not your average two up, two down. This was the official address of Cardozo's house, relating to the district in which it stood. Not until February

1815 did Esther and Aaron Cardozo have their sumptuous property on the Almeida. The cost was an astronomical figure – upwards of £30,000; an extravagant amount not just for Gibraltar but for anywhere, and it dominated the scene. He erected an elegant, well-proportioned three-storey mansion.

The interior had spacious rooms, with adornments such as tasteful carvings and marble staircases. Here they lavishly entertained the rich and the powerful, befitting his rank in society. They would have needed many live-in servants to run their huge property. Her husband was frequently away on business, sometimes for long periods, so then the smooth running of these events would have fallen entirely on her shoulders. For this she must have been an accomplished hostess and although her skills may well have been honed during the early part of her marriage, it is obvious that her education and upbringing as the daughter of a wealthy and international trader/ex-consul would have prepared her with the self-assured confidence and skills appropriate to this life. Esther would have been closely involved in entertaining guests long before their mansion was built. At her death the obituary alludes to her beauty/poise/grooming and also to the fact that she was a generous benefactress to the poor of the island, of whom there were many.

Why build such a palatial building when they had no children? There were a number of factors involved here. Isaac definitely felt in need of a suitable place to entertain the governors, high-ranking officers of the army, and important visitors to Gibraltar. The Ellicotts record: 'Elderly people in Gibraltar recall stories of lavish entertaining in Aaron's big house.'[12] Lord Nelson, his late friend and one (as was the nation as a whole) much indebted to Cardozo's huge generosity in supporting Britain's war efforts, was appalled at where he lived. Perhaps too, having waited so long to do this, Cardozo wanted to make a clear statement of his power and wealth. He had been promised some land twenty years earlier in compensation for giving up part of one of his properties which abutted Market Street. The request was made by Sir Robert Boyd, the governor, who wanted to widen the street, but unfortunately Boyd died before the land, by way of compensation, was granted. It took over twenty years of actively pursuing his claim before in May 1813 permission was granted to build on an area of land which currently housed a stable for asses. Only British Protestants were entitled to own property on the island (Aboab was a notable exception some years earlier before the Great Siege) so it is probable this matter of 'compensation' might also reflect the extraordinary assistance he had given to the garrison to protect 'the Rock'. The authority was couched in the following terms: 'All that piece or parcel of ground situated in and being at the bottom or lower end of the Almeida in Gibraltar containing an area of 3,333 superficial feet to be holden for ever.' It was also stipulated he had to build within three years 'a handsome dwelling house which would be an "ornament to the Almeida"'.[13]

The Cardozo mansion, now the Town Hall

A white elephant, or a white mammoth…

Aaron lost no time and the mansion was complete in less than two years, and most definitely complied with the decree it should be 'an ornament to the Almeida'. It was huge. It was magnificent. It was built specifically for him and his wife as a place where they could entertain the elite.

So long to wait for this house, so little time to spend in it. Gibraltar was the first ever British naval base in the Mediterranean. There were others, but these were not so important. However, following Napoleon's defeat in the Peninsular War, the British turned Malta into the main base for the Mediterranean fleet. This adversely affected everyone in Gibraltar, especially those people such as Cardozo whose trading was exclusively with the navy. is business.

Almost overnight the bulk of his business dried up, just at the time when he had invested so much of his wealth into this project, which now lost its importance and meant the running costs could not be sustained.

That wasn't his only expensive error of judgement, though that may be harsh as it is too easy to be wise in retrospect. After Cardozo's death, details in his probated will claim that he lent, in friendship, Sir John Miller Doyle £3500 for a project related to road building in Portugal. The project failed and after many years none of this loan had been returned. Cardozo claims he also lost far more than that sum as a direct result. He included this in his will in the vain hope there might be some degree of recompense along with considerable sums of money owed to him by a Mr James Ross Oxberry of Gibraltar. Sadly not.

No national health service

Gibraltar had long been seen as an unhealthy place to live and work. Where cities across the globe spring up haphazardly following a huge influx of people, then lack of planning and foresight can herald intolerable conditions. Small houses, narrow streets, lack of proper drainage and poor water supplies all lead to poor sanitary living conditions. The Levante – the suffocating, strong, fast winds gusting in across the Bay from the east – did nothing to relieve the conditions. Epidemics such as yellow fever and cholera ravished the island periodically, just as they did any populous town. Though these generally affected the poor in crowded conditions, no one would consider themselves free of danger. In 1804 the yellow fever epidemic was so bad that Aaron (and Esther) left for Morocco, then Oran, arranging food relief for Gibraltar where food was in very short supply, and not returning until its aftermath the following year. The lives of many were literally saved as a result of his activities, not just the Jews, who by 1805 comprised half of Gibraltar's population.

Years later, in 1817, two years after moving into their mansion, Esther became unwell. Her husband wanted to take her to the spa town of San Roque in Spain to convalesce (an unremarkable-looking town near Gibraltar on the bus route to Seville). However, to hear that Esther was 'unwell' does not indicate a particular kind of complaint.

Friends and Enemies

Spain was once again closed to Jews as the Inquisition had restarted there in 1814, so on 17 March 1817 he petitioned King Fernando VII for special permission to temporarily live there. This was 'The Traitor King' who restored absolute monarchy, and prosecuted and put to death everyone suspected of liberalism. Cardozo had been of considerable assistance to the Spanish in their recent wars so he had every reason to expect this to weigh heavily in his favour, especially as it was accompanied by a personal endorsement from Major-General Sir Charles Doyle, Lieutenant-General in the Spanish Services. The general reported Cardozo had donated 1200 muskets, provided clothing, donated huge sums and raised money in unparalleled generosity in aiding resistance to the attack by the French.[14] The King was not about to grant him any favours, notwithstanding those he had received himself so manifestly. The request was forwarded to the Tribunal of the Jews for consideration. From them Aaron was only granted a conditional agreement, covering himself and his wife without servants and under strict supervision.[15] Cardoza had every right to be proud of himself and his achievements. A rebuff like this would have been seen as too humiliating – Esther stayed in Gibraltar. Her health must have improved sufficiently for him to take the opportunity to travel to England on business by mid 1819.

Try getting blood out of a stone...

His father-in-law Isaac hadn't been able to make any headway with the British in the form of any recompense, even though he had been most persistent in his efforts. Why would Cardozo expect to succeed?

He had been trying to get his business together again after the devastating loss of the navy contracts. Still rich by many standards, but not in any position to continue to live in his Almeida mansion in the style he had envisaged, Aaron decided he needed to take fast remedial action before any more of the past governors and others he had assisted died. They were sadly good at doing this! Just as he felt he was making progress, they upped and died and he had to start negotiations all over again with a new person!

Cardozo had rendered numerous services over the years, without charge, but now he needed the British government to recognise this and reimburse him. He felt all his endeavours and dreams were gone forever due to Malta's elevation and Gibraltar's consequent lack of status, in spite of his own generosity over several years. At the time he was happy to be in a position to help. Now he needed help himself. He knew he had to quickly establish his case before it was too late. He would have been totally aware that his father-in-law Isaac Lara had worked tirelessly as an unpaid Vice-Consul to the official Vice-Consul for Tunisia and Arzila yet after his warehouses and property were literally ransacked then blown up during the Great Siege he received no compensation or assistance whatsoever from the government.

Aaron's solution was to request testimonials from those still living who were knowledgeable about his past activities. He wrote letters explaining his intent and received back many highly favourable comments, which he published some years later. The government, as usual, was unretractable. Aaron also offered to sell his house to the government as the maintenance for it was quite onerous, but this was not agreed either.

Aaron had not resolved his business activities and was still in London in 1820 when he heard the tragic news of his wife's death in Gibraltar. He had not seen her for two years. Apart from the tremendous loss of his wife – they appear to have been in a very happy relationship – he now had the additional loss of regular income. He had settled on her an annuity of £1500 a year (which equates to over £140,000 these days), probably considering that as his own health had been poor since around 1804 his wife might outlive him. He would have paid an enormous lump sum to receive such a high annual return. With her earlier death all of this was now also lost to him.

Sephardic cemeteries

Visit a Sephardic cemetery and the thing that will strike you is the simplicity of it all. Every tomb slab either lies flush to the ground, or perhaps at a slight tilt, and at roughly the same height as its neighbours to show we are all equal in death. It is also reputed that the flat stone was more stable at a time when cemeteries were built in swampy ground, and the tradition has continued from there. Planting is minimal. It is Jewish law that only one body may be buried in each grave, at least six foot from the surface. In theory, and almost certainly practice too, bodies are orientated with the feet towards the east. Look out for the small roundish stones gently positioned which indicate someone has visited.

In England, parish and local cemeteries are awash with a flourish of gravestones, standing tall or keeling over through the passage of time. Here you may find angels and cherubs adorning them graciously, or perhaps huge family mausoleums, especially in Victorian churchyards such as Highgate in London or Arnos Vale in Bristol. It's hard to escape the Grecian-type urns, but then there are even elaborate monuments to a person's life such as the full-size racehorse in St John's, Margate. Within reason – and according to the rules of the place – what you erect is a matter of choice and the depth of your pocket. Flowers, lovingly placed, withering after a few days indicate recent visitors. Plastic flowers – a curse of a couple of decades ago – are thankfully disappearing from sight. The six-foot or so plot in front of an upright stone (if there is one) may be planted by relatives and friends. Greenery, colour, the habitual ivy abound. This is an English churchyard. But, however we choose to respect and lay to rest our loved ones throughout the world, the one thing all cemeteries try to have in plenty is peace, calm and a certain amount of dignity. Solace for the survivors. Whether you acknowledge your visit with flowers or a thoughtfully chosen small stone, sentiments of love, respect, sadness and memories are our common link with our past treasured ancestors.

A view to die for

Sephardic cemeteries in London do not compare with the old Jews' Gate Cemetery in Gibraltar. Take a cable car up the rock and after admiring the views continue walking downhill slightly to the cemetery, the resting place of Esther, her parents and sisters.

It tumbles over to the Mediterranean Sea far below it, blue and expansive. The view is magnificent. It is the most tranquil spot imaginable. Not so long ago the whole area was overgrown (it had been closed in 1848) and in a terrible state of decay. The current caretaker, Felix Rocca, led a team who started the process of finding and restoring graves. He has continued in this task of love and devotion ever since. Religion has nothing to do with it. He is not a Jew.

And to think that the British gunners occupied this cemetery in the Second World War, realising it was a prime position for them to oversee the sea and protect the island. Once more a place of death. Rocca pointed us in the right direction for Esther's tombstone. It was quite a distance away from the entrance.

All (wo)men are equal but some are more equal than others

This place was eventually given to the Jews who were in desperate need of a cemetery. It was a huge trek up from the coastal area where most people lived. It was considered far enough away, and relatively inaccessible for no one else to want it. Over time that changed, but even then the Jews managed to hold on to it.

Esther had married a highly prominent man and on her death he ensured she had the most amazing tombstone. It would have been incredibly difficult to transport the granite there and expensive too. So, for Esther's gravestone to be different from the norm would require significant funding to bring the elaborate granite to the gravesite. There is also the factor that it is against the Jewish belief that any one person should have, in death, a more prominent position than any other. This is rarely permitted and only with special dispensation, so it is significant that her widower (albeit a highly respected individual) should even have this special request considered at all by the Mahamad. Esther herself was very well regarded too, but there would inevitably have been vociferous objections raised. Tenacious determination to overcome these odds would be needed. Only a person such as Cardozo could achieve all this.

What was so unusual about the gravestone of Esther Cardozo, other than the fact it wasn't the distinctive prostrate slab? Well, it wasn't vertical either. That would have been akin to the Christian tradition and not her widower's intention at all. It was in the shape of a trapezium, about three foot high, magnificent but not ostentatious, and all the rarer for these qualities.

On one long side is the wording in Spanish which reads:

> AQUILAZE LA BIEN AVENTURA
> SNORA DONA ESTER LARA DE CARDOZO
> FACECIO DE ESTA A MEJOR VIDA
> EL DIA 24 OCTUBRE ANO 1820

The inscription was kindly translated by the local Jewish historian, Mr Joshua Marrache. It reads:

> Here lies the blessed (or fortunate)
> Lady Ester Lara de Cardozo
> who left this life
> the 24 October in the year 1820

The opposite side was in Hebrew:

> Tomb of woman of honour and purity. Lady (dame) Ester wife of the great and honoured Señor Aaron Nunes Cardozo died 4th day of the Jewish month of Cheshvan (and later the year of her death?).

The terms Lady, Dame and Señor are honorary titles, and a class 'above' Mrs or Mr.

Obituary

The local newspapers was not generally used for obituaries, but there was one for Esther.[16]

> DIED – On Tuesday, 24th Inst., universally regretted ESTHER the wife of A. Cardozo, Esq. – In her, society has lost one of its best ornaments; and the poor, an unostentatious benefactress.

Cardozo may not have come back to Gibraltar to oversee the arrangements for her tombstone until much later, as by April 1921 he was still awaiting responses from the various high officials to whom he had written. He had no pension or new appointment as consul from the British government. It is clear he was back in Gibraltar by 1822. Once back, he settled his affairs there and left Gibraltar, leaving his nephew Isaac in charge. He was cajoled into investing with a friend in Lisbon, Portugal and travelled there next. This was a journey for which he had to apply for a passport and this was issued in 1824.[17] Sadly he lost a great deal of money in that unwise investment scheme.

Awards

A bright spot for 1824 was his award by the French of their highest decoration, for his services against Napoleon: Knight of the Legion of Honour.

Another award from a most unlikely source was the Spanish Order of Isabela la Catholica. This was granted in recognition of services which benefit the country. Cardozo was probably the only Jew to be given this.

More widely known is that one of the commemorative medallions struck for the Battle of the Nile, belonging to Nelson, was given after his demise to Aaron as a memento. The picture of this adorns both front and back cover of Benady's booklet.

Awards do not pay the bills

Where should he go next? Cardozo retired in London, but not to the West End where property prices were now above his means. Instead he lived with his unmarried sisters Judith and Rachel in Little Alie Street, Goodman's Fields in the East End.

Whilst living there he occupied himself with the printing of his collected testimonials and letters of recommendation which comprise the content, along with notes, of the aforementioned booklet. Subsequently Aaron and his sisters moved to nearby Leman Street and it was here that he died:

> Jan 12 1834: At the house of his sisters, in Leman Street, aged 72, Aaron Cardozo, Esq. late of Gibraltar, Knt of the Legion of

Honour, etc., a benevolent, active, and zealous individual, whose purse was open to the poor and needy of every clime and religion, during his residence there.[18]

This date was confirmed within the details attached to his will. It was a little while before the news reached Gibraltar, and in deference to this, the Garrison Ball was postponed.[19]

On the following Monday, 10 February 1834, the paper contained a lengthy obituary for Cardozo.[20]

He had written his will whilst at Little Alie Street, some twelve years prior to his death. By the time of the last codicil (the third) he was living with his sisters at Leman Street, where he died.[21] His portfolio consisted of three properties in Gibraltar. This may give the impression he was still wealthy, but he was not at all by his standards. Documents detailing his tax show his assets amounted to less than £800.[22] One of the properties was left to these two sisters jointly, and – bearing in mind previous government attempts at grabbing back Jewish-held property – he explicitly clarified his ownership rights and illustrated where it was positioned. Another property was described as situate in Irish Town, Gibraltar and then of course there was his mansion, 'in the public square at Gibraltar formerly called the Almeida but now the Memorial.' The ownership of this was split between his nephew Isaac Cardozo and his friend Admiral Beaulock. Upon the latter's death it was to revert completely to Isaac. As to what should happen to the property subsequently, again Cardozo clarified this absolutely – there was no room for doubt of his wishes. The problem is once you give something away, the new owner is not legally bound by what you, the previous owner, had intended (however explicitly explained and implored). Cardozo wrote:

> It is my wish that my said mansion be not sold or disposed of except to government and for a sum not less than twenty thousand pounds sterling as the same cost me upwards of thirty thousand pounds sterling besides the value of the ground…

Isaac failed his uncle on both counts. After some years he sold the property in a private sale, and for only £10,000.

At one stage it was offered as a temporary residence of Queen Victoria's third son, the Duke of Connaught. Then over time it became run-down, having for many years served as a hotel. As with numerous old buildings, exterior facades and interior spaces have since changed. The good news is that finally his mansion has reverted to the use Aaron Cardozo wished. It is still there dominating the town, in pride of place as the City Hall.

An entanglement

There is one final tale to consider here, and this relates back both to the girls' father, Isaac, and to one or even two other persons. A quick look back at the title shows it includes Sara as being one of his children. Yet there has been no mention of her until now. Why? How does she fit in?

Isaac had left London for Gibraltar in 1739. A comment in his brother Aaron's will indicates he had borrowed money from him, and it may have been for this journey. Did he have a child (or leave a mistress pregnant) before he went? If so she would have been an elder half-sister of Rebecca, Esther and Rachel. Benedy suggests that Isaac went to Gibraltar 'to avoid an entanglement with an older woman'.[23]

He confirmed to the author he had discovered from Bevis Marks records that an unmarried lady had returned from abroad with her daughter whom she alleged was the daughter of Isaac Lara of Gibraltar. Let's have a look at the situation.

Firstly there is a 'rogue' entry in the burial indexes for Bevis Marks. Here it is noted that on 10 July 1738 the son of Isaac Lara was buried.[24] Who was he? An open question.

There is also an entry in the Bevis Marks marriage contracts for the wedding of Sara, daughter of Isaac Nunes Lara to Jacob, son of Aaron Carcas on 29 March 1758.[25] If he left, having fathered a child (or possibly we are looking at a second?), then the baby would have been born in late 1739 or early 1740. Esther's father was the only Isaac Nunes Lara in London then, or at any period anywhere around this time. If she was his daughter, did Isaac marry her mother and then leave? The answer is no, confirmed by the absence of a record at Bevis Marks. To suggest she was Isaac's child is speculative, but plausible. But more detail raises this to a greater level of probability. Jacob and Sara Carcas (easily identified as the only people of that name mentioned in these records) had a son called Isaac or Joshua, circumcised at eight days old on 20 December 1767. This entry gives another link with the Laras as his godfather was Jeosuha (Joshua) Nunes de Lara and the godmother was Rachel Nunes Lara.[26] The surname 'Nunes Lara' confirms the link with the Laras of London, who were the only family to have this full surname of Nunes Lara.

Let's look at the godfather first. He was Joshua Nunes de Lara, identifiable from the Bevis Marks records as the son of Aaron, Isaac's brother. Joshua, Sara's half-cousin, was seventeen. From this entry we gather Aaron had told some of his children the circumstances of his younger brother's departure to Gibraltar.

Rachel Nunes Lara was the name of Joshua's youngest sister, and also that of his aunt, Isaac's sister. The young girl was only about ten. She might be considered a little young for this responsibility, in which case Abraham's mother would be the prime candidate.

Sara appears to be Isaac's daughter and this circumcision of her son shows some of the Laras were not only prepared to acknowledge their kinship, but knew her sufficiently well to accept the honoured status of godparents. The rest of the Laras could not have been oblivious to the situation, which may have been one which met with the deeply religious Benjamin's disapproval.

Did all of the other cousins know about their Gibraltarian relations prior to them coming to London? They were born in the mid eighteenth century, after Isaac left. If not, they could hardly escape the truth once their three cousins came to London.

Did the three sisters know about their half-sister prior to their enforced sojourn in London in the early 1780s? Even if they did not, they were here for about three years; long enough for the gossip to spread and too long for their father to keep the secret. It is unlikely a meeting could have been avoided.

Moses Lara and the Da Costas

> A well-loaded pistol or good tempered
> steel can end your existence

Here's the dilemma. We have a rich man. Strict and morally upright. He knows he hasn't got long to live so writes his will. It's very much a personal testimonial (and he's parsimonious) so he chose to write it himself rather than using a solicitor. He would leave behind a wife, two daughters and two sons. All of age. The question is: who gets the lion's share of his considerable estate?[1]

Consider the options. Benjamin Lara, for that's his name, has already paid the dowries for his daughters and most probably settled sums on his sons at their marriages. The eldest daughter has three children and has a Get, which means she is divorced (a fairly rare event within the Jewish community) and is now living again with her parents, Benjamin and Abigail. The second daughter is married to a grocer – a steady occupation, but one which would not make them particularly well off. One son is a childless widower and the other has been married for just over a year.

The traditional path would be to ensure the widower had sufficient provisions, then bequeath the vast majority of the estate to the eldest son. Benjamin Lara's much older brother, Aaron, died some years ago when many of his children were underage. He chose to part with convention, leaving his sons and daughters quite similar bequests. Benjamin's solution was also not to forego some assistance to his daughters, though his will definitely favoured his sons – but with a twist.

Benjamin was the youngest of the group of émigrés from Portugal and married in 1758 when he was nearly forty. Consequently he started his family some years after his siblings. One of his two sons was named Moses. There is no surviving register for his circumcision. This initially makes his birth year a matter of conjecture. There is one for his brother Benjamin, whose birth and circumcision records survive for 1769.

In Benjamin's will his son Benjamin was the first mentioned of the brothers; the traditional way to indicate the elder son. He received a healthy lump sum, whereas there was none for Moses, his widowed son. Benjamin Junior also had fifty pounds a year annuity from his father compared with thirty pounds for Moses. Then of the two brothers, Moses was due to receive a much smaller share of his mother's annuity once she passed away. Both were to share the residual equally, which was a substantial sum as their father had been a wealthy merchant. This meant that though Moses would still have had an excellent inheritance, absolutely everything in the will pointed to him being the second son.

For reasons best known to himself (and probably his wife and sons) Benjamin chose not to follow convention in his will. Moses was his first son!

First proof

Moses and his sister Rachel were asked to be godparents to the only son of their elder sister Sarah, Benjamin Rey (alias King).[2] This was in 1783 and a strong indicator Moses was old enough to have had his bar mitzvah by now. A further reason for supporting Moses as the firstborn son (apart from the giveaway name) was that he, along with their father, was the only son to be included in the list of elders who signed the Ascamot in 1784.[3]

Brother Benjamin, as mentioned before, was born in 1769. The two sisters, Sarah and Rachel, were the eldest. We know Moses was the third child, not Benjamin, because in 1768 (the year before his brother was born) their uncle Aaron Lara died and left an annuity of one hundred pounds to Moses, naming him as his nephew and godson.[4] The inheritance was part of a trust fund, of which the interest was to be paid to his parents for and towards his maintenance until he was twenty-one. At that time he could apply to the court to have the money transferred to his own account. His father Benjamin was one of the executors for his late brother's will, so would have ensured his son did exactly that. If found, the son's petition for full control of his inheritance should clarify his birth year.

One hundred percent proof

Chancery records show that on 14 April 1788 he petitioned the Right Honourable Master of the Rolls, requesting the transfer of his annuity from the trust fund (now standing in the name of the Accountant General) to his own account.[5] It took no time to process this for the petition was considered on the following Friday, 18 April. All the parties to the agreement had to attend the court, an affidavit to the effect that Moses Lara 'hath attained the age of twenty-one years' was produced in evidence, and everyone consented to the payment. This means he was born in March or April 1767.

The price of a one pound bank annuity on 20 October 1768 (at the time of purchase) was eighty-eight shillings and six pence, so £113 12s 9d was paid out to purchase his one-hundred-pound annuity. The master ordered the paperwork to be issued to allow Lara to receive the £113 12s 9d plus the latest interest of £13 12s 8d.

Matched, hatched and dispatched

Moses married in 1785, when he was not yet nineteen. The records for Bevis Marks show his marriage to Rebecca (recorded as Ribca), daughter of Judah Supino, on 14 December.[6] Her father had become denizened forty years earlier on 18 April 1744 – over thirty years before Moses' father did the same.

Bevis Marks Synagogue

Judah Supino had married twice. The first time was in 1752 to Leah, daughter of Haim Supino. She died three years later and in 1760 his second marriage was to Hana, daughter of Isaac Ergas. Rebecca was most likely the daughter of Judah and Hana, born in or after 1761.

Moses and Rebecca had a daughter, whom they named Sarah, born on 22 October 1786.[7] The burial register shows she survived for less than two months. Her burial was in the Children's Row on 15 December; recorded as daughter of Moses Nunes de Lara, son of Benjamin. However on the tombstone inscription for Benjamin Lara's family (written several years after Moses' death) her name was recorded as Rebecca, not Sarah.[8]

There is no doubt this is the same baby, as it is confirmed she died three days before her burial on 12 December.

Under a year later his wife also died. She was buried on 6

November 1787, also at the Novo Cemetery.[9] How sad to embark on married life, start a family, and end up alone again all in under two years. All this and not yet of age.

Moses purchased two adjoining plots, one for his wife and one for himself. He outlived his wife for several years, and with changed circumstances he passed the second plot to his eldest sister, Sarah. It was another forty-seven years before she needed it.

A dry salter

He established himself as a merchant, and became a City stockbroker, taking the precaution of insuring his premises at 38 Stewart Street, Spitalfields against the eventuality of fire.[10] He appears to have kept this warehouse all the time he traded in London, as over thirty years later he wrote to the elders at Bevis Marks from this address in Stewart Street.[11]

By 1790 we find him advertising as a dry salter in a number of trade directories, including the *Universal British Directory, Volume 1*; a major tome covering many areas in Britain. His address was 4 Browns Lane, Spitalfields and the same details appeared in the 1792 trade directory.

A dry salter has variously been the name for a dealer in food and drinks, though Moses used this term to show he was a dealer in drugs, probably because he collaborated also with his brother Benjamin who was a surgeon and apothecary.

However he described himself, subsequent mentions of Lara show he is prepared to trade in virtually anything if it would turn a profit!

He also had a brick-built warehouse in Lime Street, where spare capacity was rented out to others. In 1791 a Mr David Samuda, (who lived in Goodman's Fields close to Moses' house) took out insurance for his goods stored there. This Mr Samuda also rented warehouse space from Moses' cousin Abraham, and had a sister called Rebecca. Years later, as a widow, Rebecca da Costa benefitted from annual dividends bequeathed by Moses' second wife, Sarah, her sister-in-law.

Dealings with the Court of Chancery

Moses, his mother Rebecca and brother Benjamin were the three executors of Benjamin's will. They had to set up trust funds for his widow Rebecca and the two daughters, Sarah and Rachel. This seems to have been done. Chancery correspondence over the course of a number of years (until 1797) intimates that the dividends were indeed regularly collected by either Moses or Benjamin, but it is alleged they were not passed on to their sisters. Consequently they were obliged to present accounts to the Masters for them to consider the case. It appears that the annuities were paid after this time.[12]

First time before the beak

Moses was a defendant in the case 'Scott and another v Moses Lara' heard at the Guildhall, London on 23 July 1794. This action came about indirectly as a result of his trading as a dry salter and dealer of drugs. As it was a business matter, a special jury of merchants was called, presided over by Judge Kenyon.[13][14]

Cooking the books?

The case shows Moses Lara had agreed the terms of a partnership with David Valentine by February 1793. The month before, this same man (David Valentine) had been asked to testify as to Benjamin Lara's handwriting in order for the Grant of Probate for his estate to proceed. The court required such evidence since the will was not written by a solicitor. Valentine and another merchant testified that they were acquainted with Benjamin Lara – and with his handwriting – and it was their considered opinion that the will had been written by him.

So Moses undoubtedly knew Valentine reasonably well prior to the proposed partnership. He had inspected Valentine's books and together they agreed on 1 June 1793 as a start date. They now needed to acquire some goods on credit for their wholesale business. Without the use of credit, trade then – as indeed now – would be strangled.

Following this agreement, Valentine asked a Mr Scott for goods on credit. Scott did not know him and was wary about his ability to pay. He made the wise precaution therefore to instruct his broker, a Mr Lindo, to see if he could obtain references for Valentine, there being no formal credit rating agencies or establishments in those days.

Mr Lindo checked first with Moses' brother, Benjamin. Possibly this was because David Valentine and Benjamin Lara had been in business together as merchants. This partnership had been dissolved by mutual agreement in January 1793. Benjamin gave a satisfactory account of Valentine's circumstances and said he 'could be trusted to any amount'. He also said Moses had told him he found the situation of Valentine's affairs 'in such a posture as to induce him to enter into partnership with him'. Mr Lindo next approached Moses for confirmation of this, which was given. On the receipt of this satisfactory report Scott provided indigo to the value of just under a thousand pounds to Mr Valentine.

Needless to say Valentine's financial circumstances were not robust and did not improve – he obtained even more goods on credit, spiralled more and more into debt and borrowed heavily from his partner also. According to Moses' account, on the day he was expecting repayment for the huge advances he had given him, Valentine absconded.

A wealthy man in a good situation

Since Moses Lara had provided what proved to be a false credit rating on Valentine, Scott and others took him to court to make good the debt valued at over £1525. The plaintiffs' case was that Lara could not have been unaware of Valentine's precarious circumstances. Their barrister was Erskine, the newly elected Whig MP for Portsmouth. He said that 'the goods in question did not come unaccompanied into Lara's warehouse. Through the medium of this opulent man in good circumstances, a long and melancholy list of other goods also found their way into his possession. On those he lent money; but as the parties were Jews and it was forbidden by the Levitical laws to take interest from a brother, he only kept the goods as a deposit.'[14]

This gives us an insight into Lara's affairs. Erskine alluded to his 'good circumstances' (at a time when he was only twenty-six). It seems that the warehouse was jointly used by Lara and Valentine. It was alleged that these goods from Scott were not the only ones which 'found their way' there!

Off scot-free!

Lara claimed he also had been deceived and had lost money to the tune of £3000 on account of his dealings with David Valentine. Witness evidence suggested that Lara had not been informed by Lindo as to why exactly he was enquiring into Valentine's circumstances. Judge Kenyon observed it was Benjamin who had originally given the false character reference, and he – not Moses – should have been on trial. This was a case of misrepresentation, 'but the necessary proofs had not been adduced'. The judge ruled in favour of Lara.

Lord Kenyon was an astute, experienced judge. His decisions were always weighed to the letter of the law and figure in some of the other cases the Lara family were embroiled in over the years. He probably saw that the good business reference Lara gave a year ago may have been a lie, blinded by his friendship, but that he himself must also have been taken in. He could not have realised the true nature of Valentine's affairs. As for Erskine, he had no better success as an MP than he had with this case (losing both in no time at all), though these only proved short-term blips to the meteoric rise in the career of this capable, intelligent man.

One month earlier…

The way Lara dealt with the situation arising from his partner's defaults is another matter. A newspaper article dated the month preceding the court case sheds light on this. Other creditors were also hounding Lara. It is clear they realised he had kept the goods, which he then handled for his own benefit. The prosecution lawyers in the Scott case clearly believed this too and that subsequently some had been passed, interest free, to Jewish acquaintances of his. But it seems that he kept the larger part for himself. Perhaps he felt it was his due from Valentine and one way of recovering his own losses!

Though Mr Scott and his associate were not the only creditors believing they were crossed by Valentine and Lara, they were the only ones to take the legal route to try to redress these perceived wrongs. Others took a totally different approach. As their action occurred before the trial took place, either these creditors knew nothing of the impending trial or they did not believe it would have a favourable outcome. Perhaps they felt they had little chance in seeing their property and funds again as it was now in the hands of his ex-partner, resorting to sending an unsigned, blasphemous letter to Moses Lara.

A death threat

Not one to shirk in the face of adversity, Lara published the letter and offered the carrot of a ten pounds reward; a generous sum. The newspaper proprietors must have rubbed their hands with glee at not only having such a juicy piece of gossip to print, but having such a large column space fully paid up! When this did not get the required response, Lara took advantage of the legal status he had as an Englishman (via his father's foresight in becoming a denizened citizen) and sought assistance from the realm. The text of the letter was re-published, along with a statement of support from the government, by way of a pardon to any accomplice who brought the perpetrators to justice.[15]

A well loaded pistol or good tempered steel can end your existence

The (somewhat archaic) text is quoted in full below:

> Whereas it has been humbly represented to the King, that an anonymous threatening Letter was received, on the Instant, by Mr. Moses Lara, Merchant, in Little Alie-Street, Goodman's Fields, of which Letter the following is a Copy: 'Pity but your race were extirpated from the face of the creation – they are a disgrace to human nature – a hord of Swindlers – but your obstinacy shall avail nought – actions or indictments we are

not to be intimidated by & if by this day fen-night(?) you do not afford us an opportunity of entering your Warehouse, before midsummer day you shall behold your Warehouse and the Goods therein a heap of ashes and your claim on the Fire office shall be attached – have we got you now – you thought no one as deep as yourself and your Lawyer – but you find the property can be got out of your hands should we even be foiled there you shall not long revel in the produce of your Swindle – if a well loaded pistol or good tempered Steel can end your existence now judge for yourself we are prepared and such engines are at work as will defy discovery – men who delight in Blood and whose chief pleasure is Villainy – such are procured and such shall act for us. The creditors of David Valentine Friday 6 June 1794.'

His Majesty, for the better apprehending and bringing to Justice the Persons concerned writing or sending the Letter abovementioned, is hereby pleased to promise His most gracious Pardon to any One of them (except the Person who actually wrote the said Letter) who shall discover his or her Accomplice or Accomplices therein, so that he, or they may be apprehended and convicted thereof.

A small fortune

After the initial advertisement, subsequent ones also came with a codicil of a hefty reward:

> And, as a further Encouragement, a Reward of TWO HUNDRED POUNDS is hereby promised to any Person making such Discovery as aforesaid (except as is before excepted) to be paid, upon the Conviction of any One or more of the Offenders, by me, M. Lara.

Now we are talking real money here! This is a reward on a grand scale. Money conversion charts given on the Internet can be confusing – there is not just one method of comparing the real value of two hundred pounds in 1794 with that of today. The outcome varies enormously depending on the measure of relative value you decide to use. Just three of these – comparative wealth, the purchasing power and standard of living – give vastly different results. What we can say is that the lowest measure comes to £19,460 in 2012. The upside is so huge as to be mind-boggling.

Can Moses Lara seriously have ever intended paying out such a sum? He might have used this threat as bait to scare the writers, knowing that it would take little for someone to 'turn them in' for such a life-changing sum. What one can surmise too is that this nasty letter unsettled him more than the judicial proceedings appeared to!

A hiatus

Moses may have been relieved at his improved circumstances in the following year. No court case, no payments, no more published threats and, what's more, he was still very much alive! All quiet on the western front. For a while anyway!

Mud sticks

In 1795 events took another turn for the worst for this branch of the Laras, threatening to spiral out of control. They were caused by deceit and avarice. Singularly unpleasant, jointly repulsive. It all came about as a result of his brother's actions. Benjamin created a major scandal, which as it gathered apace threatened the well-being and reputation not only of himself, his wife, mother, brother and sisters, but would no doubt have impacted on the wider Lara family.

As Moses and Benjamin were business partners as well as brothers, many of their acquaintances would have believed he was party to his brother's plan and complicit in helping him evade capture.

What plan? The actual events unfold in Benjamin's story, but as people discussed the scandal, they would undoubtedly have recalled Moses' past indiscretions and questioned his motives.

It does look on this occasion as though Moses was an unwitting party to the events from which there was no escape. Once his brother was caught, and a trial ensued, it would be an opportunity for ill-wishers to hope for his downfall too. Would this remind him, and others, of his past? Did it give him pause to rethink his future and make him tread more warily now in his dealings? This was not the end of legal proceedings, at least those relating to family disputes. His sister Sarah started proceedings in Chancery in 1797 trying to get the annuity dividends to which she was entitled under their father's will, and which seem to have been withheld by her brothers. The various motions for this show that Moses was now living some distance from London. Pure coincidence he had moved away, or related to the aforementioned debacles?[16]

Business as usual

Moses was now advertising as an auctioneer, working from an office in Ramsgate, Kent, and premises in London. One of his these shows how successful this aspect of his business was. From his Kent office he brokered a deal for a bankrupt estate involving two adjoining freehold properties at Albion Hill, Ramsgate. They were currently residential properties, but Lara astutely hyped them up, noting they could be suitable for business as they 'are eligibly situated for trade'. The auction was to be held at the King's Head coffee room in London on 25 July.[17]

The ship swallower

Four years on we find Lara engaged in a different branch of work. An example of this was an auction he brokered at no. 8 New Storehouse on the Pier, Ramsgate, in 1809.[18] Items in this auction were saved from East India Company's ship *Admiral Gardner*, following its wreck on the Goodwin Sands some two months earlier.

A report on this freak event was made by Captain William Eastfield to William Ramsey of India House. He concluded that the *Admiral Gardner* was such a great loss because 'she was carrying a valuable cargo: 54 tons of specially minted copper coinage, destined for the East India Company's mint at Madras'. Also lost in the Goodwin Sands in the same storm was the *Britannia*, laden with cloth, lead and copper.[19]

The Goodwin Sands stretch from Ramsgate to Kingsdown,

about six miles off the east coast of Kent. Many hundreds of ships have become casualties there over the years, driven onto the sands in rough weather such as that experienced in early 1809.

The salvaged items from the *Admiral Gardner* represented a small part of its total cargo, the main body of which was in the hold and unreachable. Some of the contents have been salvaged (under licence in 1985) but owing to disagreements this work has now been suspended. Just take a look on eBay for there are often 'treasure coins' from this ship listed for auction there.

Ramsgate Pier had been destroyed in the storms the previous year, hence the new storehouses where this auction took place would probably have been temporary buildings. Lara must have profited well from this sale. Later there was a collection for 'the Deal Boatmen for their meritorious services in saving the crew of the *Britannia* and *Admiral Gardner* East Indiamen on 25 January last'[20] and Moses was one of the subscribers giving £5 5s 0d.

Who's a bigwig now?

With his business acumen, he soon took advantage of even more lucrative business opportunities, culminating with a major government coup later that year: *M Lara Esq of Ramsgate is appointed Spanish Vice-Consul at that port (the Port of Plymouth).*[21]

So we can see that by 1809 Lara's business activities centred around Ramsgate, though subsequent events, some seven years later, indicate he continued to retain a home in the City.

He formed a new company in Ramsgate, to which he gave his name (Messrs Lara & Co.) in partnership with G Hinds. They had a long association as the partnership was not dissolved until 1830.[22]

They would have been on the lookout for permanent new storehouse/auction buildings to replace those destroyed in the Ramsgate fire of 1908 as these were not rebuilt until after 1812. The perfect place presented itself on the death of Admiral William Fox in late 1810, the owner of Effingham House.

One of the company's advertisements talks of their 'extensive sales room at Effingham House, Ramsgate' where goods were displayed and sold at auction. What did they sell there? Anything that might yield a profit. Items such as 'highly modern and excellent household furniture' were advertised for sale, whilst in London, for instance, he was responsible for a completely different auction – that of a pony.

The booklet on street names in Ramsgate mentions the 'architecturally interesting' houses of Effingham Street, built between the seventeenth and nineteenth centuries. Effingham House was built in the 1700s. In 1905 it was converted into the fire station.

I don't need to be a London broker anymore

Lara had been a stockbroker since at least 1785 and continued as such for more than twenty-five years. Now he had permanent premises in a fashionable part of Ramsgate, he decided to step down from his position as a London City broker and concentrate on his activities in Kent. To facilitate this he placed advertisements in *The London Gazette* in 1810. This was *the* newspaper to read first to find out about business dealings such as bankruptcies, partnerships, dissolutions, debts, etc. This virtual monopoly ensured that no one could deny knowledge of a particular event, because if it was to be advertised, it would be found within these pages. The advert invited potential creditors to apply for final payment.

> All Persons who may have any remaining Claim or Demand on Mr. Moses Lara, formerly of the Stock Exchange, Broker, for any unsettled Balances on account of Differences arising from Stockjobbing Transactions, &c. are requested to send in Writing a particular Statement of the same within Fifteen Days from the Day of the Date hereof, to Mr. Croasdell, of No. 11, Moffat-Street, City-Road, in order that the necessary Arrangements may be made immediately for the same being paid in full.[23]

A commitment too far

He evidently had a busy lifestyle. He had attended the Bevis Marks Synagogue in London for years, and was one of the congregation's elders. His father, Benjamin Lara, had some years ago accepted the office of Gabay (Accountant) for the synagogue, and Moses, like him, had the honour of being chosen as Gabay in 1812. This is a position he never took up. Why? Did he believe he would be unable to carry out his duties to his own – and their – satisfaction as he was based so far away? Would he have considered himself too stretched with his important position in Ramsgate?[24]

A house in London, and one in Ramsgate

Lara had to divide much of his time between Ramsgate, where his main business interests lay, and London, for religious, family and social purposes. It appears he had a house of his own in London, and did not reside with his widowed mother Rebecca Lara. Their properties were close by – both in the Minories – which means they could easily have seen each other when they wanted, which was evidently the best arrangement for them both. How do we know this? These details are available because Moses Lara was unwittingly involved in an incident which went to trial. No secrets allowed there. In a trial you have to identify yourself by giving your name, occupation and address.

Before the beak again

In later years more and more data has come online, and one of the most exciting sources has been that of the trials held at the Old Bailey. It is fascinating to look at some of these; frightening too when one sees minor crimes met with the most severe punishments that the law could impose.[25]

The Old Bailey

The trial in question was indeed at the Old Bailey. Lara (identified as Moses de Lara), figured as the witness. The crime was described as 'Theft/Pickpocketing' by Richard Hurd and was held on 13 September 1815.

Mr Hurd, aged thirty, was charged with stealing, on 10 July of that year, money and property from Moses de Lara. The events of that evening are best conveyed in the exact language of the legal proceedings.

RICHARD HURD was indicted for stealing, on the 10th of July, one pocket-book, value 1s. [one shilling], three Bank of England notes for the payment of 5 l. and eight Bank of England notes for the payment of 1 l. each [one guinea], the property of Moses de Lara, from his person.

MOSES DE LARA. I am a merchant, and on the night of the 9 of July, I was returning home, towards Haydon-square, in the Minories, from Drury-lane Theatre. My pocket-book was in my inside coat pocket; my coat was buttoned, and I thought it impossible to get at it. There were three five-pound notes, and eight ones in it. I saw a fire as I was coming out of the Theatre, and I went to see where it was: it was on Tower Hill, at the back of the Minories. My pocket-book was safe when I got to the Cresent [sic]. I wanted to get out of the crowd, and in a place where there was no crowd at all, the prisoner and another came just before me, and stopped me; they said, take care, sir; and there was nothing to take care of. At that moment, I felt my coat torn open, and clapping my hand upon my pocket, found the pocket-book gone. I immediately seized them both, and held them for three or four minutes in the mob without any assistance; and at last I was obliged to let one go to secure the other, and I held the prisoner fast. I did not see the pocket-book pass between them.

JOHN HODSON. I was attending the fire that evening, near the Crescent. I did not see the prisoner until he was got hold of, and Mr. De Lara came up just after, and said, he was one that had robbed him. I knew the prisoner's person before; I searched the prisoner immediately, but found nothing on him.

The case came before Mr Common Sergeant (the general name for the magistrate in charge of the court at that time). The jury found Mr Hurd guilty of the crime, and he was sentenced to be transported for life.

Mr Hurd's partner got away with the pocketbook and with the cash too. Twenty-three pounds cash. That's a lot of money. Why would anyone carry so much cash on their person; and this after paying for an evening's entertainment at the Drury Lane theatre? No wonder Moses wanted to get away from the dangers of a crowd – it shows how affluent he was to apparently consider it as loose change to take out for an evening.

The Drury Lane theatre had been open for three years, the first to be built in the Covent Garden area, replacing an earlier structure. Everyone knows it today as the Theatre Royal. Not only would it have been within walking distance for Moses, with his house in the Minories, but also ideal for his cousin Abraham Lara (son of his late godfather Aaron) whilst he was living off the Strand.

What happened to Mr Hurd? Convict records confirmed he was transported to Australia, leaving on 16 January 1816, four months after his conviction.[26] According to the records he did not get married when he was there – convicts have to get permission to marry and this was not something he requested.

Another type of commitment

Having been a widower for many years, Moses chose to marry for a second time. The ceremony was held on Thursday 16 May 1816. Not all marriages for members of the Sephardic congregation were held within the Bevis Marks Synagogue, but it is probable this was in view of Moses' position. His bride was Sarah, the daughter of Hananel Mendes da Costa.[27] Her father Hananel was probably the gentleman of Mincing Lane who, in 1765, was party to a sale of imported precious stones to be auctioned by Moses' uncle, Aaron Lara. Marriages had to be within the Jewish community and most likely to be amongst families with whom you had already had connections.

Moses was now forty-nine. His bride figured in the 1851 census and her age then indicated she was born around 1781 in Middlesex. This year matched precisely that given in her obituary several years later, so can be regarded as accurate. Her parents, Hananel and Sarah

Esther, had registered the birth of her elder brother Moses the year previously (1780) and since girls' births could now also be registered, it is disappointing that they chose not to do this for Sarah. As she was thirty-five when they married, it is not surprising they had no children.

The Mahamad and the Haham

The Spanish and Portuguese Jews' Congregation was led by a small group (Mahamad) consisting of two wardens and a treasurer (Gabay), chosen annually from amongst the elders. The Mahamad compiled the first Laws of the Congregation (Ascamot) which were intended to maintain a pious, united and ordered community. Other responsibilities included the levy of taxes on members, the selection of the Haham (Chief Rabbi) and other officials, receiving offerings and legacies, authorising the solemnisation of marriages and distributing charity (both money and goods such as matzot, coal and blankets). As such they were hugely influential.

Following in his father's footsteps

In 1816, a few months after he married, Moses was again elected as a member of the Mahamad and this time he accepted. By then he must have felt settled and able to do full justice to this important position. The appointment was for a year; he was subsequently also elected for 1821 and 1826. Three times in all, just as his father before him. This shows how much they valued Moses, in that they chose to appoint an elder who was not a permanent local resident to such a responsible position.[28]

A Hanukkah Menorah

Moses had inherited from his parents a silver Hanukah menorah which was used in the synagogue annually at the Festival of Lights, an eight-day Jewish holiday. It was made for use with oil, not candles, with a shell and scroll border on the backplate, and was lit at the start of the festival. Eight of these lights signify each night of the holiday whilst the ninth, usually central and above or below the rest, is there for practical use. He donated this to Bevis Marks in his will.

A bust-up in the synagogue

By 1819 Moses was already one of the more prominent of the elders, a strict traditionalist, and a very generous benefactor of the community. One Sabbath he was presiding in the synagogue when he was 'grossly and publicly attacked by the Haham and his two sons'. Haham is the Sephardic term for Chief Rabbi, so clearly this was a man of great importance.

The Rabbi was called Meldola; his sons were David and Abraham. Lara made a formal complaint to the Mahamad and demanded a formal apology from the offenders, which they were not prepared to give. This is not surprising given Meldola's own poor opinion of Lara: 'Consider how much, how long and with what patience have I suffered under various unpleasant circumstances with Mr Lara and in the public synagogue as the whole congregation knows.' This refers to instances where it appears Lara had often insulted the Haham's sons (even within the synagogue) and thus incurred the family wrath in the first place. Arbitration achieved the appropriate apology.[29]

I don't want you as my valentine (but we can still be friends)

Lara announced in *The London Gazette* that his partnership with Elias Valentine was dissolved by mutual content on 24 June 1819. They had been trading together as dry salters, based in Elder Street, Norton Falgate, Middlesex. The company name was Elias Valentine & Co., so others could have been unaware Lara was his partner. Those disgruntled creditors still smarting from earlier losses may have been disconcerted to discover this, considering the families' earlier history.[30]

Admittedly he had ended up with a lucrative package after his dealings with David Valentine, but not without many associated problems. Valentine had absconded with a substantial amount of Lara's funds, along with that of others, and Moses Lara had had to endure a court case and fear for his life. Why would he trust someone from the same family? Valentine is not a common surname, so even without any proofs it is feasible to conjecture he may have been a relation to David Valentine. Nonetheless Elias and Moses remained friends throughout their lives. He was described by Moses as a 'worthy friend' and a beneficiary under his will.

In high spirits

Considering the complexity of the Treasury letters it was good to locate one from Moses. The letter in question (dated 18 August 1820) was written by M Lara of Ramsgate, Agent. He informed officers of the Treasury that in November 1819 the vessel *Elephane* was totally wrecked and little of the cargo was saved. It was his responsibility as agent for the salvage of this particular shipment, and he sought clarification about offering the goods retrieved as a regular salvage, along with any implications there might be for insurance payments. Perhaps the real difficulty here was that the cargo was Scotch spirits – easily portable and highly desirable![31]

You can't take it with you

Moses Lara administered the estate of his mother in June 1822. He was described as one of the children of Rebecca Lara, a widow, late of Prescott Street, Goodman's Fields, St Mary, Whitechapel.[32]

His brother Benjamin was periodically at sea, working as a ship's surgeon, but otherwise based in Portsmouth. He did not return to London, where he may still have been unwelcome. Why Moses chose to take out an administration is a mystery. Her effects were said to be worth less than twenty pounds and she did not consider it necessary to leave a will. Her part of her annuity from her late husband which had not been sold would not have to be declared.

The Laras were familiar with probate so this could be handled without delay. If their mother died in 1822, she would have been extremely elderly! The burial registers don't help here. Moses' father Benjamin had purchased adjacent slots, and the date of her burial should have been recorded against the number, but it was left blank. An obituary filled in the information. She had died over fifteen years previously when Moses was relatively young and energetic enough to divide his affairs between London and Ramsgate. So why leave probate for so long? Presumably the sons had originally decided there was no need for it at all, but something happened to change Moses' mind. There was an ongoing Bill of Complaint in Chancery against several persons, including the heirs of Benjamin Lara – named as Rebecca, Moses and Benjamin Lara. Could Moses have taken out probate to prove his mother's death and so have her name removed from this action?[33]

In September 1822 Moses was named as joint executor for his cousin Phineas Lara, son of his late godfather and uncle Aaron Lara. Phineas died shortly after writing his will.[34] He had no surviving brothers who might undertake the task of probate. The personal affairs of Phineas' eldest son were complex and his younger two were abroad, so he might have felt it better for others to oversee his estate. He had made donations and a trust agreement with the Bevis Marks Synagogue so his choice of two prominent elders from their congregation was appropriate, particularly as Moses was also his cousin. Handling the estate proved to be a long-running affair, with paperwork unresolved up to four years later – an obligation Moses might not have wished for at his age.

Moses and Sarah Lara had no children, so had to decide how best to dispose of their assets, whilst leaving themselves with sufficient income during their lifetimes. Moses, like Phineas, decided to assign much of his estate prior to death, rather than leave it all for his wife Sarah (his executrix) and the trustees to handle. The Lara gift, as it is known, was handed over by him to the synagogue in June 1826.[35]

Under the terms of this, the trustees of the fund were to pay him and his wife £647 4s. 0d a year during his lifetime. His widow would then receive £500 a year and on Sarah's death the whole of the fund would be distributed according to his wishes. Such a large annuity could only have been achieved from a considerable capital sum so unsurprisingly it was one of the largest gifts in the history of Bevis Marks.

His father's son

Moses wanted to put his mark on how the fund would be spent. Part of it was to be used to assist Sephardi Jews by way of gifts, loans, scholarships and dowries.

Medical attendance was one of his priorities, probably because of the family's interest in this. His father had worked as a merchant and trader, whilst being a devoted worker at the Beth Holim. This was the Jewish hospital. In all probability Moses' brother Benjamin had also been involved in this, as he was apprenticed to a surgeon and subsequently followed that profession. There were many calls on the limited finances of the congregation, and one casualty was this hospital, which had for some time become a home for the aged and infirm. The Moses Lara Trust Fund of 1827 came to its assistance to 'enable it to carry on this work free from all financial worry.'[36]

Time's up

Moses was now an elderly man and in poor health as displayed in the contents, along with shaky handwriting, of one of his letters (posted from Canterbury where the couple then lived). In this Lara says 'I am so miserably ill that I cannot take any action in the matter and I would have gone to Ramsgate…but such exertion is far beyond my power. Indeed this letter I have been obliged to address to Mr Daniels has quite overpowered me.'[37]

A follow-up letter was sent by the recipient at Ramsgate to London the next day, 3 November 1830, referring to 'Mr Lara from whom I received a letter this morning.' How's that for an efficient private postal system!

The last slow, lengthy journey for Mr Lara was in his own funeral cortège from Canterbury to London early the next year. He was buried, in accordance with his wishes, at the Novo Cemetery of the Spanish and Portuguese Jews' Congregation.[38] Moses had originally planned to be buried next to his first wife (Rebecca) but his life had changed radically since her death. For one thing he had remarried and his second marriage was long and appears to have been most contented. The plot he bought adjacent to his first wife was instead reserved for his sister, Sarah Rey (who died four years after Moses). His trustees bought three more adjacent plots: one each for Moses, his widow Sarah and his sister Rachel Mendes.[39]

Moses concerned himself with the formalities of the burial process. He naturally wished to be buried in the graveyard of the Bevis Marks Synagogue and paid for two watchers to take turns, day and night, over his grave for the next thirty days after his burial – a precaution against grave robbers. He also specified in his will that he should be buried 'in the plainest manner possible' and that his tombstone should be of good Portland or other stone, but not marble. Portland limestone is the classic material for gravestones. This is because its surface becomes harder after a few years of exposure, thus protecting it from erosion. It is not, however, good for lettering, which is susceptible to weathering unless it is cut deeply, but this would not have been an issue since he wanted it plain and unornamented. If there was any inscription at all given, it did not stand the test of time. In the 1960s (when most of the burial ground was sold to St Mary's University College) transcriptions were made of those monumental inscriptions which were still readable, prior to being broken up. A cousin's friend, working in that area, recollects seeing many of the gravestones being smashed to pieces. The available transcriptions were then reproduced in the synagogue's burial book. There was nothing there for Moses.

His will further decreed that £600 of three per cent consolidated bank annuities should be used solely for the purpose of commemorating the anniversaries of the deaths of his parents. Would funds and customs allow for this still to be part of the annual blessings?

Then again, still on the subject of burials, seventy pounds a year from the Moses Gift was to be awarded to the burial society to abolish the use of calico shrouds and to replace them with linen.

The move

His will was written on 9 October 1828. Sarah Lara proved the will and codicil in London on 15 February 1831. The quire copy made by the clerk was very hard to read, but the original was brilliantly clear. For this reason the reference to the original follows to save anyone interested the inconvenience and time of trying to decipher the copy.[40]

The codicil had been added just under a year later, on 20 August 1829, following their move from Ramsgate to Canterbury: 'Since making my Will I have purchased of Mr George Burkley a Messuage or Tenement and Garden and Hereditaments situate in the Parish of St Dunstan near and without the walls of the City of Canterbury and now in my own occupation…for use of my wife Sarah Lara her heirs and assigns for ever.'

Where there's muck there's brass

The will reveals an interesting fact: he also possessed mortgages and securities in shares of 'any Pier or Pavement or Turnpike Roads'. It seems he was able to spot an investment opportunity at a thousand paces!

Who gets what?

Moses left all the ready money he had in his house to his wife Sarah plus two hundred pounds to be paid to her as soon as possible for her immediate needs and emergencies. As is usual, household goods were left to his widow to use and dispose of, though because of their circumstances there were quite a lot of them in this case: 'And as to all and every my Household Goods, Diamonds, Jewels, Plate, Trinkets, Linen, Glass, China and other wares, print or other Books, wearing apparel and also all such provision and stocks for housekeeping wines, spirits and other liquors as shall be in or about my dwelling house at the time of my decease and likewise all such goods, chattels, articles and things belonging to me…for her own use and benefit absolutely.' As mentioned, she was also to have the annuity of five hundred pounds from the trust fund already in place. He left the same amount of money (one hundred pounds) to all three siblings, named as Mr Benjamin Lara, Mrs Sarah King (otherwise Sarah Rey Lara) and Mrs Rachel Mendes. Given his stipulation that his trust should benefit those from Sephardic marriages only, and the fact that his brother's second wife and family were Church of England, there was always the possibility he could have excluded his brother Benjamin.

Having made these small bequests, and having already disposed of a huge annuity, he was still left with a considerable estate which was assigned in accordance with his will.

The charities of Moses Lara

These were established just under two hundred years ago (in 1827) but not lost in the mists of time. The scale of his generosity was such that some of the charities either founded or supported by his legacies still operate today, just as do those from the famous philanthropist Sir Moses Montefiore. More information was provided by Cecil Roth[41] and details of the accounts and recipients over the years can be seen at the Bevis Marks Collection at the London Metropolitan Archives.[42] Application forms for the Moses Lara Fund are to be found online.

Moses knew his father was born in Portugal. He was a strict believer in pure Sephardic stock and so he stipulated the fund should assist only those persons who married others of Portuguese or Spanish origin. After the persecution in Portugal and Spain finally came to an end, the influx of refugees from these countries declined and this aspect of his fund became virtually irrelevant.

He also stipulated that following the death of his wife all sums on deposit and his houses should be sold and the money gifted to the aforementioned organisations. Not only did this happen, but during her lifetime Sarah Lara also made several important gifts of money to the synagogue.

School time

Some ten years after the death of her husband, Sarah made a generous donation to the London Sephardic community. 'In 1839, the National and Infant School [was] founded at the expense of Mrs Moses Lara.'[43] She personally opened the new premises in April 1844.

And another one bites the dust...

His sister, Rachel Mendes, died in 1840. It was his intention to record all family members on her tombstone, as a handwritten note clearly shows. Whether or not it was used in its original (or a corrected) format we do not know since neither the tombstone nor any other transcription now exists. The list was probably updated after his death and remains a valuable record of his family. Names of family members (*excluding* the errant brother Benjamin) are given. There is just a brief mention of Sarah herself (named simply as Mrs Moses Lara), but we know she was interred in one of the three purchased after her husband's death, and later her own family would ensure her gravestone had a proper inscription.

A new companion

Sarah Lara continued to live in their new house at 4 Dunstan Street, St Dunstan, Canterbury, at some point joined by her unmarried niece Abigail de Leon.[44] Both were fairly elderly by then (Sarah was sixty-nine and Abigail forty-six). They were described as 'fund holders' in the 1851 census, and able to afford three domestic servants to look after the household chores. Abigail's parents had married at Bevis Marks in 1702 then emigrated to Jamaica which is where she was born.[45]

A few years later Mrs Sarah Lara and Mr David Brandon surrendered a leasehold property to Mr John Jennings for seven years. The house was 3 St James Court, Bury Street, St Mary Axe, very close to the synagogue. In the contract Sarah is described as of Canterbury, Widow.[46] She was appointed as one of the trustees for houses in James Court in 1858.[47] The paperwork for these two items is amongst the collection of the Bevis Marks Synagogue.

Sarah outlived her husband the best part of thirty years, dying on 5 December 1859.[48] Her will with codicil was proved at Canterbury on 10 January 1860, and her date of death is given in the probate.[49] Sarah's executors were her two nephews: Hananel de Leon of Bedford and Benjamin da Costa of Brighton, Sussex with effects valued at under £5000. Her nephew Hananel was a brother of Abigail who lodged with her, and son of Sarah's sister Rachel, so probably named after his grandfather Hananel.

The Da Costas

Sarah's will paints a very full picture of her close relations. She named three brothers and two sisters, all of whom had married but by now only the widow of her brother Moses was still alive. Her name was Rebecca. She, along with Sarah's eight nieces and nephews, all had shares in Sarah's estate. An annuity was also provided for Rebecca in her lifetime, and on her decease it was to be sold and out of the proceeds a further eight hundred pounds distributed amongst four of Sarah's great nieces and great nephews, with an extra two hundred pounds going to Abigail de Leon. Rebecca died shortly after Sarah Lara and was also buried at the Mile End Road cemetery belonging to the Spanish and Portuguese congregation of the Bevis Marks Synagogue, on 20 June 1860. Her brother, David Samuda (he was denized at the same time as Aaron Lara, the uncle of Moses), was one of Rebecca's two executors. The other was the aforementioned Benjamin Mendes da Costa, so they were able to ensure the beneficiaries from Sarah's will did not have to wait long for this part of their inheritance.[50]

A reversion to a synagogue

A concise obituary: *'Canterbury Dec 5 in St Dunstan's, Mrs Moses Lara in her 79th year'* appeared in the local newspaper.[51]

On the same day, copied from the *Jewish Chronicle*, was a much more extensive report in a London-based newspaper.[52]

> There died on Sunday last at Canterbury an old lady of the name of Lara through whose decease a reversion falls to the Spanish and Portuguese Synagogue, Bevis Marks, London, which cannot be less than £20,000, but which some estimate at £40,000. The property has been accumulating ever since 1831, the year in which her husband died, the childless widow having only been allowed £500 annually out of the interest.

This report (mentioning such a huge amount of money gifted to the synagogue) obviously caught the attention of the press throughout the country, being reported more or less in full the following week by such newspapers as the *Kentish Gazette, Glasgow Herald, Liverpool Mercury, Caledonian Mercury, Birmingham Daily Post, Bristol Western Daily Press* and *Dundee Courier*. They did not mention, or seek to find out, that whilst her husband was alive the two had a regular income of less than six hundred and fifty pounds between them, so an income of five hundred pounds for one person was not as small as they made out. Added to this were the house in Canterbury and contents, plus money in her own right gifted by Moses, so it seems the newspaper was just spoiling for some unsubstantiated gossip. She would scarcely have been able to make such important gifts of money to the synagogue during her lifetime or the family bequests in her will and codicil had she been short of funds. So whilst a journalist might have felt she was forced to live parsimoniously, it seems she was very much in charge of her own finances!

Rachel Mendes

The Old Lady of Threadneedle Street?

There is very little documentary evidence about Rachel and her husband, which makes what we do have even more precious and important.

Rachel was the second child for Benjamin and Rebecca Nunes Lara and the younger sister of Sarah. She was born between 25 April 1762 and 24 April 1763, about three years after Sarah, and like her was married whilst underage.

Her husband was Moses Mendes, son of Isaac Joseph Mendes, and they married on 8 August 1781.[1] Her marriage settlement consisted of £570 worth of consolidated stock. It was a condition that this should be for her sole use: a requirement not infrequently used to protect the daughter's interests, perhaps in the event of the husband becoming bankrupt and creditors laying claim to his estate. Mendes was a grocer of Threadneedle Street, a solid occupation, but one never likely to make him wealthy.

It's highly probable that Rachel and her siblings had been educated at the Bevis Marks school. Both she and Moses were sufficiently well educated to sign their names fluently on court documents.

Difficult to think of everything

Her father died ten years after Rachel's marriage. He bequeathed cash and annuities to all four of his children. Rachel was to have forty pounds, plus a further forty pounds annuity to be invested by her brothers. They were to pay the dividends directly to her. This, he said, was to prevent the annuity being subject to any debts her husband might incur. After her mother, Rebecca, died, she would also receive a further annuity of forty pounds per annum. He also willed that the legacy of £570 consolidated stock which was the property of his daughter Rachel and currently in his own name, should be transferred into his sons' names for her benefit, again to prevent this being sold. As executor for his late brother, Benjamin would have been only too aware that some of Aaron's sons had sold on their annuities for immediate gain and he was determined to prevent this from happening with his own children. What he omitted to do was clarify what was to become of his daughters' inheritances when they died. Were they to go to their brothers (who had investment control of the annuities) or to any children of the marriage?

Godparents

On 19 April 1783, Rachel became godmother at the circumcision of her nephew, Benjamin Charles, son of her sister Sarah and husband Jacob Rey. Here she was referred to by her Sephardic title: Rachel de Moseh Mendes. The name 'Moses' was often spelt Moseh in the records of the synagogue. The baby's godfather was his uncle Moses, whose name in the register was spelt Moseh Larra.[2] Interestingly the term 'godparent' is used for both Sephardies and Christians, just at different ceremonies.

Parents

The only child of Moses and Rachel Mendes was named Rebecca and she was born in 1790.[3] Sadly hers was to be a short life, as she died before the age of four. Her burial as daughter of Moses Mendes was recorded on 8 June 1794. A footnote says the date should have been recorded as 22 June 1794.[4] Sarah and Moses had a few years to enjoy their baby daughter, though memories can be small consolation when such a young precious life is taken away. After this they, like her brother Moses, remained childless.

How can we know they had no other children apart from Rebecca, when so many birth entries went unrecorded or have been lost over the years? Through litigation! Rachel Mendes and her sister Sarah Lara wrote to the Right Honourable Alexander, Lord Loughborough, Lord High Chancellor, on 12 April 1976. Part of the petition, which essentially revolved around the non-payment by their brothers of the cash sum and dividends due to them, included the statement that Benjamin Lara had given some jewellery and money to Rachel. The brothers, Moses and Benjamin, had to give Chancery an account of the expenditure they had made as executors of their father's estate. The 'answer', made several months later in February 1797, included expenditure for mourning clothing for 'Rachel Mendes and Child' for Benjamin's burial in 1792. If Rachel and Moses had conceived other babies by then the wording would have been different. Of course they may have had more children later, but this would have been unlikely, since by now they had been married for some years. There were indeed no further births, burials or marriages recorded for this couple at Bevis Marks.[5]

Yes, but what about the money?

Did the sisters receive their inheritances in the spirit intended by their father? Sarah evidently thought not as she wrote a second time following the response from her brothers. This letter was dated 17 February 1797. On this occasion Rachel did not join forces with her, even though Sarah said her sister was also still not receiving her interest either![6] Rachel was obliged by Chancery to respond to Sarah's pleading, so she and her husband Moses Mendes attended the Public Office in Southampton Buildings, Chancery Lane on 7 November 1797 to make a joint declaration under oath.

There are some ambiguities in the statement which do not make it clear if Rachel had or had not received her dividends. What is clear was that she and her husband asked for the transfer of these investments into Rachel's name. Why would they do this unless they had, or were expecting to have, difficulty in receiving regular payments? It rather sounds like this was Rachel's careful way of not further antagonising her brothers, unlike her more aggressive sister Sarah.

The second schedule supplied by the Lara brothers related to income and expenditure. This confirmed the annuities and consols were indeed in Rachel's name and invested on her behalf. There was also an item which had not been mentioned in their father's will, under the side heading 'Unfunded property: Bond and Judgement from Moses Mendes £350'. It appears that Moses Mendes had been indebted to his father-in-law for this amount. Might this have been as payment for their living accommodation and shop?

Their mother lived for almost a decade longer, until 25 December 1806, at which time Rachel became entitled to the additional forty pounds legacy from her father's estate. Moses, her brother, did not take out an administration for their mother until very many years later. Whether or not this was to do with the payment of the final inheritance is unknown. There is no evidence to suggest the two women had to invoke proceedings in Chancery to get access to the dividends, so it seems they now received their rightful income.

Together forever?

It is clear both Rachel and her husband attended the meeting in November 1797, yet the wording in the earlier petition to Chancery implies he may have moved out of the marital home. Nine months earlier Rachel was described as Rachel Mendes of Threadneedle Street, London, the wife of Moses Mendes late of London, Grocer. Threadneedle Street was in the heart of the city, close to the home of the Bank of England. Why was her husband no longer 'of London' but 'late of London', implying he had moved away? Had they separated?

There is no trace of a burial for Moses at the Bevis Marks burying ground. He had insufficient assets to consider leaving a will, so these two factors make it hard to determine his year of death. He definitely predeceased Rachel, but there is no trace of him whatsoever after 1797. He was born and brought up a Jew, as evidenced by his name, his marriage and his daughter's burial place. Yet it seems he did not remain one, or else his burial would have been easy to locate. Bearing this in mind, the question must be asked if he and Rachel had separated. In the 1780s Sarah Rey/King, her sister, was divorced. Could this have happened to Rachel and Moses also?

Rachel's brother Moses died almost forty years after their father. He had been living in Ramsgate for several years, and latterly Canterbury, though still came to London as frequently as he could to handle his affairs with the Bevis Marks Synagogue. One presumes he took the opportunity to see his sisters on some of his visits and perhaps pass over the sums due to them. On his death he left Rachel an outright gift of one hundred pounds.[7] Her other brother, Benjamin, who had been living away in Portsmouth for several years, outlived them all. Benjamin continued the arrangement for the dividend payments from the annuities to be collected from the Bank of England by a representative on behalf of his sisters, though whether or not Rachel and her sister ever saw him again is doubtful. There is nothing at all to indicate he ever returned to London.

Moses was very wealthy so a gift of one hundred pounds to his sister was a relatively small amount. However he had also paid for Rachel's burial (whenever this should be needed) and one suspects this would have been a great comfort to her to know she would have a full Jewish burial when her time came.

The burial inscription

Her brother wrote a preliminary inscription for the family tombstone, which he wanted to be put on his sister Rachel's grave. There might already have been an inscription on their parents' gravestones, but it seems Moses wanted every immediate family member who was interred there (thus excluding his errant brother Benjamin) to have their life recorded in this way. No doubt a single stone would be the least invasive way of doing this.

His ideas were written on loose-leaf pages, now deposited in a small book which contains some of the grants made by one of the many trusts that were set up by Moses.[8]

This is the only surviving record. There is no mention of this or any other inscription in the section of the burial register for Bevis Marks which records epitaphs still decipherable in the 1970s. Anything readable was transcribed prior to the stones being destroyed (following the sale of most of the Mile End burial ground). So one can assume that the stone had weathered badly by then. All burial remains, including those of this Lara family, were re-interred at Coxtie Green, near Brentwood in Essex. Plaques, with the names of all the deceased, were erected on low fences around the burial area.

The following is the wording initiated by Moses relating to his sister Rachel. It was updated (probably by his executors) to include her details as she died several years after him:

> Beneath this Stone are
> deposited the remains of
> Mrs Rachel Mendes
> Second Daughter of the above
> Benjamin & Rebecca Lara
> Widow of Moses Mendes
> Died 22nd Nisan 5600 corresponding
> with 25 April 1840
> aged 77 years

The inscription tells us she was Benjamin and Rebecca Lara's second daughter. In fact she was also their second child, some four or five years older than Moses. As Rachel's age at death is also provided, this is the reason an accurate timeframe for her birth could be given at the start of this chapter. Seventy-seven years was quite some age to live. Where was she living then? Might it still have been at Threadneedle Street?

The official burial record, three days after her death, describes her as Rachel Mendes, widow of Moses. There is an accompanying note to say 'previously purchased…by the executors of Moses Lara'.

Her plot was adjacent to Moses and the one subsequently used for Sarah Lara, his widow.[9]

This is a clear indication her late husband either did not have the money to purchase a plot for her, or did not feel the need to do so when he was not buried there. What happened to these two? There is so much that is not known about this couple!

Benjamin Lara and the Walters

> Adventure upon all the tickets in the lottery, and you lose
> for certain; and the greater the number of your tickets
> the nearer your approach to this certainty
>
> *Adam Smith*

Past imperfect, future uncertain

1794: the year when everything changed for Benjamin. His whole life turned upside down. What's more, he – and only he – was the cause of it all…

Benjamin was the second son and youngest child of Benjamin de Nunes Lara and Rebecca de Moses Jessurum. He was born 24 June 1769 and circumcised eight days later as was the Sephardic custom.[1] By 1794, aged twenty-five, our protagonist had been married for three years, having been brought up within the strict and certain teachings of the Jewish faith. Life had not gone smoothly for him two years prior to that. In 1792 his father died and a few weeks later Benjamin's business partnership with one David Valentine was dissolved. Furthermore, in the summer of that year he and his brother Moses had been caught up in legal proceedings arising from other business dealings. How had his life panned out prior to that?

The Laras were respectable people within their community in London and they had by hard work and commitment become successful, wealthy businessmen. Good marriages were made for their children. Benjamin's chosen bride was Judith (known as Catherine), daughter of David Haim Supino.[2] They married fifteen months before his father's death, and the wedding was announced in *The Gentleman's Magazine*, where his name was recorded as Benjamin Lara Junior, of Leadenhall Street, Surgeon. He had acquired this status by completing an apprenticeship with a surgeon: Moses Garcia of Dukes Place.[3] Dukes Place was the next street to his parents' house. As he started this at the tender age of twelve he could have continued to live at home rather than moving in with his master, as was frequently the case. His father, after whom he was named, was primarily a broker and merchant, but also worked with the needy at the Beth Holim (Jews' hospital), which makes it likely he would be happy for his son to show some interest in this profession – hence the choice of apprenticeship. Even after this, Benjamin would not be fully qualified as a doctor. For that, he would have to get the appropriate degree at university, an education not permitted to Jews. Garcia had the same restrictions of course, but there was a need for medicinal aid within their community, particularly from those who could perform operations, so Benjamin was potentially well placed for the future.

Following his training, Lara now worked as a surgeon, apothecary, dealer and chapman. He became a Member of the Corporation of Surgeons of London. Some of Lara's cousins were Freemasons, still fairly unusual for Jews, so it is no surprise that Benjamin himself was appointed surgeon to the Royal Cumberland School for the Daughters of Indigent Freemasons. This sounds a grander position than it was: the school opened in 1789 with fifteen pupils and a matron in Somers Place, Euston, East London, though it was successful and numbers grew quickly.

Being only a second son, Benjamin was fortunate to become the major benefactor from his father's estate in 1792. His late father's will had urged his children to 'keep lawful connections'. Every action Benjamin was about to take was the antithesis to the way he had been brought up.

Numerous articles (including *The Annual Register* for 1794) gave snippets of the events that happened on that fateful day. They excite the imagination, picking out the more juicy aspects of the case, even as with today's news bulletins! But it is the legal records which fill in the detail. The following is derived largely from the English law reports for 1794 – even down to the conversations.[4]

A cunning plan

The character Baldrick in the television drama series *Blackadder* could always be relied upon to have a cunning plan. This was always simple and related to his passion in life – his love of turnips! Benjamin's plan was devised entirely on greed – his and others'. He also kept his plan simple. That way fewer questions would be asked. Lara wanted money now, not the promises that tomorrow might bring. Did he really expect it to work? What if things went wrong? Like Baldrick he had no 'Plan B'. A 'big idea' was just that. No other would do.

The date

Tuesday 30 September 1794 was the big day. It is probable Benjamin chose his outfit carefully as he wouldn't have wanted to arouse suspicion by dressing inappropriately. His hair and complexion were dark (that of a young adult from European stock) and he was five feet four inches tall, an average height for the times. He had in his pocket a letter to his brother Moses, ready to post, explaining his actions. It is almost inconceivable that his thoughts would not have flashed to his recently departed father. Even when it came to writing his will his father had no qualms in recording how careful he was with money and exhorted all his children 'not to live extravagantly and to model their expenses according to their incomes'.[5] This same sentiment was repeated succinctly over fifty years later by the fictional character Mr Micawber in Charles Dickens' *David Copperfield*. His mantra exhorted us to live within our means: 'Annual income twenty pounds, annual expenditure nineteen six, result happiness. Annual income twenty pounds, annual expenditure twenty pounds ought and six, result misery.'

The venue

The Royal Exchange, Broad Street, in the parish of Saint Bartholomew, London. It was both here and in the Stock Exchange where brokers conducted much of their trade.

The Stock Exchange, Walter Thornbury, in *Old and New London: Volume 1* (London, 1878) pp 473–494, British History Online

The Annual Register of 1794 says Benjamin worked as a stock-jobber which would mean he was very familiar with the premises and dealings at the Exchanges. This is incorrect. The confusion may have occurred as several family members were brokers. Also an insurance policy was taken out in the name of Benjamin Lara, broker. This was some months after his father's death, but for his widow, Rebecca. His mother, brother and a sister lived in Goodman's Fields close to the financial and business centre. The young Benjamin, a surgeon of 80 Bevis Marks, had recently moved to Bury Street in the parish of St Mary Axe. This was the street in which his parents had lived after their marriage and where they had brought up their young family. Other family members still lived there and the Bevis Marks Synagogue was close by.

The time

Eleven in the morning. Or thereabouts. Benjamin went to the ticket market in the Exchange and asked what the price was for lottery tickets. Contrary to what many people think, lotteries are not new. They have been organised for centuries in many countries. Benjamin made it clear he was interested in English lottery tickets only.

Trading

By now trading was well underway. The clamour of the participants who strove to make their voices heard, exacerbated by the sheer numbers of people on the trading floor, would make it hard for spectators and other interested parties to comprehend. The appearance of such an apparently shambolic scenario would have been quite pronounced in the late eighteenth century, and it was not until 1986 that the whole system was totally reformed.

Baiting the hook

One of the dealers, Mr Benjamin Mendes da Costa, was sufficiently interested to ask what he wanted.

"To buy."

"How many and for when?"

"One hundred for now."

Enough to make it worth his while. The trader met with others to find out the current day's price and came back with 'one hundred at £19 14s 6d'. The price generally fluctuated on a daily basis, and the rate was reported in *The Times*, in their price of stocks column. Two days later, on Thursday 2 October, for instance, the stock was listed much lower at 19L 12s 6d.[6]

Pre-decimal currency

The move from pre-decimal currency came about in 1971. The money Benjamin was quoted (the system brought in as far back as the reign of King Henry II) was often known as LSD, this being quicker and easier to say than pounds, shillings and pence. This was far removed from LSD, the thrill-seeking psychedelic illegal drug favoured by festival-goers and students in the 1960s and 70s and others since.

The L is interchangeable with £ and, just as with a lot of our language, has its origins in the Latin language: the L from the word *librae*, S from *solidi*, and D *denarii*. The amount here, £19 14s 6d, is pronounced nineteen pounds, fourteen shillings and six pence. LSD had twelve pence to a shilling and twenty shillings to a pound so a pound would have 240 pence.

The value

Lottery tickets today can be bought for a few pounds, so within the reach of many people who want an occasional or regular flutter. This is considerably less than the amount quoted above, even without taking into account inflation since 1794. How much would one be worth in today's money? A simple conversion using the Retail Price Index (RPI) as a measure suggests £2044, adjusted to decimal currency. Multiply that by one hundred tickets and the size of the potential deal becomes staggeringly large.

Can I have some more?

Mr Lara agreed the price and walked away. But not out of the building. He wanted the tickets in hand before he left. Da Costa was hooked. When he met up with his client a little later he had already found another hundred tickets to sell at the same price, and this additional business was agreed. Now the stakes were doubled.

Whilst they were conducting this second part of their business, another trader by the name of Thomas Saunders approached them and asked if Mr Lara had 'completed his quantity' to which he got the reply:

"No, I shall want another hundred."

It was agreed by the brokers that Da Costa would provide Mr Lara with the whole amount.

Early afternoon

2pm that day, some three hours after he had set foot in the Exchange, there was still no sign of any tickets. Mr Lara asked if they were now available. He was told they weren't. Da Costa wanted to know if he was going to lend money on the security of the tickets, and was apparently satisfied with the reply that he had been selling stock to pay for those he had bought. This was the sole questioning as to the financial stability and intent of his client, yet it seemed to satisfy the seller. Why did he not attempt to check out his client's credentials? Was it just complacency, laziness or the excellent commission to be had on such a large sale?

The deal concludes

2.30pm that day. Some of the tickets were ready. Lara was approached by a Mr John Spicer, yet another dealer in tickets, who said that two hundred of the tickets from Da Costa were now ready to be delivered, if he was ready to take them.

Lara replied, "Yes, but you must not take my draft immediately into the banker, as the whole money is not yet there."

Spicer responded, "No, I will not. Give me your draft and it shall go through my banker."

During this conversation Da Costa came up and said: "Spicer, you may as well give Lara fifty tickets more and then he will pay you for 250 and I will deliver him the remaining fifty."

The bank draft

Spicer, at this suggestion, made out an account for 250 tickets and Lara gave him a bank draft for that amount. He also gave a separate draft for the value of fifty tickets to Da Costa, again getting Da Costa's agreement not to present the draft immediately as he had insufficient funds at that moment. So now three hundred tickets were on offer, up from the original hundred requested.

In the late eighteenth century a bank draft, drawn on a deposit at the bank, was *the* method of business transaction. This was especially true of dealings with unknown persons as it substituted the bank's credit-worthiness for that of the person who owed the payment. The bank draft presented was drawn on Messrs Ladbroke and Co. London, dated 30 September 1794. As with cheques issued today, the initial requirement was to complete the payee's name, along with the amount in both words and figures. Hence it was completed: Pay Mr J Spicer, or bearer, two thousand one hundred and fifty-seven pounds 10s. In the payment box was inserted the figures £2157 10s. The signature 'Ben Lara' completed the process.

The bank

In recent times banks have been forced to tighten up their security to safeguard the funds of their depositors as fraudsters seek more ways of separating people from their money. These include devices such as banknote detector pens (used for checking if a note is counterfeit), and counteracting credit or debit card fraud where the card itself or the account is compromised. The use of cheques is limited these days and for this reason alone it is rare for people to receive a cheque which 'bounces'. A 'bounced' cheque is one which is returned unpaid, overwritten in red with the words: REFER TO SENDER, often due to inadequate funds in the account holder's possession. Lara's cheque did not just 'bounce' – it was a total damp squib. It was not a case of him having insufficient funds with Ladbrokes. He didn't even have an account with them!

The pawnbroker

At last, with the lottery tickets in his possession, Lara left the building and hurried to a pawnbroker called Edward West. There he pawned the tickets for £2550, saying he was temporarily in need of funds, but would return to repay and buy them back. The money Lara received was in the form of two bank drafts. West's bankers were Messrs Hankey.

An etching by the caricaturist George Cruickshank of a pawnbroker's shop in London was used as an illustration in *Sketches by Boz*. Boz was Charles Dickens' pseudonym and his friend Cruickshank fashioned this in 1838. The pawnbroker in Monmouth Street showed it had separate booths for privacy of clients, rather than open counters.

The Bank of England

The Old Lady of Threadneedle Street, as it is fondly known today, is situated close to the Exchange. Dangerously close I would imagine for Lara, whose circumstances would require him to distance himself from Spicer and Da Costa as quickly as possible. But he had no choice. Hankey's bank had given him two £1000 banknotes and one £500 banknote in exchange for the bank drafts. These high value notes would be useless to him. He needed lower value notes and only the Bank of England could exchange them for him. And this they did.

Time to run

Lara chose to go home next. Did he have personal belongings to pack or to pick up? If his wife was home did he want her to come too, or had he intended to leave her? Whatever his reasons this action lost him more valuable time. From Exchange to pawnbroker, pawnbroker to Hankey's bank, Hankey's bank to Bank of England and finally home. It all added up to a number of time-consuming journeys. Time he could ill afford to lose.

Post-chaise away

He had summoned the post-chaise to be ready for him, perhaps with a newfound sense of urgency. The post-chaise was a rapid means for transporting mail (hence the word 'post'). The word 'chaise' originated from the French word for 'chair' indicating that seating was hired out to passengers also. Depending on the size, two to four persons could be accommodated inside the carriage. This had four wheels, was generally closed and hooded, with yellow bodywork. To get the necessary speed required either two or four horses were used. These were usually rented and fresh ones were substituted at the stage posts. On this occasion the post-chaise had four horses. This being the case it is probable that the driver would ride on the near horse of the pair attached to the post-chaise. When two horses were used the coachman would usually sit at the open front of the carriage.

Did Lara think he had accomplished his goal? Succeeded in swindling a couple of brokers out of lottery tickets and in so doing lining his own pockets substantially? Did he think that a sunny future awaited him, a colourful life as bright as the outside of the chaise? So where did he plan to go to escape his vengeful pursuers? Somewhere distant no doubt. How about Essex? No, not a misprint. Essex it was. Romford in Essex to be exact! Romford was a coaching town in the eighteenth century, so there would have been regular post-chaise timetables which might have influenced this decision. Had he anticipated that the number of tickets he could get would snowball? If not, his unexpectedly large haul might not have been taken into account when planning where he might go.

Now would be a good time to have a name such as John Smith

Mission accomplished. After such a stressful day, time to unwind and start to relax.

He was no longer alone. On the road he met with a young man by the name of Mr Cleland and they began to talk. They introduced themselves, exchanging names. Lara let his defences slip and he made a big mistake, a real whopper of an error. He gave his name. His real name: Benjamin Lara. He didn't think to use an alias.

Now Mr Cleland was familiar with the events in London. He knew that the draft for Mr Spicer hadn't been paid, that the Royal Exchange was in an uproar and also that Benjamin Lara had no cash at that particular bank. News had travelled incredibly fast. Mr Lara was sufficiently self-possessed to act surprised and to wonder how such a mistake could have happened. With such an uncommon name as Lara, how could he pretend he was not the man at the centre of all this attention? He assured Mr Cleland he would sort it out as soon as he returned to London Town.

That response might satisfy most people. Or, even it if didn't, how many would pretend otherwise? There's no end to the reasons why one would not want to be inconvenienced and tangled up with someone else's problems.

But that wasn't how Mr Cleland reacted. He was adamant that the business should be settled without any delay at all. He was a 'man of principle'. No protests to the contrary were countenanced. Denials and refusals were useless. He decided that they were to return to London now to settle the business.

Mr Cleland took a degree of personal interest in this above the ordinary, and, for the young man that we are led to believe he was, had a remarkable degree of self-assurance and determination. For all we know he may have been sent by one of the injured parties (possibly Mr Spicer as he referred to him by name) in the hope of waylaying Mr Lara. Whatever the reason, it changed the course of events that day.

Mood changes

Lara must have been rather incredulous. Why would someone take this degree of interest? A biblical Good Samaritan? Surely this man wasn't really prepared to go all the way back to London? There must be a way out. How would he have felt? Possibly hot anger that anyone outside the law should presume to interfere so. Cold fear of what that could mean. Fitful hope he could still turn this around. Thinking time…that's what he needed…

Lara had daydreamed that he was safe already. He forgot the long delays that had plagued his journey to make that less certain. Also that others might be zealous in getting their balances cleared. He thought the drafts would not be presented to the bank until later, perhaps even the following day, buying him precious time. But now it was clear this had not happened. Da Costa and Spicer had been to the bank already. When they agreed to a delay, their understanding of the length of time a 'delay' meant was not the same as Lara's. So Da Costa went to Ladbrokes. Ladbrokes wouldn't pay the draft.

They confirmed Lara had no account with them. The fraud was discovered. The news spread rapidly. Benjamin Lara had to be found and the money returned.

An unhappy awakening. The surrounding landscape was a mix of autumnal colours, summer foliage giving way to yellows, oranges, reds and browns; browns especially. The year of 1794 had heralded a dry, warm summer; now a distant past. That fine weather had sucked out moisture from the trees and plants, leaving them brittle and faded. It is likely his own mood swung in concert as if to mock him. From yellow to brown, to red and back again, reflecting the scenery and the desolate, cheerless grey of the weather, as fear and a sense of imminent doom pervaded.

Throughout September the weather had changed as if to make up for the last months and the heavens had opened. Rain, rain and still more rain fell.

We must go back

Realising he had no option Lara returned with his unwanted companion. He could not run from here as his whereabouts were now known. Cleland would raise the alarm. The only thing to do was to go back and somehow escape his clutches. Lara asked Cleland to accompany him to his home, in Kensington, where he ushered him into a front room. Lara promptly went to the back door and absconded a second time with the money. This time he had to avoid the route to Essex.

The Annual Register for 1794

A summary was also recorded in *The Annual Register* for 1794 for the month of October.[7] Much of the account is similar to that given in the newspapers of the times, concentrating on those elements which would most likely interest its readers. A confusing, conflicting element is where the article says that upon the fraud being discovered quickly by Da Costa, he went to Lara's Peckham house. There was a post-chaise and four waiting at the door. Peckham was a long way from the City and no other reports mention this address. The article also says Da Costa's son had seen Lara a little while before and had mentioned that his father had gone to Lara's house. The son was unaware at this stage that Lara's actions had been fraudulent. Was it this knowledge that allowed Lara to escape by the back door, leaving the post-chaise, Da Costa and Cleland by the front?

Off again

This time there would be lots of people searching for him. By now, as the law report confirms, there were handbills printed and 'circulated throughout the Kingdom offering a large reward for the apprehending of him'. No smartphones or Internet, yet very fast communication nonetheless.

He was the one person everyone wanted to know about. They gossiped in the coffee houses, at the theatre, at the synagogue, everywhere. It wouldn't have been a good time to have the surname Lara. One can imagine some of his relations would have been very upset to be associated with him, and his direct family would need to hunker down. Handbills and newspaper articles fed the appetite for savoury news stories.

Now aware of the speed of the news coverage, Benjamin knew there was no point in going the same direction as before. So where to this time? Portsmouth. Portsmouth would have been known to him, at least conversationally. It was a huge naval port and the point of entry of many travellers from abroad. His own uncle had come to Britain in a naval convoy some ten years earlier, escaping from the siege of Gibraltar. So it is unsurprising that he thought he might do the opposite, particularly now as the enormity of the situation must have made him realise that it would be very difficult to escape capture if he remained in the country.

The Portsmouth Chaise

The chase was on again. From stage post to stage post, the post-chaise continued from London to Portsmouth, changing to fresh horses at each stop. The police were apparently in hot pursuit, but that possibly sounds grander than it actually was. On arrival Lara found there were no immediate sailings from Portsmouth. He knew that remaining there would be risky. He decided there was no option other than to return to London to enlist the aid of his family. Discretion took him on an alternative route back to the capital.

The swindler apprehended

The Morning Herald takes over the tale here with the headline THE SWINDLER APPREHENDED.[8] Lara had written to his brother, Moses Lara, and sent the letter some time that day. On his return to London he booked himself into an inn called The Golden Cross, at Charing Cross, under the pseudonym of Mr Jennings. This was a major coaching inn, opposite St Martin-in-the-Fields Church; the area now famous as Trafalgar Square. It was from here that he sent another letter to his brother, signing it Christopher Jennings, asking him to meet him at the Golden Cross Inn. Unbeknown to either of them, a description of Moses Lara had been provided to the Bow Street officers, along with the address of Mrs Rebecca Lara, their widowed mother. She lived in Alie Street, Goodman's Fields. Two officers, Miller and Kennedy, discussed the situation and thought they might get some valuable information from Mrs Lara, so they set out for her house.

Brothers arrested

It just so happens that Moses Lara, on receiving the second letter from his brother, decided to see their mother and apprise her of the situation. She only lived a short distance from him, so he started walking to her house. The article continues, 'When they had got near the house, they met with a person whom they supposed, from a description they had previously received of him, to be the offender's brother, and took him into custody.' On searching Moses' pockets they found the letter from Christopher Jennings. They were convinced, judging from the contents and the tone of the letter, that Mr Jennings and Mr Lara were one and the same person. Miller immediately went to the Golden Cross and enquired for Mr Jennings. Lara was unsuspecting as he thought his brother had arrived. Miller searched Lara's possessions and found everything – all the banknotes and money for the whole of the sum received for the tickets, apart from about forty pounds which had been spent that day. He arrested his suspect and escorted him to the Public Office at Bow Street.

Before the Justice of the Peace

Mr Justice Addington was the Justice for the Bow Street office, so it was before him that Lara was taken for examination. William Addington is reputed to be the first regular Bow Street magistrate. He heard that the offence had been committed in the City of London, which was outside his jurisdiction. Consequently he ordered the officers to conduct him to the Lord Mayor. It was a short matter before the Lord Mayor decreed that he should be locked up and Lara was flung into the gaol at Poultney.

The end of the longest day

It didn't stop raining. The rain which started in earnest in September was to continue for a couple more months with little relief. Though indoors, away from the continuous drenching, rain, the incessant drumming on the roof of the building, would have been a depressing sound. From the night of 30 September to 7 November 1794 he remained in Poultney Gaol. This would have been a very small local jail, accommodating those awaiting trial. There was no electricity or even gas in those days; and for the prisoners no candles either. Any semblance of light would come from those lit for the officers, flickering and playing with the unsettled emotions of the cell occupants.

Home Office documentation shows that on Friday 7 November Benjamin Lara was brought to the November court sessions for Middlesex.[9] From there he was transferred to the notorious Newgate Prison. A regular 'List of Felons' at Newgate, indexed under the month the person was committed and according to the crime, was kept and is now also housed at the National Archives. The first entry for him was one week later, on 14 November, in the 'Prisoners for Law' section. Subsequent entries for him (with the comment that he was a doctor) were made more or less monthly.

Penny token, Newgate Prison, 1797
Birmingham Museum and Art Gallery

At the time of his imprisonment his business was recorded as: Surgeon, Apothecary, Dealer and Chapman. He could not carry out his trade whilst in prison – unless to aid his fellow prisoners – and as it was a specialist business there was no one else to run it for him. Doubtless any attempt to continue would have met unbending opposition from his prosecutors. As early as 8 November 1794 *The London Gazette* (a paper which specialised in businesses and reporting bankruptcies) gave notice that creditors were required to come forward to prove the amount of outstanding debts due them. Lara, for his part, was given more time to make a 'full discovery and disclosure of his estate and effects'. The proceedings for this had started very quickly after Lara's capture. Had this been instigated so promptly by his prosecutors and creditors, as they anticipated a summary judgement and wanted closure on his business too? Or was this procedure already in hand, and thus a factor in Lara's planning? *The Gazette* again, on 27 December that year, signified creditors should come forward to prove their debts, prior to the certificate being used on 10 February 1795.

Newgate Jail in which he languished has had a chequered history. Originally it was housed in a gatehouse on the Old London Wall. This building to which Lara was sent, designed by George Dance the Younger, had only been constructed eleven years previously. Even so it would have been filthy and overcrowded, as were the other prisons of the day.

There was no escaping criminality in jail along with drunkenness, gambling, violence and disease. Whether his family had been able to afford to pay the jailers some bribes to defray some of these conditions and allow him a little comparative luxury are unknown. It is certainly probable he had food taken in, judging from the time he spent in Newgate. To start with, he was there for a month prior to the case coming to court.

Predicting the unpredictable

The Times reported that at the Old Bailey, 'The Sessions House was very much crowded on Saturday afternoon in expectation of the trial of Mr Lara, the Jew, who is indicted for obtaining a number of lottery tickets by fraud...'[10] Just imagine how jam-packed it would have been, with trial officials, the plaintiffs and their supporters, plus those who squeezed in for the amusement, the entertainment, the grudge, the anger, for retribution, justice or family support. Possibly more than a few were waiting and willing for the black cap to be placed on the bewigged head of the judge.

Trials at the Old Bailey in the eighteenth century were notoriously short. Judge and jury listened to such evidence as was available, counsel cross-examined the witnesses and defendant, statements and addresses were made. They came to a quick verdict whilst remaining in the courtroom (with little or no discussion before coming to a vote). A punishment according to law was meted out by the judge.[11]

Such was the legal system of the day. Punishments were swift and hard. Finding a way through the twists and turns and legalese of this case would not be easy. It appears Mr Common Sergeant speedily came to that conclusion.

The indictment (the formal accusation of a crime) was that of obtaining a number of lottery tickets by fraud at common law. Before the Lord Mayor retired for dinner Mr Garrow, for the prosecution, said he was prepared to delay the case. Mr Fielding, the prisoner's counsel, wanted to proceed so the trial time of 5 o'clock was booked. They were running late and it was not until 7 o'clock that the recorder was relieved by Mr Common Sergeant. He looked around at the crowded courtroom, the plaintiffs and their eminent prosecutors, and decided pretty quickly the case was beyond his capabilities. According to *The Times*' report, he observed that 'as he should be the only judge on the bench, he did not think himself competent to decide a trial of so much weight. He had considered also of the evidence to be produced, and was of opinion that it was too late an hour to enter on so complicated a business. Another reason why he wished to defer the trial was that, the indictment being perfectly new, many questions, altogether novel, might occur for his decision, and he should not have the assistance of any judge. He did not think it right to stand in that predicament.' It was his opinion that the indictment ought to be referred to a higher court: the King's Bench.

This unusual case went against all the 'rules'. Most of the company present must all have been hugely disappointed that the trial was not to be held then.

Mr Garrow, for the prosecution, declared again that he was happy to delay the trial as it was of extreme importance to the great commercial city. The name Garrow might be familiar to those who have watched *Garrow's Law* on television. This was a legal drama inspired by the pioneering skills of eighteenth-century barrister, later judge, William Garrow. The cases televised were 'enriched' scenarios from Old Bailey cases. Ultimately this particular trial for Lara never took place at the Old Bailey, hence it is not even mentioned in their proceedings.

Garrow had proposed the case should return to the Old Bailey at a time when there would be three judges on the bench as well as the recorder and Mr Common Sergeant to give their opinion; unlike the judge he did not want to move the case to the Court of King's Bench. He argued that would mean a lengthy delay until the next sessions took place. But that was exactly what was decided. The case was to be postponed until next session. Mr Lara would continue in custody at Newgate. He was entitled to 'British Justice' as his father had the foresight to take out denization in 1771, which confirmed these rights for himself and his heirs.[12]

There are four legal sessions each year: Michaelmas, Hilary, Easter and Trinity. This initial foray at the Old Bailey was towards the end of the Michaelmas session. Trials to be held at the Court of King's Bench would have been already agreed for the Hilary session. So it was that the prosecution at the Court of King's Bench was not held until Easter term 1795. The start of the Easter term depends on the date of Easter Sunday; though variable it falls roughly mid April to very early June. Mr Garrow was correct in stating that this would mean a lengthy delay. Benjamin Lara had to languish in Newgate awaiting a new trial date some five months distant. Originally his name was near the bottom of the List of Felons, though unsurprisingly by 26 May 1795 his name was seventh from the top.

Brrr…

Not only was Newgate, under any circumstances, an unpleasant place to reside, this was especially so over the winter of 1794/95 when the weather was exceptionally severe. A specialist historical weather site shows that very cold conditions settled in by Christmas Eve 1794 (though it had been cold since November).[13] The frost then lasted, with some breaks, until late March. The cold was most intense during January, which resulted in January being the coldest month in the instrumental era (which began 1659). This era has since been styled the 'Little Ice Age'. On 25 January an extreme temperature of (minus) 21 degrees Centigrade was recorded at an unspecified location in England, though some references give this as London. A rapid but temporary thaw, accompanied by heavy rain, began on 7 February, causing much flooding and extensive damage to bridges. The severe cold returned after February 12 and by 23 February a number of rivers, including the Thames, were frozen with 'frost fairs' being set up there. Frost fairs were prosperous business opportunities, centring on such entertainment as puppet shows, roundabouts, and fairground booths. Walking on the deep frozen water, cooking stalls, horse-riding and skating were amongst the other pastimes to amuse the populace and to take some advantage of the weather. Freezing cold and snowy conditions with easterly gales continued well into March.

Fresh indictments

10 February 1795, the date the certificate for winding up Lara's business was due, came and went. As the court case dragged slowly on, so his business closure moved in concert. *The Times* once more was the best source of information on subsequent dealings of the King's Bench with Benjamin Lara.

On 2 May 1795 they allocated a substantial footage of this action to their law report.[14] It was stated that the prosecution case of Mendes da Costa was to present new accusations against Lara. Once more William Garrow was his legal representative. The case was heard at the Court of King's Bench on Saturday 1 May with the defendant, Lara, present. It was reported Mr Garrow moved that the defendant might be charged with two new indictments.

Benjamin Lara pleaded 'not guilty' on both counts. The reason given for fresh indictments was there had been 'an ingenious alteration between the charge and the evidence which might have entitled him to an acquittal and this fresh indictment was designed to ensure that that did not happen.'

Lara was asked if he had any bail. "No," he said, but he asked what amount of bail would be required. The Lord Chief Justice found out that the money from the fraud had been restored to Da Costa who was therefore scarcely out of pocket. Bail was set at £200 on each of the indictments and two more of £100 each on each of the indictments, adding up to £600, a substantial sum. There was no chance of this money being found. The prosecutor had wanted it pitched at such a high level as a deterrent, as he clearly did not trust Lara from absconding. The court ordered Lara to be remanded until the bail was found, so once again he went back to Newgate Prison. By now he had been there as one of the longest detained prisoners under charges of fraud.

Both *The Times* and the law reports state that just over a month later, on 20 June, Lara was required to return to the CKB again; this being confirmed by a note in his prison record.[15] His two attorneys, Shepherd and Knapp, had two indictments to defend. The first concerned John Spicer, who it was alleged was defrauded, having passed on lottery tickets belonging to Da Costa. His defence was to clarify the evidence that these tickets actually belonged to Spicer, who had purchased them from Margary and Co. These particular ones did not belong to Da Costa at all. The jury accordingly acquitted the defendant on this first count.

The second count was that he did cheat and defraud Benjamin Mendes da Costa by 'making the false pretence that was used on one man and by which he was deceived, operated to the prejudice of another.' In other words, only Person A was actually deceived by Lara; Person B was taken in by the information passed to Person A. On this count the defendant was found guilty.

Following this verdict, Shepherd, one of the defence attorneys, requested an 'Arrest of Judgement'. A 'Rule to Arrest' the case is a motion asking the court to overrule the judgement in a civil or criminal case, on the grounds that it was granted in error. They were successful in this request as they were able to assert that the defendant hadn't used any token or shown false evidence to prove that he had the funds and was willing to pay for the tickets. He had merely said that was the case. Shepherd submitted that common prudence should have been used when passing over valuables to an unknown person. One would expect individuals to be on their guard under such circumstances. Furthermore, he submitted that this was merely a private transaction between two parties. It was not a matter for public concern. That being the criteria under which indictments for fraud at common law are based, this particular case should not have been treated as such.

Lord Chief Justice Kenyon agreed that the defence should prepare a rule to that effect, and that the case would be held over to the next term.

Lara was returned to prison yet again as he had no bail, and the prosecution was clearly of a mind to ensure he was never released on bail, even if he had the funds.

Mr Shepherd obtained a rule as had been instructed by Kenyon. Now he had to bring it before the court. The date agreed was 23 November 1795. Benjamin Lara came to the court under a writ of habeas corpus obtained by Mr Vaughan. Habeas corpus is a Latin term, meaning 'you should have the body'. So the writ of habeas corpus was the legal action summoning the prison authorities to present the prisoner before the court. The court would then determine whether there was sufficient lawful authority to keep the prisoner in detention.[16] This did not mean it was all over. The court needed time to consider the rule. So back to Newgate for a further winter.

Newgate records confirm Benjamin Lara, a doctor from London, was still held there on the dates that the counts were taken: 7 July, 25 September, 31 October, 7 December 1795 and 21 January 1796, by which time his name had moved up to fourth place.[17]

With no verdict after all this time, would Lara have allowed himself to dream of a future life on the 'outside'? He was sufficiently astute to realise that he had to plan for a different lifestyle from the one he had lived prior to his imprisonment.

What might he do? How could he prepare for an uncertain future?

Lord Kenyon's verdict

From now on the Guildhall was to be the preferred place for judgement. Lara's case was due again at court for full discussion and hearing on the rule set for the Hilary Term (mid January to early April). The date fixed was Monday 8 February 1795. The presiding judge remained Lord Kenyon, Chief Justice. Either he or his clerks had checked previous similar rulings for guidance. The judge was able to use the ruling from a previous case to come to a conclusion on the evidence presented here. He needed to establish the boundary between frauds which are indictable at common law and those which were not. The case quoted was The King v Wheatley.

As the case had gained in momentum without (for the prosecution) a satisfactory conclusion, four worthies were lined up in their attack. These were Erskine, Garrow, Wood and Knowlys. They all argued for the necessity to frame this indictment at common law. The alternative had been to prosecute under statute which they had felt was inappropriate as the lottery tickets were neither money nor goods.

Lord Chief Justice Kenyon pronounced that 'the defendant's conduct was certainly grossly immoral and highly reprehensible, but as he used no false token to accomplish his deceit, the judgement must be arrested.' He stated also that 'other judges gave similar interpretations that (Lara's) actions had been wholly based on a bare naked lie.' As a man the bench decreed: 'It was not a matter criminal, but it was the prosecutor's fault to repose such confidence in the defendant.'[18]

Da Costa, now out of pocket from considerable legal fees, also had this added embarrassment heaped on him. The pronouncement that he should have checked out the credentials of the prisoner put him at fault. He was publically shown to be at blame for just accepting what he had been told at face value.

The following day, 9 February, *The Times* reported on the Lord Chief Justice's words.[19] He had made it quite clear that he had arrived at his decision for the sake of justice, though he had an extremely low opinion of the prisoner. He had declared: 'This was a very bad man, and if the Law had reached him and involved him in an offence of a higher nature he should not have been very sorry for it. Though in future he must be driven from Society of all honest men, and could never expect to have any commerce with Society or to be trusted again, yet the Court were not to reach him where the Law did not. The indictment ought to have been founded on the Statute.'

The judgement was arrested.

February 1796, and the records detail Benjamin Lara's imprisonment at Newgate for debt was over. His barristers, especially Mr Shepherd, had achieved the seemingly impossible. He was not sentenced to death. He was not transported for life. He was a free man.

What next?

In all he had been in prison for just over one year four months. During that time presumably his wife, mother and brother, possibly also his sisters, had visited him and taken him food and other necessities. He, for his part, had intended to abscond, leaving them all to face the backlash. Had he considered what his family would think when they discovered he had left? Would he see them again? Did he care that much?

During that period he was the talk of the town. London Town naturally, but also elsewhere: Gloucester, Oxford, Leeds, Edinburgh, Norfolk, Derby, Bath, Northampton, Chester and Winchester to name just a few. Provincial newspapers all reported on events in the capital which were considered newsworthy for their readers. His exploits ticked all the boxes.

His reputation was in tatters, and his business ruined. All he had was his liberty – and time to work out another plan…

Three months after his release Benjamin's business dealings had been sorted. *The London Gazette* regularly updated creditors of the progress.[20] His new address was now listed as Kennington Green, near Vauxhall, Surrey, some distance from the city. The commissioners had met on 14 May 1796 at 10am at the Guildhall, London, to receive the proof of the debt. On 16 July of that year it is recorded that unless 'cause by shewn to the contrary on or before the 6 day of August next' this certificate would be confirmed according to the Act. It was, and he was officially bankrupt with a Commission of Bankruptcy awarded and issued against him.

Building on his medical experiences he wrote and published his first paper on midwifery in the year of his release. The following year, 1797, a major undertaking was published. This he called *A Dictionary of Surgery or the Young Surgeon's Pocket Assistant*. He may have started work on this whilst imprisoned as one way to keep himself mentally active, up to date with his profession and to generate hope. He might also have expected some income from sales.

But his future life could not be played out in London; people have long memories. He would need to move away from his notoriety and start anew. A new place, a new job, a new Benjamin. A person who might even seek redemption for the actions of his past? That's where our story goes next…

Portsmouth ahoy!

Once more Portsmouth was his destination, for the simple reason it was the largest naval seaport of the time and further away from London than Chatham docks.

Where there were ships, there were ship's surgeons. This was a time of political unrest in Europe so there were plenty of employment opportunities within the substantial fleet. Lara was successful. It is recorded in the navy lists that on 26 March 1798 he took up his appointment as ship's surgeon in Portsmouth and confirmation of this date was subsequently found in his service record.[21]

Now let's go back a bit, even before his earlier exploits in London.

Just weeks after his father died, Benjamin split up from his business partner David Valentine, and this was formally announced in *The London Gazette*.[22]

When asked to give a reference for his ex-partner, who had applied for goods on credit shortly after, he provided a satisfactory one.

Valentine subsequently absconded, leaving huge debts. As a result of this Benjamin and his younger brother Moses were embroiled in a court case to prove they were not party to misrepresentation.[23]

Benjamin and Moses had two sisters – Sarah and Rachel. Though he was the youngest of the four, Benjamin inherited most when his father, also Benjamin, died in December 1792. His mother, Rebecca, had a lifetime annuity of one hundred and fifty pounds, of which seventy pounds would pass to her younger son on her decease. Benjamin decided he wanted the regular income now, and wished to buy out his share of her legacy outright. His mother and brother appeared to agree, but the arrangements proved problematic. So he wrote to the Lord High Chancellor asking for a ruling to allow him to have access to the money. The other parties were required to state their positions and considerable legal correspondence from him, his mother and siblings ensued until it was resolved.[24]

Benjamin and his wife Catherine moved to Portsmouth, 'the principal seaport of the Kingdom', where they started their family. Pigot's trade directory for the Portsea area of Portsmouth for 1823/24 reports: 'There is also a Hebrew Tabernacle for the Jews who are very numerous here.' This was the synagogue whose elders had welcomed the Jewish refugees from Gibraltar following the Great Siege, giving them temporary respite and relief. They corresponded with their counterparts in London – the final destination for many including Isaac Lara, Benjamin's uncle. His nephew, then about ten years old, would have met his uncle and three cousins during their protracted stay, if only at the synagogue.

It was at this London synagogue that he had married Catherine. Both husband and wife had come from devout Jewish families so one would expect them to continue to worship at the Portsmouth synagogue. Though there is a surviving circumcision book for Levi Isaacs. This contains an entry for their (unnamed) son who was circumcised on 14 March 1800.[25] The baby boy was one of only thirty-six entries over a seventeen-year period. He was described as being the son of Simhah Levi 'Doctor Lara'. Probably the boy was also buried there along with an earlier baby sister.

A Dickens of a coincidence

When Catherine died in 1816 aged forty-nine she was not interred there. She was laid to rest in the churchyard of St Mary, Portsea.[26]

The current St Mary's was built in the 1930s, following several rebuilds. Catherine probably had her ceremony in the original building. The route to St Mary's went via Queens Street and Edinburgh Road, then along a path known today as (guess what?) Church Path. It was at this early church that Charles Dickens was baptised in 1812. The place of worship was one-and-a-half miles from Portsea and generally known as Kingston Church, after the district in which it stood. It was the only church for the sprawling Portsea area until the 1820s, when two chapels of ease were built.

Catching the post

Queen Street, mentioned above, was a main thoroughfare in Portsea. Here was the Post Receiving House of William Chubb (no. 52) where letters to London, the north and east were dispatched every evening at 7.15pm. Literature in the Dickens bi-centennial exhibition of 2012 suggested it took ten hours to reach London from Portsmouth by the Royal Mail post-chaise. London was seventy-two miles away and regular coaches travelled the route to the capital, most departing from Queen Street, a few from High Street. The coaches had distinctive names such as The Hare, The Rocket and The Nelson. The final stop in London was at Charing Cross or Gracechurch Street, depending on the coach company.[27] In some respects travel then was no different from now. Ask a person for directions and you'll expect to hear of landmarks en route, especially pub names. The names of inns were even more important in the past as travellers would need overnight rest and recuperation before completing their journey. The route from The George in High Street, Portsea finished at the Golden Cross at Charing Cross. For Gracechurch Street passengers started at The Golden Eagle.

Known to be operating in 1798 was the True Blue coach, leaving at 6pm from The George Inn, Portsea and setting down at the Golden Cross, Charing Cross. This sounds like the coach to London that Benjamin had boarded with a heavy heart some years earlier expecting to meet his brother Moses, having failed to get a quick passage across the Channel to complete his escape.

Jump forward again to 1816 when he was settled in Portsmouth and a widower. He did not take out probate for his late wife until over a year after her death, and this was a month after his second marriage! Why the delay? Was he at sea when she died?[28]

Some time after his wife's death Benjamin returned to London, presumably with the sole intent of finding a bride. He could not enlist the help of his brother Moses who regularly returned to the City from his home in Ramsgate, since he was a staunch traditional Jew, whereas Benjamin clearly was not any longer. Perhaps this was a factor of life at sea. A surgeon had to be on hand to tend the sick even on the Sabbath. Also it would take a man of strong religious convictions to stand apart from the rest of the crew. Benjamin may once have considered himself such – his father had left him his sermons, rather than his first son – but he was living as an ostracised outsider, far from the close circle of family and friends and often at sea. He may, metaphorically, have lost his way.

Benjamin's choice of second wife was Rachel, the daughter of Thomas and Anna Walters. The church where they married, St John at Hackney, was quite close to Benjamin's old haunts so he may have been drawn back to familiar territory. They married on 20 October 1817, five days after the marriage licence was granted.[29]

In the fullness of time Benjamin and Rachel had three children, all baptised at St Mary, Portsea. First was Mary.[30] She never married. All three censuses in which she figured (1841–1861) show her living initially with her parents and siblings, then with her mother and sister (both widows). There is an indication Mary may have moved away from the family home for a short period before late 1843. Her father wrote his will in that year, in which he recorded he had lent her £400. It is difficult to know of another reason she may have needed so much money. On his death this sum became due to the estate.

Two years after Mary's birth they had their only son, Benjamin Walters Lara, named after both families.[31] As his son grew, Benjamin Senior would have made good use of his connections and income to allow him to pursue a career in medicine. The boy would have needed an excellent education throughout his youth and this may have been at Portsmouth Grammar School, founded 1732 and still thriving today. This cannot be substantiated as no school records survive prior to the mid 1800s. Apart from this school there were many academies for children from better-off families. There was also a Seaman & Mariners' Orphan School to which it is recorded that Dr Lara MD made a donation of ten shillings in 1835.[32]

At the age of eighteen Benjamin Walters was still at home.[33] His father died in 1847 by which time the young Benjamin had moved to 14 St John Street, Adelphi, St Martin-in-the-Fields and remained there until at least 1856, as confirmed by the UK Poll Book, Westminster Rates and the 1851 census.[34] His occupation was given in the census as a medical agent, so it appears he chose to use his medical expertise in a less hands-on manner than his father. He may have temporarily gone abroad as he applied for a passport in 1855.[35] He became a partner in a business, now styled Messrs Lane & Lara, which had been established in 1828. Benjamin Walters went on to study at King's College then on 1 November 1856 he was admitted to Gray's Inn. He continued to study part-time, combining his academic studies with paid employment. 1857 saw the publication of *The Medical or English Medical Dictionary* which he edited and jointly published from the firm's new premises.[36] This work was the subject of an unsuccessful law suit with the General Apothecaries Company.

Benjamin Walters lived at Gray's Inn as a student and surgeon in 1861, along with two of his cousins, one of whom was also in a related line of business: an agent for Church property.[37] He started a new business, called B W Lara & Co., and meticulously kept copies of his replies to potential clients for the purchase and sale of Church properties. One of these copy books – which indicates how much work was generated – can be seen at the Wellcome Institute, London.[38] In 1863 the commission on one of his sales was disputed, taken to court, and won by Lara.[39]

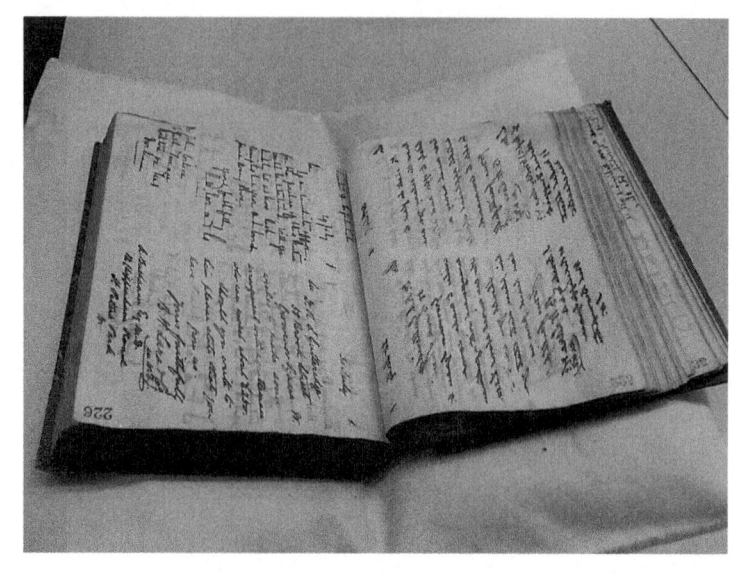

A letter book of B W Lara & Co.
Wellcome Library, London

It was not until 1865 that Benjamin Walter's marriage to Marianne Elizabeth Gatehouse took place at St Mark's, Tollington Park. Marianne's cousin conducted the ceremony. The Church of England was important to this family – her younger brother Thomas John was also a rector.[40]

The truth will out

A stressful time for the couple came two years later when Benjamin was cited as a co-respondent in a divorce. This seems extraordinary as they were only relatively recently married and this was late in his life; he did not seem to be the type of person to be caught up in an extramarital liaison. The court case makes fascinating reading and is a good example of the growing integrity of the British legal system in its pursuit of truth. Benjamin was not the only person named in the action by Francis Godrich against his wife, Adelaide Fanny Godrich. Three other co-respondents were also named. She was one busy lady! The evidence showed that Mr Godrich had lied about all their involvements to take revenge on his wife as she wanted a divorce. The case was dismissed and the judge decreed Godrich was to be tried for perjury. Justice for all![41]

A few years prior to his marriage, and certainly by 1861, his elder sister Mary moved to Brompton, Kensington with his mother Rachel and a younger sister Elizabeth. This was several years after the death of his father. Rachel Lara was by then blind, so this may have precipitated the move. Their new home would have been much nearer her family and also closer to her son. She was fortunate to have her two daughters to care for her. Not for long though. Her firstborn, Mary, died on 24 May 1863 aged forty-three.[42] All three had been described in the census as being fund holders: each daughter had a one-thousand-pound inheritance (from which they received annuities). Rachel also had regular annuity dividends, in addition to a naval pension.

The Admiralty papers held at the National Archives include the pensions for widows of navy officers. It was not until 1808 that surgeons had been raised to 'wardroom rank' which meant that from thereafter they were, for all practical purposes, treated as though they were commissioned officers. As such his widow, Rachel, was able to apply for a naval pension. The death certificate of her late husband confirms he was a physician, indicating he died at 2pm on 28 December 1847 at his tenanted home, 3 Queens Place.[43] Rachel received her widow's pension from the first day of the New Year. It was noted she had a private income of £66 per year, whereas most other applicants had 'nil' against this heading.[44] She outlived her daughter Mary by two years, dying in 1865 a few months prior to her son's marriage and was buried at Brompton Cemetery.[45]

Unlike his father, Benjamin Walters did not make old bones. He was just fifty-two when he died on 6 May 1875 and was also buried at Brompton Cemetery.[46] In his will he gave his occupation as 'conveyancer'. Probate was granted to his widow Marianne on 31 May.[47] Fortunately some years earlier he had taken the precaution of buying a life policy, so this would have proved invaluable for his widow when he died unexpectedly young.[48]

Marianne remained at their home in Palgrave Place, St Clement Danes for some years after his death. She was eleven years younger than her late husband, and outlived him by fourteen years, being buried in the same grave as Benjamin. She also left a will. As they were childless, her brother, Reverend Thomas John Gatehouse, was chosen to be one of her two executors.[49]

The end of the line

Outliving all her siblings was Benjamin and Rachel's youngest daughter Elizabeth (known to the family as Bessie). She was five years younger than her brother, born on 26 February 1827 and baptised the following month at St Mary, Portsea.[50]

Her birth notice in the local newspaper was worded unusually: 'the Lady of Dr Lara of Portsea, a daughter.'[51]

She had stayed in the family homes at St George's Square and Queens Place until sometime after her father had died, by which time she was nearly thirty. At such an age she had probably resigned herself to remaining single. Bessie went to London to stay with relatives. This might have been her cousins, the children of her uncles Gregory Seale Walters and Charles Walters, but more likely her brother. It was there she met James Philip Doyle and married him at Hammersmith Church.[52] Hammersmith is a district close to the end of the M4 motorway and a stepping-stone for the city nowadays, but would have been considered some distance away in the mid nineteenth century. Like her brother, James was also of Middle Temple and knew Benjamin reasonably well, for it was Doyle who had represented him in the 1857 law suit.

It was a short marriage, for Bessie was widowed just four years later. She was childless and did not remarry. An entry for her in the 1871 census gives her age as forty-four, a widow living off annuities. She died in 1880 and was buried in the same grave as her husband, at the same cemetery as her mother and brother.[53]

In summary, Benjamin the fraudster/surgeon had one son and two daughters. He had been named after his father Benjamin (a refugee from Portugal) and in turn gave the name to his own son, Benjamin Walters Lara.

Benjamin's only brother was Moses, who also had no surviving children. Nor did his sister Rachel. The only descendants from the branch of the family emanating from the Portuguese-born Benjamin all came from the brief marriage of Sarah to Jacob Rey (known as John King), whose fascinating story is the subject of the next chapter. But there were no more Laras from this branch of the family.

But for now let's return to Benjamin, the subject of this chapter. First of all, a reminder that he died in 1847. Having lived to the ripe old age of seventy-eight, with a medical practice in Portsea for over forty years in tandem with his naval duties for almost fifty, Lara would have been well known by many locals. Newspaper reports of his death circulated mainly – though not exclusively – in the Hampshire area.

The navy lists are on display at the National Archives and there is one for each year. The first entry for Benjamin was on 1 April 1798, this date appearing in subsequent entries as well. In the July 1847 and January 1848 editions he was listed amongst those surgeons declared 'unfit for service at sea'. By then he was the surgeon with the greatest length of service. Also in this last edition (1848) for Benjamin was the report of his demise, on page 269, recorded as Benjamin Lara MD. This was the only time where MD was included against his name in any navy list, though Benjamin used the title from time to time.

He wrote his will in late November 1843 when he could no longer ignore his failing health. Many years earlier, in 1831, he had reported himself as 'unfit for duty', having tremulous hands, with his general health impaired. Following this he was reduced to half-pay. Was this a form of Parkinson's or Huntington's disease? If so, how had he managed to continue working for so long?

In his will he described himself not as a surgeon or resident physician but by the title of Doctor of Medicine.[54] Small bequests were made to two of his brothers-in-law, as a mark of esteem, with the rest of his estate to his wife and three children. Just a few months after his demise there was a serious cholera epidemic in Portsmouth which caused the death of some 860 people. His widow and daughters remained there throughout this time and were apparently not affected.

Where will we put you?

Where was Benjamin buried? It might seem obvious that it was at St Mary's where his three children were baptised, but such is hindsight; easy when all the facts are neatly assembled. Bearing in mind his Jewish upbringing there was always the possibility he might choose to be buried in a Sephardic cemetery. The one belonging to Bevis Marks can be ruled out, as no such entry appears in the burial register – and their record-keeping is exemplary. Nor was he found in the registers of Fawcett Road cemetery, Portsmouth, a peaceful haven hidden behind high walls. His first wife was not buried as a Jew and his second wife was brought up within the Church of England. She would be the person to arrange the interment. This question of place had also taxed Sir Thomas Colyer-Ferguson, the eminent Jewish genealogist, who had written to the superintendent of Highland Road Cemetery in Portsmouth asking if Benjamin was buried there. The reply dated 3 October 1946 was no, as the cemetery had not opened until 1854. The suggestion was that he should try St Thomas' Churchyard. Whether or not he did is not clear. There is no evidence to suggest he took it further.[55]

His burial record at St Mary, Portsea reads: 'Benjamin Lara of Queens Place, Portsea, buried on 5 January 1848 aged 76 years'.[56] The age at death was two years out. The priest performing the ceremony was surnamed Walters. He was definitely not the vicar or any of the usual curates, so probably a relative of Rachel since there were clergymen in her family.

St Mary, Portsea is now a church of almost cathedral proportions, surrounded by an extensive grassed walking/playing area, presumably the site of the original burial ground. There are scarcely any extant tombstones. The curate said some had gone in the 1887 rebuilding and the rest when the current church was built. Few tombstone inscriptions were taken down; those which survive (nothing for Benjamin) are to be seen at the Hampshire Record Office, Winchester.

Lara's ceremony was held in the rebuilt church of 1841, Thomas Ellis Owen being the architect. The work took seven months and cost £5000. He didn't make a very good job of it. The ventilation was inadequate and internal lighting so poor that not everyone could even see the pulpit from their seats. Not surprisingly this church was rebuilt again within the next fifty years.

Dr Lara I presume

So Lara described himself as a Doctor of Medicine in his will. Dr Lara? He may have had the experience, but did he actually have the qualifications to justify this title?

Let's have a look. Lara was apprenticed to a surgeon as a boy and listed his positions prior to 1794 in his medical dictionary:

Member of the Corporation of Surgeons of London
Surgeon to the Royal Cumberland Freemason School
Late Surgeon to the Portuguese Hospital

An advertisement in *The Morning Chronicle* for an anniversary fundraising dinner on behalf of the London Lying-in and Inoculating Charity includes Benjamin Lara Esq. as one of the stewards. This was earlier in the same year as he conducted his lottery fraud.[57]

This shows he had experience of midwifery other than with just those women he tended at the Jewish hospital; enough to consider himself sufficiently knowledgeable about the subject to write a paper on this aspect of medicine in 1791: 'An Essay on the Injurious Custom of Mothers not suckling their own Children with some directions for choosing a nurse and weaning of children'.[58]

What else do we know of his medical experience prior to his move to Portsmouth? His *Dictionary of Surgery*, mentioned before, was printed in 1797 and reprinted as recently as 2012. An original volume, leather-bound and in excellent condition, can be seen at the British Library. There is also a copy at the Wellcome Institute in London, and one at the Medical Library of Pennsylvania Hospital in America.

Lara might have believed that his standing in the medical world would improve once he was published and he did not shy away from this opportunity. His book was published by Ridgway and sold at 5s. 6d. An original was seen for sale recently on eBay at $300. Not bad for an obscure book first published more than two hundred years ago. Pity Lara never got the prices charged today – he would have been able to give up his day job!

The book is a pocket-sized edition, intended for young practitioners and designed to be carried easily at all times. Its small size would necessitate omitting much information and require great skill in selecting what to include, along with sharp précis and editing skills. Some initial reviews were good, commenting on the convenience of its small size and his use of specific source referencing. Another review at the time – so lengthy as to almost rival the word count of the book itself – concluded that whilst there was much which was praiseworthy, the book was unbalanced by a poor selection of material, including the superfluous, did not always have concise explanations, and was lacking in modern medicine.[59]

Such were his experiences at the turn of the century when he applied to the navy for a position as surgeon. Then, surgeons were examined and appointed by The Sick and Hurt Board (lovely name). This board also appointed surgeon's mates from those applicants with less experience and lacking the qualifications needed. Entries for Lara in the Naval Service Registers show he was never regarded in this capacity.

His name in the registers, like all the others, was beautifully scripted in large lettering across the page. The magnificent effect of this is spoiled as each was struck through with a bold black line once the surgeon had died. These are the only records seen by the author where a stroke of a clerk's pen was his shortcut to terminate the record of a life.[60]

On the first page were Lara's date of enrolment and his date of death, and a note that it was his daughter who notified the Admiralty by letter of her father's decease. The second page was more interesting as it contained periods of half-pay (when he was on sick leave) and some of his addresses.

Some luxury and status

He moved very little – between Prince George Street and St George's Square for the most part and finally to 3 Queens Place, Southsea; all close to the docks. The dates he was at each street are fully detailed in an annual set of rate books held locally.[61] Entries for the Pigot's directories corroborate these and also point to his having a local doctor's surgery, which might well account for the proximity of all these addresses. A thesis entitled 'The Origins and Growth of the Town of Portsea to 1816'[62] includes photographs of Queen Street and Prince George Street. No. 2–4 St George's Square is the oldest surviving dwelling house in Portsea. Lara was at number 64. Cramer says there were no building firms as such in Portsmouth then – a builder would get tradesmen to help out. John Monday of Portsea (later spelt Munday) built many houses in the St George's Square area. The houses appear to be large and suggest that Lara had achieved a degree of affluence.

Proof that he had managed to gain acceptance as a 'worthy individual' came in 1820 when he became one of a group selected to produce an Address to the King. 'The reading of the Address produced a spontaneous burst of applause, followed by nine distinct huzzas from hundreds of people who crowded into the Hall.'[63]

Accepted as a surgeon for the Royal Navy and later having an established practice as family doctor brings us back to the question: when and how did he gain the professional qualifications for these positions? First a reminder that as he was born and brought up a Jew, in England this was just not possible.

If not England, then where?

If you seek hard enough there's always a way round a vexing problem. Lara was fully aware that his apprenticeship came with no formal qualifications. He might have seen this as a problem, since the navy was reforming its practices and the checks on academic status were becoming more rigorous. Men in established practices sought to gain full qualifications to enhance their status and careers and of course to improve their earning power. So too did Lara.

In the first half of the eighteenth century medical graduates were a select group, the majority coming from Oxford and Cambridge (617) whilst those from Scottish universities numbered 406. A mere one hundred years later, in the first fifty years of the nineteenth century, the number of graduates had escalated sixfold, but of these 7,989 were from Scottish universities and only 273 from Oxbridge.[64]

Why did this reversal of fortunes from England to Scotland occur, and how was it so many more people were eligible to enter this profession?

Just as there were two prestigious competing universities in England, so there were two rival institutions in Scotland. These were Marischal College and King's College, both in Aberdeen. Their degrees could be awarded as legal recognition of service given to the medical profession by reputable and experienced physicians. England had long guarded entry to its universities, whereas in Scotland there were no religious tests put in place to restrict Jews and other dissenters. Their requirements were considered by many – especially the English – to be extremely lenient. These included a minimum registration fee of ten pounds and at least one reference certifying the skills of the candidate. Lara sent in two testimonials to Marischal College. One was from Dr Jamieson of London and the other was Dr Thomson of the Haslar hospital. The Royal Hospital Haslar was a Royal Navy hospital dating from 1753. At the time it was built Haslar was the biggest hospital and largest brick building in England, and it was sufficiently modern to include an asylum for sailors with psychiatric disorders.

The Royal College of Physicians in Edinburgh confirms that

Benjamin Lara received his diploma on 17 May 1802 and that his licence to practice followed, some years later, on 18 February 1814. On 2 August that year he was admitted as a Fellow – possibly the first Jew by birth to be awarded that distinction.[65]

Did he go to Scotland for study? Highly unlikely, bearing in mind the distance and the disruption this would cause for his work. Like very many students it appears he received his degree 'in absentia'. This 'Scotch degree', as it was known, was regarded with hostility and suspicion in England. Certainly the requirements were not as stringent as for the English universities, but that was because they recognised practical experience rather than just academic prowess for the select few. Perhaps a little like the National Vocational Training of today?

A jingle of the time expressed a sceptical view of the qualification:[66]

> Ne'er doubt my pretensions I am a physician,
> See here's my diploma and in good condition.
> From Aberdeen sent by coach on my honour,
> I paid English gold to the generous donor.

Be that as it may, this Lara became fully qualified within a few years of arrival in Portsmouth and so *was* entitled to use the initials MD.

Keep on writing

Benjamin clearly had a well-rounded education. He had the ability to write fluently, to publish, and became party to the process of improving medical treatment. He would have had no doubt that this might further his career, but it also indicates a certain dedication to the profession. Part of his naval 'job description' was to keep an annual medical journal, noting the dates, illnesses and treatment of those in his care. These journals were foolscap size with pre-printed headings. Few have survived, but some of Lara's are amongst them. His had been meticulously completed.

A Seaman's Wager or there must be safer ways to gamble

'A Seaman's Wager'[67] is a fascinating account of a seaman called John Cummings, who was treated by Lara whilst on HMS *Isis*, some details of which came from the medical journals at the National Archives.

And the nature of the wager? Lara was on board the *Isis*, having joined two years after Thomas Masterman Hardy left to serve with Nelson. Yes, that's Horatio Nelson. He completed his medical journal of HMS *Isis* for the year from February when the *Isis* was employed in the North Sea and on the Newfoundland Station.

One of the last entries, and one which clearly interested him, was for seaman John Cummings, where he expressed a wish to know if there were any later reports.[68] He found out at first hand. The following year, in Lara's next journal for the *Isis*, he notes he had to attend the same seaman again for a similar predicament. His successor on the *Isis* continued to send him reports until Cummings was discharged as unfit in June 1807.[69] What had interested Lara so much? Well, the American sailor complained of 'excessive pain in the stomach and intestines, incapacity of retaining anything in the stomach and pain on walking or standing erect'.

When questioned, he admitted to 'having swallowed on the preceding day 19 or 20 clasp knives'. It seemed he had done this several times before (often when drunk) after bragging of his exploits to shipmates, who had demanded proof. It was not difficult to get supplies of alcohol since grog – naval rum and water – was available as a daily allowance on board. Lara prescribed castor oil and thick gruel as enemas along with opium for the pain. This sounds sensible enough, since an operation was not feasible, but proved ineffective. The subsequent treatment was daily drops of sulphuric acid hoping to dissolve the iron! Cummings must have been doubly relieved when the knives eventually dropped. Sorry for the pun, it's a short cummings...

On leaving the *Isis*, Cummings went to Guy's Hospital, London for treatment. He wasn't initially believed, and it was only when his condition deteriorated even further that he was taken seriously.

Again the treatment was acid, mucilage and opium, which he suffered until his death in March 1809. The autopsy revealed a knife blade, spring and various fragments of knives in his stomach. These were kept and displayed in a glass case. When he heard this further report on Cummings, Lara wrote to Dr Curry, the physician at Guy's, to update him on the history of this man.[70]

Journal cover for B Lara MD for the *Isis*,
The National Archives

Lara's first appointment had been a short stint on the HMS *Penguin*. The ship may not have left port, so he would have had plenty of time to see the prison hulks in Portsmouth Harbour. These were redundant ships permanently anchored in rivers and harbours. Convicts were required to do hard labour by day and slept in chains at night in dreadful conditions. Would he have wondered that he might have endured a similar fate had he not been released for his offence back in London? A salutary thought.[71]

Lara had several other postings; those to 1806 are listed in the books showing Officers Full Pay.[72]

Ship's Name	Payment from	Payment to
Penguin	4 Dec	13 Feb 1798
Vesuvius	4 April 1798	20 Aug 1799
Camilla	21 Aug 1799	12 Mar 1800
Syen	13 Mar 1800	28 Nov 1800
Princess Royal	7 Feb 1801	17 April 1802
Minorves	25 Mar 1802	6 May 1803
Prince of Wales	7 May 1803	22 Jan 1805
Isis	17 Feb 1805	30 Nov 1806

The most significant collection of records

In 2010 the National Archives indexed the few surviving log books of the navy surgeons. When the project was complete, and the news released to the press, Bruno Pappalardo, the naval records specialist there, said 'The journals are probably the most significant collection of records for the study of health and medicine at sea for the nineteenth century.' As they included the names of many seamen seeking treatment the indexes are a quick method of locating naval ancestors. The expectation was that the books would be more extensively used in future. Amongst these log books were three of Lara's, checked previously by this author.[73]

Hitting the news again

Once more he was making headlines. What exactly had Lara been up to this time? Nothing more than many other doctors of the time. When the press took up a storyline, hey presto, he was in the news again, some 170 years or so after his death, finding international fame as the doctor who used to blow smoke into the mouth of a patient to try to resuscitate him, amongst other remedies.

Rum, baccy and turps: the Royal Navy's cure-alls

Banner headlines are designed to grab the reader's attention. And which surgeon did they select for reader gratification? None other than Benjamin Lara – time to hit the sensational press again. The headline above came from an Australian newspaper.[74] The logs show the use of tobacco smoke as a cure for drowning, rum as a tonic for tarantula bites and brandy for basically anything! (My husband could agree on the latter.)

An online blog entitled 'Naval Surgeons' Journals reveal peril of life at sea' talks of bloodletting, blistering, and burying to the neck in sand as some of the treatments used with varying degrees of success by surgeons of Britain's Royal Navy.

The sailor who refused to die and the man who did his utmost to ensure he lived

The example used to show how tobacco smoke was employed came from Lara's log book when he was ship's surgeon of HMS *Princess Royal*. He reported that one of the seamen was brought on board 'without any symptoms of animation', having fallen overboard from a launch, been submerged for twelve minutes and then run over by two boats. This was in the early days of Lara's career, in 1802. He tried to resuscitate him for nearly an hour, without success. However in another half an hour the man was able to speak, and within four hours it appears he was perfectly recovered. Stamina, determination and skill – a life saved. Excellent. And what of the methods used? Lara indicates these were based on the recommendations of the Royal Humane Society. First he warmed Seaman Calloway with heated plates wrapped in flannel in an attempt to raise his body temperature. When this failed to revive him, he used a pipe to blow tobacco smoke into his lungs. This final resort was in the hope he might choke and restart breathing. It worked.

The earliest of his accounts to survive was for the year starting February 1802, when Lara was stationed on HMS *Princess Royal* (later renamed HMS *St George*). In this he wrote of his formation of a 'sick mess' – an area where the sick could be segregated from the rest of the crew. To think that they were not separated from the healthy may today seem surprising.

Minor punishment in the Navy

A letter from him is stored as part of a collection dated 1808–1852 assembled by Sir George Ballingall at the Wellcome Institute. As Professor of Military Surgery at Edinburgh University he was clearly the person to contact about medical concerns within the armed services. Lara's letter is tantalising because the first part of the document, which might have given the date, is missing. However, his reference to HMS *Bellerophon* means it was written between 1808 and 1815. After that the vessel served as a prison ship at Sheerness, before being renamed *Captivity* in 1824. The *Bellerophon* was a ship of repute; it was aboard her that Napoleon had his formal surrender to the British in 1815.

The bulk of Lara's account, given without trace of emotion, condemnation or agreement, is reproduced below:

> There are also whimsical punishments constantly invented by 1st Lieutenants. One I have seen which very soon had the effect of preventing the men spitting about the deck. Holes were bored in the rim of a common spittoon through which a cord was passed and it was suspended round the offender's neck during the smoking hour, when every man requiring its use was obliged to summon the bearer to receive the deposit, under the penalty of changing the burden to his own shoulders. Again, a steward for not keeping his pantry clean has been compelled to walk the deck for a couple of hours with his head encased in the plate basket.
>
> In The Lancet of last week it is stated that the Assistant Surgeon of the Bellerophon was lately desired by the 1st Lieutenant of that ship to have a man who was incorrigibly dirty in his person thoroughly anointed with strong mercurial ointment, with a further injunction that it should be well rubbed in.
>
> This however has been deemed so tyrannical both to the Medical Officer and the culprit that it will probably be taken up by the Admiralty.
>
> Junior officers such as Mates, Midshipmen 2nd Masters and Masters' Assistants are now generally punished by being put in watch

and watch, or in other words are kept on deck for 12 hours out of the 24, or (as are also Assistant Surgeons and Clerks) by having their leaves stopped, or in serious cases by being turned out of the mess, and compelled to take their meals by themselves on their chests.

Flogging even Petty Officers is now prohibited. No man above the ranks of A.B. is subject to this punishment, and he cannot, except by order of a Court Martial, receive more than 48 lashes. Two dozen is the average number administered. In every case, as far as I know when the offence is perpetrated at sea, the man is kept in irons till this punishment is inflicted which is generally about 24 hours afterwards.[75]

As a ship's surgeon Benjamin would have witnessed much at sea that would churn today's stomachs. The difference between harsh treatment then and unacceptable behaviour today is about two hundred years!

A bunch of primroses

When one thinks of primroses, it is usually the delightful delicate yellow flower which comes to mind. However it is occasionally used as a person's name. One such was a doctor's wife. As a direct result of her husband's despicable actions the coroners' courts were recently reformed and checks for the registration of deaths were increased. Another 'used' a doctor to her own ends. It is the latter Primrose of Portsmouth to whom we next look.

She was poor and illiterate, and wanted a letter to be written on her behalf. There were people who made a living by writing letters for others. She went to such a person, Kitty Boyes, who wrote to the dockyard, claiming money said to be due to Martha Primrose, with Dr Lara purportedly signing the letter to this effect. The truth came out. The sick person had died the previous day, so no money should have been paid. The case went to court. Dr Lara was called and professed his ignorance of the whole affair. It was shown that the signature on the letter was nothing like his assured flourish. Primrose and the letter writer were tried for fraud and the latter was acquitted. Not so Primrose. She was found guilty and sentenced to death. We are talking here of eighteen shillings – less than one pound – for which a death sentence had been imposed. Just thirty or so years earlier Dr Lara himself was tried for fraud for an infinitely more serious offence, for which he was acquitted. But then his family could afford a good lawyer and he had luck on his side. Primrose had neither wealth nor luck. But she had some relief from her harsh sentence as it was subsequently commuted to one year's imprisonment.[76]

Supplementary pay

In his 'second life' Lara showed he was prepared to work for a living. This might be a reason why he also took on a local practice in addition to his naval appointment and the reason why Martha Primrose had heard of him. It seems there were frequent times when he was not at sea so this made it feasible. He also became an agent for the Asylum Life Assurance Company of Cornhill, London.[77]

Once he was called out to assist the household physician of a Donna Francisca, the wife of Don Carlos (the pretender to the Spanish throne) who was suffering from a bilious fever, for which he received a twenty-pound note![78]

Money matters

How much did he earn whilst working for the navy? A basic rate of five pounds a month (sixty a year) was the rate, according to 'Naval Records for Genealogists'.[79] The author also records the complex way in which surgeons' additional pay was assessed. The factors included the number of men on board, an annual allowance which varied from war to peacetime and the class of ship.

Lara does not appear to have received any of these additions, at least until 1807, as his records in General Officers Full Pay indicate he was paid the basic fifteen pounds a quarter (sixty a year) until 1806, when it was increased.[80]

However, he would have been entitled to payment from Queen Anne's free annual gift to surgeons. This was determined by whether the country was at war or not, along with the classification of the vessel on which they currently worked. There were six categories for this. As an example, the highest rate in war for the highest category was £62 6s 10ds, whereas the lowest category rate in peacetime was £21 4s 9d. Lara's rate was likely, at least initially, to have been closer to the lower rate.

And let's not forget he was still getting annuities from his father's estate. His two elder sisters, Sarah and Rachel, were also entitled to dividends, the money for these being invested on their behalf by Benjamin and Moses. When Rachel died childless this extra income fell into Benjamin's hands. But when Sarah died she had a son who outlived her, Benjamin Charles King, as well as grandchildren from her late daughter Charlotte. Would they be entitled to her inheritance? Benjamin Charles thought he was and wrote to his uncle Benjamin following her death asking why the payments had been stopped. He believed he was entitled, as her son and heir, to have the money, and when his request was turned down, he took his uncle to court.[81] Benjamin believed he had no obligation to continue paying the annuities once his sister had died. Though no ruling of the court has been found, it is likely they upheld the will as it stood, effectively giving him sole access to the money in the years to come. It is a sad note to finish on that Benjamin appears to have felt no moral obligation to his wider family, a throwback to when he had taken the law into his own hands decades before.

Sarah Rey King

> When you have eliminated the impossible, whatever
> remains however improbable, must be the truth
>
> *The Sign of the Four,* Arthur Conan Doyle

Sarah seems a tough woman to like. Hard and determined to press for what she perceived as her rights. Was she always this way as a young woman, or was this simply the person she became?

She was the eldest child of Benjamin Nunes Lara, a strict, religious, hard-working Jew. She married young. It may not have been a love match, but that was rarely the case within her society in eighteenth-century London. She would at least have the opportunity to know her intended quite well and might well have been pleased at the match. He was only a little older than her, had probably attended the same Sephardic school, was single and of the same religious persuasion. He also had sound career prospects and finances. All in his favour. What could possibly go wrong?

Her parents had married in March 1758, which makes it likely she was born within the next two years. Apart from the youngest couple of children of her uncle Aaron, her other cousins were some years older than her, so she and her younger sister may have seen little of them during her childhood. Her marriage, on 8 May 1776, was in accordance with the Jewish scriptures, and with the same traditions as her parents before her. She was no more than seventeen when this took place.

Sarah was described in her marriage ketubah (contract) as Sarah de Benjamin Nunes Lara and her husband-to-be as Jacob Rey (alias John King).[1] She died in 1835 and in her short will Sarah King stated she was a widow and left everything to her only son, Benjamin Charles King Esq.[2] Her address was given as Bagnio Court, Newgate Street, London, so named after the Bagnio, or Turkish bathhouse (though according to those who verified her signature on the will she had since moved to The Haymarket, St James, Westminster).

Her brother Moses had, many years earlier, bought and reserved a grave for his own use next to that of Rebecca, his daughter by his first wife. He subsequently left this for Sarah. Moses died before his sister, leaving notes for a tombstone inscription which mentioned not just her but all the family members. The part of the inscription relating to Sarah read:

Mrs Sarah Rey Lara
Eldest Daughter of the above named
Benjamin & Rebecca Lara
Died 1*st* of Rosh Chodesh Tebet 5595[3]

The Jewish date in the inscription, Rosh Chodesh Tebet, is a Fast day for mourning and repentance. It falls on 1 or 2 January. On this day the armies of Nebuchadnezzar commenced a siege on Jerusalem. Months later the walls were breached and the people were banished to Babylonia, an exile lasting seventy years. In view of the significance of the date, her burial was a few days after her death, on 5 January 1835, not earlier as was customary.

So that's the short synopsis about Sarah. What else is there to say? Researchers are often able to provide the odd extra snippet of interest about their ancestors. One such is that in her will she called herself Sarah King formerly Sarah Lara, but for her burial she was called Sarah Lara, other name Sarah Rey.[4] But that's not new information, as Rey and King were the names used by her late husband at the time of their marriage.

Why would he choose to have two new names, both first and

last? Perhaps there was something to be found here? Other than that, what could be simpler than this tale? She was one of Abraham Lara's younger cousins, many of whom had chequered lives. Although there is that slightly unusual element of a complete name change for her husband, there are enough instances of people changing their names, even several times, not to be unduly surprised by it.

Is that it then? Born, married, died. Nothing of note in-between? No, there's more to this story. A lot more.

Back to those names. In his will her brother Moses had bequeathed her one hundred pounds in 1831 when he referred to her as his 'sister, Mrs Sarah King otherwise Sarah Rey Lara'.[5] But surprisingly, when her father Benjamin had written his will in 1791, he referred to her as 'Sarah Nunes Lara, a spinster' of Poland Street, Westminster.[6] This was fifteen years after her marriage. There was no trace of a burial for her husband, and in any case if he had died why did her father refer to her as a spinster? Curiouser and curiouser…

Four years after her father's death, there were a series of legal petitions concerning the allocation of his estate and how it was to be administered (actions of her brother Benjamin's making) in which she was little more than a bystander. She responded in her letter to the Treasury of 1796 in the same terminology as her father had used in his will, calling herself 'a spinster of Poland Street, Westminster'.[7] She appears to have been living with her parents at Russia Court in 1791 at the time of her father's death. After this her widowed mother moved house, though the above address for Sarah shows she did not go with her. However, in another case she said her father had willed that she should remain in his home. If her mother chose to move elsewhere, why did she not move with her? Perhaps there was a mystery to be solved, after all.

Intriguing!

What better than a snowy February afternoon to hole up for some initial research? A reference to Jacob Rey read: 'Hardly less spectacular was the romantic career of Jacob Rey. Four years after leaving the Sephardic Orphanage where he had been brought up he sent it a donation of £100 as a token of his gratitude.'[8]

Now how would Jacob Rey have managed to accumulate such a huge sum (with presumably enough left over to ensure he could continue his business activities) in such a short period of time? And what was romantic about his career? Roll over Sherlock Holmes – 'the game is afoot'.

As the stories unravelled, it became clear that the compelling characters in this dramatic tale of Sarah's life were her husband and daughters. The two daughters both predeceased her; the reason why neither of them was mentioned in her will. Her husband's name, that by which he was known during his early years anyway, was Jacob Rey. Hyamson declares that he was looked after in the Sephardi Orphanage for seven years, from 1764 to 1771. There are slight differences of opinion surrounding Jacob's birth year but generally around 1753 is most often quoted. So does this mean he was orphaned at the age of eleven?

Was he orphaned as a boy?

Yes. His father was called Moses Rey. The records show that he died in 1763, which corresponds with Jacob's admission to the orphanage shortly afterwards.[9] According to Jewish law, when Jewish boys become thirteen years old, they become accountable for their actions, this being celebrated by a bar mitzvah. Jacob had not yet reached this milestone.

He attended the Spanish and Portuguese Charity School for his religious and academic education. This may have been partly financed by his father, whilst he was alive. Mr Rey was assumed to have been born in North Africa as he was known as 'the Sultan' and chose to dress as a Turk. This may have been in deference to his own upbringing, a ploy to attract attention, or to be easily recognised as a trader. His business was supplying frequenters of coffee houses with a range of cheap commodities. In common with other poor families in London, his wife also had to work to help support them. She made candy, which their son sold in the streets for a good profit.[10]

An apprenticeship to a clerk in a Jewish business house was

arranged for Jacob, with the Sephardic community paying the premium of five pounds. How long he stayed there is not known, but it is astonishing that he should find himself in a position to be able to make a contribution of one hundred pounds to Bevis Marks so soon after starting his career as a financier. No doubt this was given in gratitude to the community for all the assistance they had given him. If this money was indeed paid four years after he left the orphanage/school in 1771, then it was in 1775, the year before his marriage. At this time he was living at 27 Charlotte Street, Rathbone Place, Middlesex, and placed newspaper advertisements offering his services as a financier to 'the nobility, gentry and other persons'. He was reported to deal at a number of the 'best' coffee houses, such as Garraway's in Change Alley and Old Slaughter's Coffee House in St Martin's Lane.[11]

John King

As a young man Jacob Rey decided to rebrand himself, but in a totally different way from the approach his father took. When he married Sarah in the Bevis Marks Synagogue, it was as Jacob Rey, alias John King. For everyday life, he forsook the Sephardic name Jacob Rey, and became known simply as John King.

The Jew King

How soon he first became known by the expression 'the Jew King' is not known but this was indeed regularly used by others either in deference to his achievements but more probably to describe him in a derogatory fashion. Why? Why would people feel the need to do this?

Firstly, because he was financially successful – or at least he was (in-between bankruptcies) for much of his life. Many people desire success but are unable to achieve it for themselves. Some inevitably become resentful of those who do prosper where they have failed. King had decided to start out on his own as a financier, or money-lender, and soon became a leading figure in this line of business.

What made John King so exceptional and a real achiever? His

skills were initially played out as a poor young boy selling in the streets of London, where he would have practised and refined his natural aptitude as a salesman. Not unlike Alan, now Lord Sugar. An extensive biography on King suggests he became articled to an attorney for a short period after his clerkship ended. In this capacity he would have been introduced to the mechanics of the informal credit system which solicitors operated at that time.[12] Perhaps he learned more of this line of business from Sarah's father, though Benjamin Lara was first and foremost a merchant. Lara had come to London as a refugee in the same party as his cousin Clara Mendes Furtado and her children. So John King would undoubtedly have known her three sons, all highly successful merchants and financiers to the upper classes. The fact he was living at Rathbone Place (where one of her grandsons lived) is another indicator they knew each other.

Innate intelligence, total self-confidence, independence of thought and personality with a capital 'P' appear to be dominating factors in his success. Money-lending was not an easy business, nor one for those with moral inhibitions or little insight into financial affairs. One of his wife's older cousins, Aaron Lara, had married his cousin Sarah D'Israeli (the daughter of Benjamin D'Israeli, grandfather of our famous prime minister Benjamin Disraeli). D'Israeli had also tried to make his living as a moneylender. The kindest comment might be he was just not suited to this kind of work! A bit like Abraham Lara, another cousin. You may recall he was the victim of a money-lending scam in 1775, the year when John King so obviously was starting to do well!

King rapidly became well known, but fame often comes at a price. As he became established and successful he took on work for members of the nobility in order to assist them in financial matters until their circumstances improved. If they did. Not all loans were repaid. The results of court action against the nobility – especially by a Jew – were unlikely to be successful (as has been seen with other relations) so alternatives had to be considered. It seems that on one known occasion King was not averse to resorting to blackmail when a client defaulted.

His success as a financier could have made him a target for jealousy from a quite a few people. This particular trade was not permitted to Christians whereas it *was* one of the few permitted for Jews. This created bad feeling in people who would have liked to work in this field but were excluded. Likewise there would be others who might have felt it beneath themselves to be beholden to a Jew, but had little choice in the matter if they were to have the financial resources they needed. Then there would have been other established moneylenders who might have wanted to operate in this superior league, but just didn't move in the right circles.

Critics of the day – of whom there were many – gave a united impression of disgust at his absolute ruthlessness in both personal and business dealings. How much truth there is in this is difficult to assess, especially when the comments are often accompanied by strong anti-semitic language. An example of this comes from the July 1787 edition of the *Town and Country Magazine*: 'This fellow sprung from the dregs of the Jews, who are the dregs of the people'.

Mad, bad and dangerous to know

Two well-known figures who engaged his services were Lord George Gordon Byron (known simply as Lord Byron) and the poet Percy Bysshe Shelley, both leading figures in the Romantic movement. Some reviewers have suggested that Byron's aggressive criticisms of the published works of King's elder daughter Charlotte (who wrote poetry under the name of Rosa Matilda) may have been partly due to his desire to get back at both King and her. She wrote in a style Byron had earlier adopted, which had earned Byron poor reviews. One instance was his parody of her work *Hours of Solitude* under the title *Hours of Idleness*. Ouch…

Moneylenders knew they were open to attack by all sides of society. They inevitably dealt with the dissolute, the gamblers, the shameless, as well as those hard-working men and women whose circumstances had sadly changed. It was an unforgiving trade for many.

An encounter with Sir Henry Paget led to a duel between the two. The latter's father, when asked to stop the fight, said, "Never mind it, Townsend, let him fight. He is no son of mine if he can't fight." Fighting apparently was in the blood for this flamboyant, extravagant man who was later involved in another duel. At the Battle of Waterloo, he lost his leg to a cannon shot reputedly: "By God, sir, I've lost my leg," to which Wellington replied, with equal restraint, "By God, sir, so you have."[13]

The drama king

Let's not stop there. Not just with success, fame, court actions, blackmail and dangerous adversaries. King appears to have been a spirited, opinionated, resourceful person, confident in his own abilities, quite at ease with entertaining and working with Christians. As an entrepreneur he identified gaps in the market and seized the opportunity to benefit from them. One particular business illustrates his range of interests. The rich and/or the noble had to find suitable life partners. Unlike the poor they could not just marry anyone they chose. So he started a marriage bureau to discreetly address this and help match up clients, in the way that a matchmaker would do in other communities. The bureau was advertised, with a respectable lady as frontsperson. Another such, on similar lines but for the masses, was set up a century later in the 1940s. This was the source of material for a recent book described (inaccurately as the above information indicates) as the first marriage bureau.[14]

As for politics, his strong views were propounded in his radical articles. Hyamson lists some, including (in 1783) King's address to Charles James Fox, the rival of William Pitt the Younger. Others throughout his lifetime are well documented.

His interest in politics appears to have been growing for some years. As a young man he met Tom Paine, one of the Founding Fathers of the United States. Paine was happy to discuss with King his own political ideology, many aspects of which were included in his authoritative *Rights of Man*, written in 1791 in Paris. Tom

Paine had emigrated to America in 1774, so this places their original acquaintance at a time when John King was about twenty and Paine about thirty-seven. Two years after he wrote *Rights of Man* Paine wrote to King from Paris, recalling his impression of him, saying: 'I noticed you because I thought I saw in you, young as you were, a bluntness of temper, a boldness of opinion and an originality of thought that portend some future good.'[15] How about that for a commendation!

Notoriety

King was not shy at keeping out of the public eye. If he did not agree with something, he said so. Nor was he prepared to allow the character slights made about him to pass by unchallenged. For instance when an article in 1798 referred to him as 'the King of the Swindlers' he took the publisher John Parson to court for which he was awarded a judgement of fifty pounds.

A paragraph from his obituary in *The Gentleman's Magazine* sums up his attitude and approach:

> His transactions being carried on in a peculiar way, he was constantly before some of the courts of law or equity, as plaintiff, defendant, or witness, in which latter capacity he was often roughly treated by the Gentlemen of the Bar, which induced him, in 1804, to publish a pamphlet entitled 'Oppression deemed no injustice towards some Individuals.'[16]

Heartless monster or hopeless romantic?

So now we see there was a whole raft of political personalities whom he managed to disaffect. Yet there's more. As if this was not enough, he upped and left his wife. Sarah had just had their third child. This baby boy was their first son, so she would have had every reason to suppose he would be delighted at the birth. Any personal troubles they might have had would normally be put aside under such circumstances, so this action was possibly unexpected by Sarah. John left his family for another woman, well over twenty years older than his wife, and at least fifteen years older than himself! To be discarded for someone old enough to be your mother would add insult to injury to most women! His new amour was an Irish Catholic widow with two daughters which effectively meant John King ended up substituting one family for another. And she was not just any woman! Like him she was accustomed to the good life; to wealth, high living and mixing with the elite wherever she went in Europe. Reputedly she was a beauty and surviving prints of her prove the point. She was stunning, so much so that her admirers styled her Countess (lovely) Lanesborough. She captivated John.

Jane, Lady Lanesborough
Courtesy of Westmeath County Library and
Archives Services and Leo Daly

But with this one action, he managed to morally outrage members of the Jewish and Christian communities. Quite a feat! If he wasn't well known to 'anyone who was anyone' in London society before, all that changed now. His personal life played out on the international stage as if it was one huge drama.

Nothing much changes

A measure of how much a person is known is by the publicity surrounding them, not only in their own lifetime but long after their death. This is the case for John King. Not to be missed is the substantial tongue-in-cheek article published in *The Times* in 1790.[17] But there are no shortage of recent articles to be seen, mainly written by and for the Jewish community, but also including Wikipedia and the *Oxford Dictionary of National Biography*. These are well worth a read for those interested in the nitty-gritty.

Footballers, artists and royalty are just three examples of people who all have one thing in common: other people are interested in them. What they say, what they do, what they look like. John King was one such person. An engraving of him, said to be a strong likeness, was included with the article in the *Town and Country Magazine*. He was portrayed as 'The Fugitive Israelite'. Next to it was another engraving entitled 'The beautiful portrait of the Degenerate Countess'. There were other unflattering caricatures of him, as well as an engraving of him as a much older man held at the Jewish Museum, London.

Now for a look back at Sarah and John's family life. They had children soon after marrying but the births of both daughters were not recorded, or if they were, not kept.

Charlotte was their first baby, born in 1772, if one is prepared to accept the consensus of the first critiques on her life. Later writers suggest her birth was some ten years later, in or around 1782. This year was the possibility suggested in the article about her in the *Oxford Dictionary of National Biography*[18] and in a Wikipedia article on Charlotte (under her better known pseudonym of Charlotte Dacre). A burial entry for Charlotte shows she died in 1825. The misinformation concerning her year of birth appears to have been generated from two entirely different sources. One was the age at death given at her burial. This was held on 11 November 1825, at St Mary's, Paddington Green Churchyard, four days after she died.[19] Her mother was still alive, but it is more likely her husband would have provided the details for the burial entry. Her recorded age was fifty-three. So it is evident those persons propounding her birth year as 1772 deduced it from this. But this takes no account of the year of her parents' marriage! Could she have born four years *before* they married? Oh no! Apart from the fact Sarah would have been chaperoned by her strict and highly religious parents prior to her marriage, it would have been virtually impossible because of her youth at that time. She would have been just thirteen! So it had to be later.

That brings us to the alternative birth year of around 1782. Surprisingly, this is equally implausible, even though the year was derived from a comment made by Charlotte herself. In *Hours of Solitude*, 1805, Charlotte clearly states she was aged twenty-three, which means she was born in or around 1782.[20]

Since this is the year Charlotte has told her readers she was born, why can't we believe this? The answer is straightforward. She was the eldest of three children, all born by the time her father left them in 1783. The mathematics is indisputable, but not necessarily surprising. It is not uncommon for people, women in particular, to 'lose' a few years the older they become, especially if the pretence of youth might have been regarded as a selling point for the book.

When you have eliminated the impossible, only the truth remains

Based on their marriage date, the earliest birth year would be January 1777. Allowing a two-year window, Charlotte was likely to have been born between 1777 and 1779. In her book Charlotte included an engraving of herself taken (she says) when she was twenty-three. It was a most attractive portrait and so unlikely she would have felt the need to have another taken just a few years later.

A *Blue Peter* moment?

So the author's suggestion is that having written her poetry over a few years, she saved herself the need to explain the conflicting information by simply confirming her age when her portrait was produced – one taken earlier!

Charlotte had a fascinating life which will be considered in more detail later. Her sister Sophia is also often reported with the wrong birth age, almost certainly to try to 'fit' her in with the assumed year of birth for Charlotte. She was born in mid to late 1781 according to what one might assume was a very reliable source: herself! But was she inclined, like her sister, to say what she thought readers would want to hear?

Like other members of this family she was a writer and poet. In the preface to her poetry entitled *Unknown Warrior* published 1801 she described herself as a 'weak sapling of nineteen years' growth'. Prior to this the two sisters had jointly published a book of their poetry in 1798 in which Charlotte's name (Rosa Matilda) is given first. This is generally the position taken by an elder sibling.

The third and last child of the marriage was named Benjamin Charles Rey. He was born on 12 April 1783 and circumcised on the nineteenth of that month.[21] His godparents were Moses Lara (Sarah's eldest brother) and sister Rachel Mendes. He was born almost seven years after his parents were married. Benjamin Charles King (as he was called in his mother Sarah's will) was the only son of John and Sarah. Charles King, as he was more generally known, is reported to have distanced himself from his father. This is not surprising when one considers that he was born in 1783 – and it was in that year his father left the newborn baby son, his wife, and two young daughters for another woman. The fact he took her children with them must have added insult to injury.

Sarah and her young family returned to live with her parents after her husband deserted her. Having experienced a life of some luxury with John, to move back to her parsimonious parents must have been painful for everybody. However it did at least mean that when her estranged husband got into serious trouble with the authorities and fled the country to avoid imprisonment in 1784 she was not involved in this.

There is a lot of discrepancy and misinformation written about John King's marriage to Sarah and of their children. Sarah's name has been fabricated as Deborah and this was subsequently reproduced in other books, showing how easily a simple unsubstantiated inaccuracy can gain momentum, and some credibility.[22] Even within King's lifetime there was a scurrilous article by Thomas Martyn published in 1798 entitled 'King of the Swindlers', an assessment of which is submitted as an Internet blog in recent years with totally inaccurate details of his alleged children. John King is such a common name that it is easy to confuse one person with another unless careful, independent checks are made.

A countess is a lady

The *Oxford Dictionary of National Biography* records that John King met Jane Isabella Butler, the widowed countess of Lanesborough, in 1783, the year of his son's birth. Information on her family's ancestral tree shows Jane was the only daughter and eldest child of Robert Rochford, the first Earl of Belvedere. She was born on 30 October 1737, followed by three younger brothers. Her father imprisoned his wife Mary on his estate, following suspicion of her infidelity with his brother Arthur, and did not allow her to see her infant children. How sad!

Jane became Countess of Lanesborough on her marriage to Brinsley Butler, the Second Earl of Lanesborough. She is often somewhat confusingly referred to as Lady Lanesborough. This is because 'Lady' is the common address for a countess. They had two daughters (Lady Mary and Lady Catherine) and she was widowed in 1779, four years before she met John King.

Got to get a Get

Both contemporary and official sources indicate that King had fled abroad with her to escape imprisonment following his failed financial dealings in this country. In 1784 King divorced his wife at Livorno,

Italy (known by the English name of Leghorn) before a rabbinical court. As it was a Jewish divorce, parliamentary approval was not required for a Get. The countess could not have continued to entertain and be accepted as a lady in society whilst she was known to be the mistress of a married man, so for her a divorce was essential. For Sarah (who may have wished not to divorce, and possibly preferred to stop her husband's remarriage) the finality of such a move would at least have freed her from the ambiguity of her position. It would also allow her to remarry should she wish to. A Get may have been considered vital for all parties.

It is said variously that either Sarah pursued him to Italy for a divorce (perhaps with her father) or that he took her there for that purpose. If she went on her own accord, it would indicate a particularly indomitable spirit on Sarah's part.

Where's my money?

In 1791 Sarah's father died. Sarah Lara and her children were all bought mourning clothing for his burial, and this was paid out of Benjamin's estate. This description of them was included in the list of expenses his executors produced.[23]

These expenses were provided as a requirement by Chancery and were dated 17 February 1797. Sarah, using the name Sarah Lara, had petitioned the court to force the transfer of the annuity left to her by her father, along with payment of the outstanding dividends due on this. The Bank of England responded, saying they had followed the instructions of the executors and the accounts showed the interest being paid out at regular intervals to Benjamin, and also (though less frequently) to Moses Lara, and their mother Rebecca. There is no doubt the bank paid out the interest due when it was due. Whether or not it was actually then transferred to Sarah and her sister Rachel is another matter. Benjamin and Moses said they paid it and Sarah said they did not. It was their word against hers.

Of his four adult children, Benjamin Lara left the least to Sarah. Since her separation, Benjamin had probably been supporting her and his grandchildren, both financially and emotionally. Could he have believed the others now deserved more, especially as she was not entirely dependent on him? For one thing is clear: King did not leave his wife and children penniless.

Fatherly love

In 1798 Charlotte and Sophia jointly published a volume of poetry entitled *Trifles of Helicon*. It included a dedication to their father which is affectionate, indicating they still had a close relationship with him. It is also possible to deduce from their comments that the three children were all very well educated at his expense. The dedication reads:

> To John King Esq. Instead of the mature fruits of the Muses, accept the blossoms; they are to show you that the education you have afforded us has not been totally lost – when we grow older, we hope to offer you others with less imperfections.
>
> Your Affectionate Daughters
> Charlotte King
> Sophia King
> January 14 1798

Though on the surface, this might also appear one way of endeavouring to show their support for their father in a year in which he was arrested for bankruptcy, it was actually published before this event took place.

John King lived in upmarket areas of London with his countess, where they entertained lavishly.[24] King was recalled as being a 'man of wit and elegant taste whose dinners were attended by the rich, powerful and aristocratic'.[25] It was not until around 1817 that they lived permanently in Florence. Although he and the countess travelled extensively throughout Europe it is likely he saw his children as they grew up, though in his later years his visits to London became more infrequent. Maintaining affectionate relations under such conditions would have become increasingly difficult for them all.

Did King marry his lady?

There is no consensus on this. If they were, as seems likely, this probably took place in Italy. The important consideration was for 'society' to believe they were married so that they would not be ostracised. So it may be considered relatively unimportant if they were or were not. Without waving around authentication of the marriage, there would be plenty of people who would believe the opposite anyway. A witty and sharp report, referring to their current court case, suggests they *were* married: 'The elegant and accomplished Lady Lanesborough and her highly esteemed husband Mr John King have lately been introduced to court on their recent marriage, but it was to the Court of King's Bench.' Since the King's Bench was the place for judgements, this type of court would have been far from the sort of court they would have preferred to attend![26]

Some years later, King and Lady Lanesborough were mocked in a caricature: *New Roads to the Temple of Fortune* by De Wilde, published in the New Year of 1811 in *The Scourge*. This depicted the couple and others with the satirical comment: 'On the left fleeing from justice…higher up the hill are John King and his wife. King, real name Jacob Rey, was a Sephardi Jew, and was accused of money-lending, fraudulent banking, forgery and blackmail.'[27]

The following year (1812) there was a report in a London newspaper whereby learned counsel quoted as 'evidential' the divorce of Sarah and John King ('nisi prius') in an action he was defending in the case of Gainer v the Countess of Lanesborough. It was admitted in evidence that 'Mr King was discharged from this alleged marriage by a divorce pronounced by the Synagogue of the Jews at Leghorn.' The judge required proof of the law on this subject at Leghorn, and Sarah Lara herself was then offered as a witness, being the 'very alleged wife herself'. Although her presence was not allowed, her testimony was admitted 'as to the recognition of sentences of divorce by the Jewish Synagogue, and that she had been actually divorced from Mr King'.[28]

It seems King and the countess lived a somewhat unusual life veering between the extremes of poverty and magnificence. Their fortunes finally changed many years later on the death of her brother George, the Second Earl of Belvedere. George Augustus Rochford was two years younger than her. He was the eldest son so received the title on the death of their father. He also inherited the estate and released their mother from very many years of captivity. George was childless, as were his brothers. On his death in May 1814 he left much of his fortune to his second wife. Under the terms of their father's will, the part of the estate which was entailed (more than 2500 acres) was passed to his sister Jane. This is a larger acreage than might appear since Irish acres are larger than English ones, and the estate provided a large income for her.

King and Lady Lanesborough, as 'society people', moved from one country to another. It was in a comment in a Scottish newspaper of all places (in 1819) that mentioned their visit to France: 'Amongst the late arrivals in Paris is the Countess of Lanesborough and the celebrated Mr John King.'[29]

For most of his life King lived amongst Christians, but in the late 1790s he 'reversed course and began to re-embrace his Jewish identity, eventually becoming a spirited defender of his ancestral faith.'[30]

King died in 1823, so that is the 'technical' reason why Sarah King could now describe herself as a widow. The following news report (again from Scotland) says: 'At Florence, John King Esq., well known under the designation of Jew King and who married the Countess of Lanesborough.'[31]

Similar entries in newspapers across the land dated between 20 and 30 August 1823 indicated the interest the newspapers gave to him in death, as well as in life. The extensive reporting included, amongst others: *Bath Chronicle and Weekly Gazette; Royal Cornwall Gazette, Truro; The Examiner, London; Derby Mercury; Bristol Mercury; Hampshire Chronicle; Lancaster Gazette and Durham County Advertiser.*

These items all appear to stem from Irish newspapers which were first to hear of the news. Now he was dead some newsmen felt freer to express the contempt felt about him, such as 'We have neither time nor inclination to enter more into the biographiana of Jew King, but many traits of this extraordinary individual are likely to survive the oblivion he would otherwise have been consigned to.'

He did not forget the congregation of the Bevis Marks Synagogue, as it is said King left them a small legacy in his will. Although she was some years older than him, Jane, Countess of Lanesborough outlived him, reaching the grand age of ninety. Announcements of her death (said to be on 1 January 1828 in Leghorn) appeared more than two months later in newspapers throughout Britain.

An example of these is a lengthy comment in the *North Wales Chronicle*: 'Lately at Florence, at a very advanced age, the Right Hon Jane Isabella Countess of Lanesborough. By her demise the estate of Belvedere, in the country [sic] of Westmeath in Ireland [which she inherited by the will of her father, the Earl of Belvedere], devolves upon her grandson, the Earl of Lanesborough, and is entailed by the same document upon her daughters Lady Mary Ponsonby and her sons, Lady Catherine Marley, Col. Marley, etc. Her other grandson, Mr Butler Danvers, is heir presumptive to the earl, and committee of his family estates in the counties of Cavan and Fermanagh, etc.'[32]

Romantic poetry...

Having briefly introduced the children of John and Sarah King, it is now fitting to take a closer look at the three of them. Both daughters seem to have inherited the literary skills of their father. Charlotte started with poetry, writing verses under the pseudonym Rosa Matilda, publishing in *The Morning Post* and the early joint work with her sister Sophia (*Trifles of Helicon*, 1798).

Seven years later, in 1805, she published her collection of poetry entitled *Hours of Solitude* under the pseudonym Charlotte Dacre. As Rosa Matilda she had a loyal readership, and she chose to build on that base to introduce a new nom de plume. In the frontispiece she linked the two names, publishing under the name of 'Charlotte Dacre, better known by the name of Rosa Matilda'. The engraving she chose to include was entitled Rosa Matilda (not Charlotte Dacre) – a further indication it was not as recent a picture as might otherwise be believed! The fact she included such a glamorous portrait of herself also set the scene well for her brand of writing.

This use of the name 'Charlotte Dacre' was not introduced on a whim, nor as late as 1805 as *Hours of Solitude* seems to suggest. She had actually rebranded herself at least four years earlier. When her younger sister Sophia married (as a minor) in 1801 Charlotte was one of her witnesses, and she signed the record in the name of Charlotte Dacre.

Her poetry was highly sentimental, and alluded to love as an all-consuming, life-changing experience. Was Charlotte head over heels in love at the time?

The romantic themes of complete abandonment are so strong as to indicate that this mirrored her personal life at that time. This four-line poem from the book, entitled 'Simile', is an example of this:

> The little Moth round candle turning,
> Stops not till its wings are burning:
> So woman, dazzled by man's wooing,
> Rushes to her own undoing.

...and pornography

In the same year (1805) the first of her novels was published. *Confessions of the Nun of St. Omer* was a tale in three volumes, and 'sold by all respectable booksellers in the United Kingdom'. In the following year (1806) came *Zofloya*. Though she was a prolific writer it would hardly have been possible for her to write two novels so close to each other, as well as her poetry. In fact Charlotte claims she wrote the first when she was eighteen, some years earlier, after which she had travelled abroad for a while, so left it untouched for several years.

...or at least a minor scandal

These novels were in a different style from her poetry. She is most well known for *Zofloya* which has attracted much critique over the years. This novel was considered pornographic by some contemporary critics. In spite of this (or perhaps partially because of it) the book sold well and was translated into French and German. It was in three volumes, and sold for twelve shillings in boards (now known as hardboard or hardback copies).

Charlotte Dacre remains one of Britain's more obscure writers. In more recent years, with greater interest in gender issues and a Gothic revival, her work has been reprinted and brought to the attention of modern readers. The reading lists for university studies of Gothic writers often includes Dacre's name alongside Dickens and Brontë. The University of Stirling, for instance, has conducted courses on Gothic Studies for over twenty-five years now. Their Masters Degree in Gothic Imagination is one which includes a study of Dacre, especially pertaining to *Zofloya*.

Her initial offerings to *The Morning Post* newspaper appear to have been made with the support of the poetry editor there, but as a reasonably regular contributor it could not have been long before she met Nicholas Byrne, the editor. He was several years older than her and married. They became lovers. As Charlotte was much younger than Nicholas, this might be a reason for him to hide her true age as he might not have wanted it known she was so young when they were first together.

Byrne did not divorce his wife. That was not an option as it would entail an Act of Parliament, a hugely expensive and public business. He could well have set his wife or mistress in premises of her own and for all we know his wife may well have been happy with this arrangement. Did Charlotte move in with him? It does seem so. He and Charlotte had three children together at a time when he was still legally married to another. The eldest was William Pitt Byrne. He was born in 1806 and given the middle name as a show of admiration for the politics of William Pitt who had died earlier that year.

The dangers of lust

Her highly romantic poetry has all the hallmarks of a time when she first became besotted and seduced by Nicholas. They went on to have two other children: Charles and Maria. All three were baptised at St Paul's Church, Covent Garden on 8 June 1811. The couple presented themselves as a married couple using the names of Nicholas and Charlotte Byrne. Possibly Nicholas's wife had lived far longer than they had expected and possibly they felt they could no longer delay the baptism of the three children from their liaison. The vicar at St Paul's was more rigorous than many and recorded the dates of birth along with the baptismal dates. For instance, the birth date of their eldest, William Pitt Byrne, was given as 12 September 1806. The record is now searchable online, but mistranscribed as William Pill Byrne; an easy error to make as the thin line across the 't' is now barely visible on the original record. The baptism following that was for Charles, born 6 November 1807, then finally Maria, born 12 July 1809.

Her novel, *Zofloya*, was published the year of her eldest son's birth. The storyline has underlying moral messages, warning young women against 'the dangers of lust'. This was completely different to her poetry. It was a dark Gothic tale, a relatively new way of thoughtful writing at that time. Gothic writing was still in its relative infancy, and so it was brave for Charlotte, a woman, not to publish under a male pseudonym. This type of work was obsessed with people's natural feelings. Until then the State and the Church had together led the way for sexual repression. Sex outside marriage was to be punished by society as being against God's law and as late as the previous century (seventeenth) people were still being hanged for adultery in Scotland.

Was it coincidence that Charlotte wrote about seduction and sexual liberation? Was it linked with the knowledge that her sister had married as a minor, and more importantly the knowledge of her father's relationships and of her own, from an early age, with a married man? King's three children had been largely brought up by their mother Sarah, as a single parent. These circumstances may have given them a good deal of awareness into human behaviour at an early age. Because of the position in which she found herself,

Charlotte would have had a better insight than many of her contemporaries into the sexual desires of men. Her father was so swept away by another woman that he left his wife and young family, and now she too was under the spell of a married man and had, by now, his first illegitimate child. How much of her writing was linked with this could not be acknowledged publically, but appear to have influenced the tone of Charlotte's work.

Immortal beloved

Her lover, and later husband, was the editor of *The Morning Chronicle*, which (surprise, surprise) frequently printed her poetry, under the name of Rosa Matilda. Here follows one example of the bias this publication showed towards her. In 1812 a large column was printed on two consecutive weeks, ostentatiously reviewing (but in reality just praising) her latest work: 'This lady, whose words have made the name Rosa Matilda as immortal as the works themselves...'[33] An assertion such as this was open to ridicule. Not everyone agreed with this blatantly absurd introduction. A correspondent to *The Examiner* refers to 'the ridiculous and absurd rhapsodies of Rosa Matilda and her friend' (presumably her sister with whom she jointly published some poetry) and to *The Morning Post*, 'a paper which is treated with contempt by every thinking person.'

Wed at last

Charlotte could not legally marry the father of her children until the death of his wife. This burial has proved elusive. The only viable one found is for (uncompleted first name) Byrne in June 1815 at St James, Westminster.[34] The complication here is the deceased's age is given as seventy-six, so if this person was indeed the wife of Nicholas, she would have been considerably older than him – a possibility as they had no children. Whatever the truth of this, Nicholas and Charlotte were married a week after this event, in the same church of St James, Westminster, by licence.[35] He gave his details as Nicholas Byrne Esquire, a widower (rather pretentious, as where the term 'Esquire' is used, it is generally in the abbreviated format). The bride gave her birth name of Charlotte King, confirming she was a spinster.

There were two witnesses and it is interesting that her mother, Sarah King, was one of these. This would suggest that though her daughter had married a non-Jew, Sarah was not only at the church to show her support, but as a witness indicated her consent and encouragement. It seems unlikely that John King would be unaware that his daughter was getting married, but it also seems unlikely he attended.

...and then they died

Charlotte was married for ten years, having been his mistress for a similar amount of time. She died the year after her father and some ten years before her mother. The Byrne children were well-educated adults and financially safeguarded, so it is unsurprising they were not mentioned later in their grandmother's will.

The obituary, surprising for the lack of mention of her name or her literary career, states baldly: *Nov 7 1825. In Lancaster-place, the wife of Mr N Byrne of The Morning Post.*[36]

The Times gives her a little more justice, but does not allude to her literary past.

> On Monday evening – in Lancaster Place after a long and painful illness which her purity of heart and sublime greatness of soul enabled her patiently and piously to endure, Mrs Byrne, wife of Mr N Byrne of The Morning Post.[37]

There did not appear to be a report in *The Morning Post*. Four days later she was buried in the churchyard of the Parish Church of St Mary, Paddington Green. The entry was recorded as 'Charlotte Byrne of Lancaster Place, Savoy, Strand, buried 11 November 1825 aged 53'.[38]

Though much older than her, her husband did not die until 1833, reputedly aged seventy-two. If correct, this would make him sixteen or seventeen years older than his late wife. William was the sole executor for his father's estate and proved the will and codicil on 2 September 1833. A note on the original will indicates Byrne died on 27 June 1833. His will, and especially his codicil, revealed a couple of surprises.[39] Firstly, he was not simply the editor of *The Morning Post*. He was in fact the sole proprietor of the business and had been from 1803 until his death in 1833. The paper was published from his leasehold house in the Strand. He left three-quarters of the newspaper copyright, the printing presses and stock employed in printing plus the same proportionate share of the house to their eldest son William Pitt Byrne. The other quarter was passed to the second son Charles, along with an annuity of two thousand pounds, increased by another three thousand pounds in the codicil. The paper was eventually sold and absorbed into the *Daily Telegraph*.

Byrne had bequeathed their daughter Maria a substantial sum of ten thousand pounds bank annuities and solicited his beloved son William 'having the fullest confidence in the kind goodness and affection of his heart that he will watch over and pay attention to the interest and comfort of my dear Maria, his sister.' A codicil two years later appears to have made little change, yet four months later on 14 April 1832 Byrne not only had second thoughts, but a new codicil shows a complete and utter turnaround in his wishes. He was not a man to be crossed, and patently fumed at what he regarded as his daughter's decision to marry 'against my wishes and in direct opposition to my most earnest entreaties and frequent and most serious remonstrances'. Her direct inheritance was changed from an outright gift to interest only, with a hefty reduction to two thousand pounds. This was designed not only to punish her but to ensure 'the same shall be free from the disposition control intermeddling debts and engagements of her present and future husband'. On her death the lump sum was to be divided amongst her children. Poor Maria. Let us hope her husband was able to make his own way in the world, and had not expected to married an heiress!

William went on to become a barrister, married and had two children called Maria E and Charles Edward Wadsworth Pitt. He was sufficiently wealthy to have a footman, two housemaids, cook and nurse as well as a foreign professor to tutor his children.[40] After his death in 1861, William's widow Julia Clare had a memorial fountain erected in his honour in Bryanston Square, Marylebone, which is still there today.

The third writer in the family

Sarah's second daughter Sophia not only published a joint work of poetry with Charlotte in 1798, but also a novel in the same year. She was a quick, prolific writer. Two more novels – *Cordelia* and *The Victim of Friendship* – came out the following year, with a further novel in 1800 and yet a fourth in 1801. All these whilst still underage! She was still a minor when she married Charles Fortnum, which meant the couple required a special licence to prove her father's consent. This was given and the entry is as follows:

> Charles Fortnum of this parish bachelor and Sophia King of the same parish spinster a minor and with consent of John King father of the said minor were married in this Church by licence this 19 July 1801 by me Chas Brent Barry. Signatures: Chas Fortnum and Sophia King. Witnesses were Wm Abbott and Charlotte Dacre.[41]

This is fascinating on two counts. Here's proof John King agreed to Sophia's marriage, and since her elder sister Charlotte chose to sign as a witness with her nom de plume, it shows she had totally renounced her birth name of Charlotte King by now.

From the pathos of her writings it has been suggested that Sophia was childless. Such evidence as there is supports this. They had a son, named Charles, who was baptised on the first day of November 1803 at the church where Sophia and Charles had been wed. The entry was annotated to comment this was on the day he was born. Baptisms are generally held from at least a few days old, so an early event appears to indicate that the baby was probably weakly and not expected to live, as indeed he did not.

Like her sister, Sophia chose to write some of her poetry under a pseudonym. She chose the name of Sappho. Sappho was a Greek poet who lived and studied on the isle of Lesbos in the ancient world. To choose to associate with an ancient Greek poet is a further indication of the thirst for knowledge and wide-ranging education of the King sisters.

Her last known work was *The Adventures of Victor Allen* in 1805, published under the name Mrs Fortnum (late Sophia King). No poetry or novels were published after this date.

It is inconceivable that she gave up writing; therefore the only explanation is that she died shortly after this time, perhaps during a foreign holiday. Extensive searches have not yet revealed a burial in this country under any of the names with which she was associated.

What about Charles Fortnum?

Charles was the son of a gentleman called William Fortnum, a close relative of the Fortnums who owned the Fortnum and Mason store in Piccadilly, in which locality they lived. He inherited from his father's estate in 1801,[42] and went on to establish a business dealing with stationery, sealing wax, laces, hosiery and other such diverse objects. It was later in that year he had married Sophia. It is said that Charles had exported goods to the Continent and was imprisoned in Paris, escaping in 1804.[43] On his return to Sophia in England he found his business had been mismanaged during his absence and he lost everything to his creditors. That was another low point for the couple, though his fortunes were restored later.

Some years after his wife's death, Charles remarried. This was to a widow named Letitica Basden, née Stephens.[44] Their son, Charles Edward, became a great Victorian collector and benefactor, and recorded notes of his ancestry.[45]

An aside

An interesting find came to light when seeking a will for Charles Fortnum, checking from the date of Sophia's death. Though Charles did not actually die until many years later, there were others with the same name as him who left wills, all of which were checked. One such was in 1845. In the box of wills for the month of March 1845 assigned to surnames C to G[46] was one for Prince Joseph Bonaparte. One would expect to find it in the 'B' box, but was presumably filed under C for Comte as his alternative title was Prince Joseph Napoleon Bonaparte Comte de Survilliers. He was the elder brother of Napoleon Bonaparte, and he died in Florence. The will was translated from the Italian and probated in this country as he claimed lands in England, along with some in America and France.

Your will be done

Charles King was the youngest child of John and Sarah King. A number of sources state that he later took over his father's business interests. It therefore appears he did have some contact with his father, and at some stage in his life dropped his first name of Benjamin. However he sensibly used his full name as late as 1835 when dealing with the law, thus ensuring there would be no problems as to his true identity. His action, in the name of Benjamin Charles King of Bolton Street, Piccadilly, Middlesex, Esquire, was against his uncle Benjamin Lara, a physician living in Portsea, Hampshire.

Charles's mother, Sarah, outlived both her daughters. She died on Rosh Chodesh Tebet, which according to her son was on 2 January 1835 that year. He gave this date when he took out a court action in an attempt to prove his legal entitlement (as her sole son and executor) to the annuities which were paid to her until her death. These had been bequeathed to her by her father, his grandfather and namesake, Benjamin Lara.

Charles's uncle Benjamin was the only surviving sibling of his deceased mother. The complaint centred on the cessation of interest payments on his mother's death. Two payments (of thirty and twenty pounds) were made annually by her brother Benjamin Lara from investments he had been directed to invest for her benefit. Charles considered that, as her legal personal representative, he was now entitled to the whole sum, or at least to continue receiving the dividends. His uncle was now the sole surviving executor of Charles' grandfather's estate and refused to comply with the request.

In order to consider this case, the Court of Chancery needed information from Benjamin. He gave his legal answer on 10 April 1835, from Portsea. Benjamin agreed with much of his nephew's comments, confirming that both his sisters had received their respective legacies during their lifetimes, but his defence relied on his inability to remember dates of any events and his belief that the annuities were now vested to himself. He agreed he had 'declined to continue to pay' as he felt the construction of the will was doubtful, and he would need specific direction from the court if he was to transfer these sums. In conclusion he asked for the case to be dismissed and claimed reasonable costs and charges.[47]

The problem of a homemade will

No doubt Sarah's father felt that he was doing the best for his daughters with his bequests, and believed he need not employ a solicitor to write his will when he was clear about his objectives. Benjamin must have thought he covered everything but he did not anticipate what might happen to both his daughters' annuities when they died, or direct what should happen to any of their surviving children. Wills are often contested when there are ambiguities to be explored or exploited. Would Benjamin Senior have expected his grandchildren to inherit once his daughters had died? Study the will and indeed you will find no mention of what should happen to the money after his daughters' deaths. He wrote his own will (it appears without legal advice) and omitted to include the right of his grandchildren to inherit, at a time when he had four. And what might have happened if either of his daughters outlived both sons? We'll never know. All he wanted to do was protect the annuities from the grasp of their husbands. As it happens his younger son Benjamin assumed he would keep both sisters' monies after they died, and probably did exactly that.

Epilogue

The name 'Lara' has continued in our family for generations. It's been a first name, a middle name and a last name. For example, it's been combined with the surname Bell for a family who emigrated to New Zealand, saying "if there was any truth in the tale of the fortune and the diamonds, they would stand more chance of inheriting some". Please queue here! My daughter was christened Lara to perpetuate the name in our branch of the family.

So did the family legend prove to be fact or fable? A bit of both really. It was based on truth, but became distorted over time. Henrico de Lara (the man in the picture) did not come from Andalucia, nor was his real name Henrico.

And Abraham (Henrico) was never really wealthy. However at one time he was a jeweller with assets. It is clear he lost much of this and therefore became impoverished. We are now sure his partner was Rebecca Bell, but they were not able to marry for religious reasons. Their children were known by his surname of Lara, but as adults usually as Bell. Their son, baptised as Henry James Bell, frequently referred to himself as Henry James Lara.

Let's return to Abraham's reputed name of Henrico. His grandmother was Maria Henriques. The spelling and Portuguese pronunciation of Henriques (with the stress on the ending) is not dissimilar to Henrico. Her daughter, Rachel (Abraham's mother) was brought up with the last names Henriques de Lara, as was his aunt Clara Henriques de Lara.

So perhaps the name in the legend was simply that of the

Portuguese surnames, rather than representing a first and last name as has been assumed.

The siblings and cousins herein are some of the children of the refugees - the Lara family who sought a new life in England.

The life and times of more of the 'famous' Lara family (as they have been referred to in the past) will be explored in further volumes, as well as revealing the identities of others who joined them. A further eight cousins (the children of Aaron Nunes de Lara and his wife Rachel - the eldest daughter of his cousin Clara Mendes Furtado) all have fascinating tales to tell. Then it will be time for the truth about the Furtado family, their close relations. They were also in the public eye but for them it was music and theatre, rather than literary works that made them famous.

Finally their grandparents' flight from Spain, their parents' entrapment in the Portuguese Inquisition and subsequent escape to England is a case study in the endurance of the human spirit in the face of the most appalling circumstances.

Notes

Preface

1 LMA, Magistrates Session, against William Mitchell, MJ1827.
2 TNA, B/70, B8/18.
3 BL, Manuscripts, Letter HJ Lara to Earl of Liverpool, 25 October 1819, Add. 38280, ff 213–14.
4 BM, Burial Register, Notable Burials and Epitaphs, xxii.

Abraham Lara and Rebecca Bell

1 BM, Marriage Contracts, Part II, Daniel Nunes de Lara and Rachel Nunes de Lara, Vindos de Portugal, 6 Elul 5495 (24 August 1735), no. 557.
2 BM, Register of Burials, 3 October 1800, s de Abm de Daniel Nunes Lara, no. 6737.
3 LMA, St Leonard, Shoreditch, Baptisms, 6 July 1785, P91/LEN/A/004/MS07496.
4 BM, Register of Burials, 15 May 1816, Abm de Daniel Nunes Lara, no. 5004, Grave 49, Row 49.
5 *The Star*, Civil Action, 25 February 1791, p3.
6 Gedalia Yogev, *Diamonds and Corals*, p137.
7 *The Times*, 28 April 1791, p4, also *Evening Mail*, issue 339.
8 TNA, KB168/35.
9 BL, Manuscripts, Letter HJ Lara to Earl of Liverpool, 25 October 1819, Add. 38280, ff 213–14.
10 TNA, Treasury Letter Book, 6 Nov 1811–9 Aug 1812, T2/61, no. 740. Letter dated 20 Jan, received 22 Jan, minuted 24 Jan and reply sent 30 Jan. See 1812 box file.

11 TNA, PRO30/8/137.
12 Saō Pedro, Covilhã, born 14 and baptised 27 April 1714, fol 79 & 80v.
13 LMA, Middlesex Quarter Sessions, MJ 182.
14 John Drinkwater, *A History of the Siege of Gibraltar*.
15 LMA, St Stephen, Coleman Street, Baptisms, 20 May 1789, P69/STEI/A/003/MS04450.
16 TNA, 1841 census, HO107/693 folio 55 Book 3; 1851 census, HO107/1539 fol 267 p44.
17 LMA, St Leonard, Shoreditch, Burials, 9 February 18376, MS7499/21, no. 1995.
18 TNA, Volunteers records, WO13/4467.
19 HA, Watchmen's Book, appointed 1823. Last entry February 1830, P/L/R/8 He was already a watchman on 9 October 1722 giving evidence on Thomas Short, Old Bailey, t18221023-64.
20 Beattie, J M, Policing and Punishment in London 1660-1750.
21 *The London Gazette*, 24 May 1842, Issue.
22 House of Commons, Parliamentary Papers, 17 October 1842.
23 *The Gazette*, 21 June 1842, Issue 20112.
24 TNA, Petitions of Prisoners (Town) 13 August 1841-28 February 1851. B6/70.
25 LMA, St Leonard Shoreditch, Baptisms, MS7496/45 p273.
26 GRO, Death, Alfred Lara, West London, December 1838, 2, 194.
27 Corporation of London, Coroners Inquest, London, 1838, No 129 Alfred Lara. There is also a lengthy report in The Examiner, 14 October 1838, Issue 1602.
28 Holdens Trade Directory, 1802, Abraham Lara, watchmaker, 14 Brick Lane, Whitechapel.
29 BM, Burials, Abraham de Daniel Nunes Lara, 15 May 1816, row 49, grave 49, no. 5004.

Judith and Ester Curry

1 TNA, Will of Aaron Nunes Lara, 4 July 1768, codicil 22 July 1768, PROB11/943 Proved 14 Oct 1768.
2 BM, Marriage Contracts, Jacob de Judah Ancona and Jeudit de Daniel Nunes de Lara, 20 February 1771, no. 1031.

3   BM, Burials, Judith Ancona, 20 January 1778, no. 3450, Row 36, Grave 23.
4   BM, Marriage Contracts, Elias Cunha (alias Corre) and Ester de Daniel Nunes de Lara, no. 1038.
5   Report, 99–20 from a source compiled by E H Phelps-Brown and Sheila Hopkins.
6   TNA, C33/454 f110, January 1780.
7   BM, Circumcision Register, Isaque son of Jacob Soares, 15 February 1765, no. 1223.
8   BM, Circumcision Register, 3 June 1772, no. 1387.
9   BM, Burials, no. 2364 BM, Row 10, Grave 47.
10 TNA, Patent Roll 14, Geo III, p3.
11 LMA, MS11316/246–64.
12 BL, James Picciotto, *Sketches of Anglo-Jewish History*, pp 207–208.
13 Solomon Northup, *Twelve Years a Slave*, 1853, p106.
14 ERO, All Saints West Ham, Baptisms 1746–1799, D/P256/1/3.
15 BM, Burials, Behind the Boards, 5 August 1792, no. 6712.
16 BM, Burials, Introduction, p xxi.
17 LMA, MS11316/265–283.
18 TNA, PROB 11/1220.
19 BM, Marriage Contracts, 14 Nisan 5553 (27 March 1793), no. 1314.
20 LMA, MS11316/286–289, Fourth Quarter.
21 LMA, MS11316/313, £5 0s 9d.
22 BM, Burials, 2 July 1815, no. 4979.
23 BM, Marriage Contracts, Moses Curry (alias Moses Mendes Cunha) and Sara de Paz, 25 January 1795, no. 1335.

Jacob Lara and the Buzaglos

1   TNA, CO324/55.X.62.
2   BM, Marriage Contracts, Jacob de Daniel Nunes de Lara and Lea de Jacob Buzaglo, 2 September 1778, no. 1117.
3   The Bible, Genesis 28:23.
4   BM, Marriage Contracts, Jacob de Moseh Busaglo and Elisebah de Jahacob Salom Morenu, 26 July 1730, no. 472.
5   BL, José Maria Abecassis, *Genealogia Hebraica: Portugal e Gibraltar: Sécs XVII a XX*, pp 483–4.

6   BM, Marriage Contracts, Ester de Jacob Buzaglo and Moseh Masias, 5 December 1764, no. 963.
7   BM, Marriage Contracts, Rachel de Jacob Buzaglo and Semuel de Moses Cohen, 31 March 1779, no. 1121.
8   Cecil Roth, JHSE Vol 23, 'The Amazing Clan of Buzaglo'.
9   BM, Burial Register, Eliseba Buzaglo, 2 July 1758, no. 1660.
10 BM, Marriage Contracts, Abraham Buzaglo and Rosa Ester de Salom Buzaglo, 16 March 1763, no. 930.
11 *Daily Advertiser*, 30 October 1744, *General Evening Post*, 13 August 1751, *Gazetteer* and *New Daily Advertiser*, 11 October 1765 and 24 January 1780.
12 TNA, Patent Roll 12 Geo III, pt 3.
13 LMA, BMC, Minute Book of the Mahamad 1754–1828, 4521/A/01/04/003.
14 LMA, Land Tax Assessment, MS11316/276.
15 LMA, Fire Insurance Policy Register, 1777–86, Rachael Nunes de Lara, MS11936/263.
16 TNA, PROB11/1220.
17 TNA, PROB11/1227.
18 BM, Burials, no. 4260, Row 42, Grave 56.
19 BRO, Reading, *Commonplace Book of William Savory of Berkshire, 1786*, pp 126–127, D/EX/2275/1. Also see Rev Daniel Lysons, *The Environs of London*, 1795, for an excellent report on Jewish funeral ceremonies.
20 BM, Burials, s of Moses Vintura, 1 October 1786, no. 3320.
21 LMA, MS11316/306.
22 BM, Burials, no. 5132, Row 51, Grave 32.
23 TNA, Local & Personal Acts 1973, Elizabeth II, B667. Queen Mary College Act, Chapter xii entitled: An Act to authorise the disposal of the Nuevo burial ground in the London Borough of Tower Hamlets…18 July 1973. This comprised around 1.9 hectares, most of which fell within the meaning of the Disused Burial Grounds Act 1884. There was to remain 0.4 hectares to be fenced off as a restricted area (burials until 1953). The College transferred land for re-interment in the Brentwood, Essex burial ground, and was responsible for the removal of the gravestones of the existing burial ground.

Esther Cardozo, Sisters and Sara Carcas

1. GNA, Civil Secretary's Register, proclamation for a new return of all Jews to be made to the Jury's Office.
2. GNA, Civil Secretary's Register, no. 4, p133, 22 April 1781.
3. TNA, printed leaflet 'The Humble Petition and Memorial of the Inhabitants and Proprietors of Houses in the Town of Gibraltar', CO91/30.
4. GNA, Civil Secretary's Register, no. 43, p153, 20 May 1781.
5. JHSE, R D Barnett, letter from Portsmouth to Bevis Marks, Trans Vol XX, p15 and note.
6. GNA, list of Jews and date of return, 1784.
7. Ed Tito Benady, *Aaron Cardozo: Life and Letters* (a very full account of Cardozo's activities).
8. Mr Belilo, a member of the Mahamad and one of the guardians of the synagogue said in response to an enquiry about Isaac Lara: 'Oh I know him. He had a daughter called Esther who married Aaron Cardozo. Lara was a witness to a Will. I have a paper I can show you. There are no Laras in Gibraltar now.'
9. Benady ibid..
10. ibid..
11. ibid. pp 3–4.
12. JT and DM Ellicott, *An Ornament to the Almeida, being the Story of Gibraltar's City Hall*, p24.
13. ibid. p21.
14. Ed Benady, ibid., letter no. 11, pp 13–15.
15. ibid. pp xi–xii.
16. GNA, *Gibraltar Chronicle*, Saturday 28 October 1820, no. 44 p353.
17. GNA, Books of Passports ceded by Governor's Permit, 1824.
18. GM, p339 1834, part 1 ibid..
19. GNA, *Gibraltar Chronicle*, Thursday 6 February 1834, no. 3922.
20. ibid. no. 3925.
21. TNA, PROB11/1828/392 written 17 December 1822, three codicils, latest 25 October 1833, proved 26 March 1834.
22. TNA: Death Duty Register, IR27/1347 fol 114. Effects sworn under £800.

23 Ed Tito Benady, ibid., p vi.
24 BM, Burials, Index 277.
25 BM, Marriage Contracts, no. 864 19 Adar 11 5518 (29 March 1758).
26 BM, Births, MS162 Sheet 2 (birth recorded as Isaac, with a note that he was circumcised as Joshua) 12 December 1767, and Circumcisions, no. 1282, f 90.

Moses Lara and the Da Costas

1 TNA, PROB10/3228, H-P, January 1793.
2 BM, Births, Sheet 41/172. Benjamin son of Jacob and Sarah Rey, circumcised 19 April 1783. Godfather Moses Lara, Godmother Rachel, wife of Moses Mendes. They would have to take these duties seriously as their sister Sarah would have needed a lot of support in the harrowing weeks to come.
3 Rev Moses Gaster, *History of the Ancient Synagogue of the Spanish and Portuguese Jews*, 1701–1901, p157. The Ascamoth/Escamoth (the Laws of the Congregation) was compiled by the Mahamad. These were intended to ensure the community were united in decision making under these religious precepts.
4 TNA, PROB11/943, Proved 14 October 1768.
5 TNA, C33/470, fol 360 (Easter term 1788).
6 BM, Marriage Contracts, No 1221, Moses de Benjamin Nunes Lara and Ribca de Judah Supino, 13 Tebet 5546 (14 December 1785).
7 BM, Births, Sheet 22 and Burials, no. 3327.
8 BMC, LMA/4521/B/28/003/002.
9 BM, Burials, no. 3439, Ribca de Mos Nunes Lara, 6 December 1787.
10 LMA, Sun Life Records, MS11936/334/515595. Insured: Moses Lara, no. 38 Stewart Street, Spitalfields. Stockbroker. On his household goods in his now dwelling house only situate as aforesaid. Brick except a small part timber not exceeding two hundred and fifty pounds. Wearing apparel therein only not exceeding one hundred and fifty pounds. Plate therein only not exceeding one hundred pounds (total £500), 16 January 1786.
11 BMC, LMA/4521/A/01/07/008, no. 16, Elders Papers 1817–1819, 7 November 1819.

12 TNA, C12/1996/41, C12/226/20.
13 *The Times*, Civil Action, Guildhall, Scott and another v Moses Lara 28 July 1794, p3, col. B.
14 TNA, Law Report, King's Bench, Wednesday July 23 1793, Scott and another v Moses Lara.
15 *The London Gazette*, 10, 14, 15, 28 June and 1 July 1794.
16 TNA, C33/498, Lara v Lara ff 379 and 389.
17 Holden's London Directory, 1802, Auctioneer of 8 Fieldgate Street, close to Whitechapel Road; *The London Gazette*, 17 July 1804.
18 *Kentish Gazette*, 17 March 1809, advertising auction on Monday 20 March 1809.
19 BL, Oriental & India Collection.
20 *Kentish Gazette*, Tuesday 16 May 1809.
21 *The Times*, 25 September 1809, p3.
22 *The Morning Post*, 31 March 1830.
23 *The London Gazette*, 17 March 1810 p412 and 27 March p470.
24 Albert M Hyamson, *Sephardim of England: History of the Spanish and Portuguese Jewish Community 1492–1951*, Appendix V, List of Members of the Mahamad.
25 Oldbaileyonline.org, t18150913–154.
26 TNA, Australian Convict Transportation Register, imaus1790a-081474-00011.
27 BM, Marriage contracts, no. 1540, Moses de Benjamin Nunes Lara and Sarah de Hananel Mendes da Costa, 18 Iyar 5576.
28 Albert M Hyamson, ibid., List of Members of the Mahamad, pp 440–442.
29 ibid., pp 228–229.
30 *The London Gazette*, 20 November 1819, issue number: 17536 p2068.
31 TNA, T1/1957/20121.
32 TNA, PROB6/198 Middx June 1822.
33 TNA, C13/2349/9.
34 TNA, PROB10/4636 for J-S Sept 1822, Will of Phineas Lara, Proved 23 September 1822, in London, by Moses Lara & Isaac Foligues. For much more on Phineas and his family see the next book.

35 Cecil Roth, *Anglo-Jewish History*, pp 316–7 (1938).
36 Albert M Hyamson, ibid. p326.
37 BMC, LMA/5421/A/01/16/007, Mahamad papers, 1830–1832, Letter to Mr S Almornino of Ramsgate, dated 2 November 1830 for onward delivery to Mr Daniels of Bevis Marks Synagogue concerning the Bond.
38 BM, Burials, 3 January 1831, no. 5553, Row 55, Grave 51.
39 BM, Burials, no. 5554 & 5552, Row 55, Grave no. 52R and 50).
40 TNA, PROB10/5219 (L-O, Feb 1831).
41 Cecil Roth, ibid., pp 316–317.
42 BMC, LMA/4521/B/28/003/002.
43 Albert M Hyamson, ibid., p271.
44 1851 Census, HO107/1625 f91 p1.
45 BM, Marriages, no. 1303, 5 September 1702, Solomon de David de Leon and Rachel de Hananel Mendes da Costa.
46 BMC, LMA/4521/A/03/039, Lease signed 17 October 1855 with Mr John Jennings, a bricklayer, for £18 per annum rent.
47 BMC, LMA/4521/A/3/01/001.
48 GRO: Sarah Lara, December 1859 Blean 2a 341.
49 GovUK Find a Will, Will of Sarah Lara with codicil, 10 January 1860, Effects under £5000.
50 Rebecca Mendes da Costa PCC 28 September 1860.
51 *Kentish Chronicle*, Saturday 10 December 1859.
52 *London Standard*, Saturday 10 December 1859.

Rachel Mendes

1 BM, Marriage Contracts, no. 1151, Moses de Isaac Joseph Mendes and Rachel de Benjamin Nunes Lara, 17 Ab 5541 (8 August 1781).
2 BM, Births, Sheet 41/172.
3 BM, Births, Sheet 28, Rebecca d Moses and Rachel Mendes, 20 October 1790.
4 BM, Burials, no. 3775.
5 TNA, C12/1996/41 Lara v Lara, 12 April 1796.
6 TNA, C12/226/20, Lara v The Bank b.r.r.r. (1797).
7 TNA, PROB10/5219 (L-O, Feb 1831) Will of Moses Lara.

8 BMC, LMA/4521/B/28/03/003/002, Recipients of payments: aged and decrepit, poor and deserted children.
9 BM, Burials, no. 5552, Row 55, Grave 50, 28 April 1840.

Benjamin Lara and the Walters

1 BM, Births, Sheet 3, p2 and Circumcision Register, no. 1372, f95. Sarah Furtado, a relation, was the Godmother.
2 BM, Marriage Contracts, 7 September 1791, no. 1287.
3 TNA, Register of Duties paid for Apprentices' Indentures, 2 March 1781, IR1/31.
4 TNA, Rex v Lara, Court of King's Bench, 2 June 1794, 2 Leach 647, 168 ER 425.
5 TNA, Will of Benjamin Lara, Proved 8 January 1793, PROB10/3228.
6 *The Times*, Thursday 2 October 1794, p3 Col C, Price of Stocks: Lottery Tickets.
7 *Annual Register* for 1794, October, p33.
8 *The Morning Herald*, London, 3 October 1794, issue 4853.
9 TNA, November Court Sessions, Middlesex, HO26/4 p25, Newgate.
10 *The Times*, Monday 15 December 1794, p3, Col C, Old Bailey.
11 Proceedings of the Old Bailey, 1674–1913, www.oldbaileyonline.org.
12 TNA, Denization, Patent Roll II, Geo III, Part 5, C66/3732, no. 17.
13 British Weather from 1700 to 1849, *Memoirs of Pascal Bonenfant*.
14 *The Times*, 2 May 1795, p2 Col D.
15 *The Times*, 22 June 1795, p3 Col C, Law Report.
16 *The Times*, 27 November 1795, p4 Col A, Law Report.
17 TNA, List of Felons, Newgate, PCOM2/181 [entries from 13.12.1794-02.1796].
18 TNA, Rex v Lara, 6 Term Reports 565, 101/ER/706, 1795 and 8 February 1796.
19 *The Times*, 9 February 1796, p3 Col A, Law Report.
20 *The London Gazette*, 8 November and 27 December 1794; 21 May, 11 June and 16 July 1796.
21 TNA, Service Registers of Surgeons, ADM104/12.

22 The London Gazette, 19 January 1793, issue no. 17536, p64: 'Messrs David Valentine & Ben Lara of Church Street, Spitalfields, Merchants. They wish to dissolve their partnership by mutual agreement, Mr Lara retiring from the business. Signed David Valentine and Ben Lara jun.'
23 *The Times*, Civil Action, Guildhall, Scott and another v Moses Lara 28 July 1794, p3, col B.
24 TNA, C12/647/4, Lara v Lara b.r. 6 December 1793, and C33/486 folio 43, 12 December 1793, Judgement.
25 JHSE, Henry Roche, Portsmouth Circumcision Register, no. 93.
26 HRO, fiche 959, no. 634, p80 CHUU3/1E/3.
27 Pigot and Co.'s National Commercial Directory 1823/24, Portsea section.
28 TNA, PROB6/193 fol 171, Catherine Judith Lara. 15 November 1817, Southampton.
29 LMA, St John at Hackney, Marriages, P79/NJ1 no. 893.
30 HRO, fiche 1245, p67, no. 535, 4 July 1820.
31 HRO, fiche 131, p63, no. 500, June 1822.
32 *Hampshire Telegraph and Sussex Chronicle*, 23 November 1835, p28.
33 1841C, HO107/415 f19, p3.
34 1851C, HO107/1481 f329, p38, Westminster Rates for St Martin-in-the-Fields 1849–1856.
35 Benjamin W Lara, Passport no. 24473, date of application 11 July 1855.
36 BL, Publishers Lane and Lara, Chandos Chambers, 22 Buckingham Street. Shelfmark PP2487.fb.
37 1861C, RG9/184 fol 95 p1.
38 WC, MS.3170.
39 TNA, Lara v Hill, Common Bench, N8 45, 143 ER 699, 23 June 1863.
40 *Hampshire Telegraph and Sussex Chronicle*, 18 October 1865: Lara Gatehouse. On the 3rd inst (i.e. 3 October 1865) at St Mark's, Tollington Park, by the Rev E Hyde F. Cozens, M.A., cousin of the bride, Benjamin Walters Lara Esq of Gray's Inn and C, (i.e. Court) Pump-court, Temple to Marianne Elizabeth, second daughter of Charles Gatehouse, Esq, Holloway. No cards.

41 TNA, J 77/75/451, Divorce Court File: 451.
42 *The Morning Post*, Tuesday 28 May 1863, GRO, Deaths: Mary Lara, Kensington, June 1863 1a 81.
43 GRO, Deaths, December 1847, Portsea, 7, 116.
44 TNA, ADM 23/106 1830–1859 Pensions to Widows.
45 GRO, Deaths, March 1865, Kensington, 1a 105; Burial, Brompton Cemetery, 31 March 1865.
46 *Hampshire Advertiser*, 19 May 1875, Page 2 Death notices 'On the 6th inst (i.e. 6 May 1875) in his 53rd year (i.e. aged 52) Benjamin Walters Lara Esq of Palgrave Place, Temple, London, only son of B Lara Esq M.D. and F.R.C.P.E. late of Southsea'. Also GRO, Deaths, June 1875, Strand, 1b 369; Burial Brompton Cemetery, 11 May 1875.
47 GovUK Find a Will, Benjamin Walters Lara, 31 May 1875, fol 420. Effects under £600.
48 City of London life policy, no. 19032, dated 28.09.1869.
49 GRO, Deaths, Marian (sic) Elizabeth Lara, age 55, Mar 1889 Kingston (Surrey) 2a 195; Burial Marianne Elizabeth Lara, Brompton Cemetery, 27 December 1888; Will proved 6 February 1889, £1385 0s. 9d.
50 HRO, St Mary, Portsea, fiche 145 p27 no. 214, 24 March 1827.
51 *Hampshire Telegraph and Sussex Chronicle*, 12 March 1827.
52 *The Standard*, 14 May 1856 (married 13 May 1856), GRO, Marriages, June 1865 Kensington 1a 31; 1871C, RG10/868 f120 p36.
53 GRO, Deaths, James Philip Doyle, June 1860, Holborn, 1b 303; Burial Brompton Cemetery 12 June 1860; GRO, Deaths, Elizabeth Doyle, 58, March 1880, Marylebone, 1a 451 (she was five years younger than age quoted); Burial Brompton Cemetery 2 February 1880.
54 TNA, PROB11/2071, Proved 25 March 1848.
55 SoG, Jewish Museum Small Collection, Box 36, Item 33 under Furtado. The Furtados were close relatives to the Laras. The generation before had come to England together as refugees.
56 PCRO, CHU3/IE/30, fiche 1 of 6, p1, no. 7. The registers are held here, but there are copies on fiche at the HRO in Winchester.
57 *The Morning Chronicle*, 9 April 1794, Ticket 7s 6d, at the Paul's Head Tavern, Cateaton Street.

58 WC, Printed for William Moore, no. 8, Leadenhall Street, 1791, reprinted by James Ridgway, York Street, St James' Square, Sixth Edition 1796, Price 1s.
59 BL, *Dictionary of Surgery* by Benjamin Lara, 1797, Ridgway Press, 783.a.36; Critical Review, Vol 20, edited by Tobias George Smollett.
60 TNA, ADM104/12, List of surgeons and surgeons' mates, p61.
61 Portsmouth History Centre, housed in the public library.
62 ibid., J Cramer, 'The Origins and Growth of the Town of Portsea to 1816'.
63 *The Morning Chronicle*, 30 September 1820.
64 Kenneth E Collins, Jewish Medical Students and Graduates in Scotland 1739–1862, quoting from *The Evolution of Medical Education in Britain*, ed F N L Poynter, Table VI by A M T Robb-Smith.
65 *Historical Sketch and Laws of the Royal College of Physicians*, Edinburgh. 1925, p7.
66 Kenneth E Collins, ibid..
67 Journal of the Royal Society of Medicine (*The Lancet*), 'A Seaman's Wager'. Jonathan Goddard FRCS, July 2003. See also a detailed summary in *The Gentleman's Magazine* of 1809. Part I, p384.
68 TNA, ADM 101/105/3.
69 TNA, ADM/101/105/4.
70 *The Times*, 20 April 1809 (following letter from B. Lara to Dr Curry at Guy's Hospital on 27 March 1809).
71 Visit Portsmouth Museum, an 1828 engraving by William Cooke depicting these ships.
72 TNA, ADM 24/53.
73 TNA, log books for *Isis*, no. 42, 43 ibid., and ADM/101/115/3 for *Princess Royal*.
74 *The Australian*, online report, 30 September 2010.
75 WC, Ballingall Papers, Memorandum by Lara, naval surgeon, on minor punishments in the Royal Navy, Western MS.6905 no. 44.
76 Crown Court, Western Circuit, Winchester, 2 March 1832.
77 *Hampshire Telegraph and Sussex Chronicle*, 1 November 1824.
78 *The Morning Post*, London, 1 September 1834, from the *Hampshire Telegraph*.

79   N A M Rodger, Naval Records for Genealogists, HMSO 1988.
80   TNA, ADM 24/53, folio 20.
81   TNA, C13/1077/31.

Sarah Rey King

1   BM, Marriage Contracts, no. 1093, Jacob Rey (alias John King) son of Moses Rey and Sara de Benjamin Nunes Lara, 19 Iyar 5536 (8 May 1776).
2   TNA, PROB 11/1841, Will of Sarah King formerly Lara, Widow of Saint James West Middlesex, Proved 13 January 1835.
3   BMC, LMA/4521/B/28/03/003, Recipients of payments: aged and decrepit, poor and deserted children (as a folded sheet of paper, loose inside the front cover).
4   BM, Burials, no. 3438, 5 January 1835, Row 36, Grave 11.
5   TNA, PROB10/5219 (L-O), Proved February 1831.
6   TNA, PROB10/3228, Proved 8 January 1793.
7   TNA, C12/1996/41 Lara v Lara (1796) 12 April 1796.
8   Albert M Hyamson, *Sephardim of England: History of the Spanish and Portuguese Jewish Community 1492–1951*, p209, 1951.
9   BM, Burials, No 1966, 23 September 1763, Row 22, Grave 22.
10 Michael Scrivener, *Jewish Representation in British Literature 1780–1840: After Shylock*.
11 *The Morning Post* and *Daily Advertiser*, 7 February 1775, 6 June 1775.
12 Todd M Endelman, *Oxford Dictionary of National Biography*, John King (formerly Jacob Rey, c 1753–1824).
13 *The Times*, 1 November 1827, Police – Bow Street.
14 Penrose Halson, *Marriages are made in Bond Street: True Stories from a 1940s Marriage Bureau*.
15 Hyamson, ibid., pp 210–211.
16 GM, 1824, p184.
17 *The Times*, 25 December 1790, John King Esq of Duke Street, Westminster.
18 Paul Baines, *Oxford Dictionary of National Biography*, Charlotte Byrne, 1782?-1825.
19 St Mary's, Paddington Green, Burial Register 11 November 1825, p235, no. 1880.

20 *The Morning Chronicle*, Advertisement Section, 16 August 1805, Hours of Solitude, Price 14 shillings, with a portrait of the Author.
21 BM, Birth Register, Sheet 17 and no. 41/172.
22 Christopher John Murray, *Encyclopaedia of the Romantic Era*, 1760–1850 (which erroneously refers to Charlotte's mother as 'Deborah').
23 TNA, C12/226/20 Lara v The Bank b.r.r.r. 1797, Second Schedule.
24 LMA, Land Tax Assessments at St Marylebone and Westminster.
25 Captain Gronow, 1794–1865.
26 *The Times*, Wednesday 29 December 1790, News Section, p2, Column C.
27 *The Scourge, 1* January 1811. *New Roads to the Temple of Fortune*, by De Wilde.
28 *The Morning Chronicle*, 17 November 1812, Law Intelligence section.
29 *Caledonian Mercury*, 3 June 1819.
30 Todd M Endelman, ibid..
31 *The Aberdeen Journal*, 27 August 1823.
32 *North Wales Chronicle*, 20 March 1828. Also in *Jackson's Oxford Journal*, 22 March 1828, *Newcastle Courant*, 22 March 1828 and *Caledonian Mercury*, Scotland, 27 March 1828.
33 *The Morning Chronicle*, 2 and 3 September 1812, Arts and Entertainment section.
34 St James, Westminster, Burials, 22 June 1815, p66, no. 592.
35 St James, Westminster, Marriages, 1 July 1815, no. 238.
36 GM, 1825, p2.
37 *The Times*, Wednesday 9 November 1825, p4, Col A.
38 St Mary's, Paddington Green, Burials, 11 November 1825, p235, no. 1880.
39 TNA, PROB11/1821/50, Will of Nicholas Byrne, Saint Mary le Strand, Proved September 1833.
40 TNA, HO107/1489 f437, p48 (1851C) and RG9/77 f89, p9 (1861C).
41 St Mary's, Marylebone, Westminster. Marriages, p41, no. 123.
42 TNA, PROB11/1353/321, Will of William Fortnum, Gentleman of Upper Berkeley Street, Portman Square, Middlesex (who died 6 February 1801). William and Charles, his two sons, inherited equally

stock, share in a Tontine, household furniture and mother's wearing apparel (at her request). Administration granted with Will, as no executors named.

43 Eds Ben Thomas and Timothy Wilson, *C.D.E. Fortnum and the Collecting and Study of Applied Arts and Sculpture in Victorian England.*

44 Parish of Kingsbury, Middlesex, Marriage, 17 April 1819, p3, no. 8, Charles Fortnum, widower and Letitia Basden widow by banns

45 Eds Ben Thomas and Timothy Wilson, ibid..

46 TNA, PROB10/6299, March 1845, C-G, Will of Prince Joseph Bonaparte.

47 TNA, C13/1077 folio 31 King v Lara stored off-site (three days delivery), 3 February 1835 – a huge, thick, very dirty roll, boxed.

Abbreviations

BL	British Library
BM	Bevis Marks Synagogue
BMC	Bevis Marks collection at the London Metropolitan Archives
BRO	Berkshire Record Office
CKB	Court of the Kings Bench
CO	Colonial Office
D&C	Diamonds and Coral, Yogev, Gedalia
ESO	Essex Record Office
GM	*Gentleman's Magazine*
GNA	Gibraltar National Archives
GRO	General Register Office
HA	Hackney Archives
IOL	India Office Library
JHSE	Jewish Historical Society of England
LMA	London Metropolitan Archives
PCRO	Portsmouth City Records Office
SoG	Society of Genealogists
TNA	The National Archives
WC	Wellcome Collection

Bibliography

Abecassis, José Maria, *Genealogia Hebraica: Portugal e Gibraltar: Sécs XVII a XX*

Baines, Paul, Charlotte Byrne, *Oxford Dictionary of National Biography*

Ballingall, WC, Papers, *Memorandum by Lara, naval surgeon, on minor punishments in the Royal Navy*, Wellcome Institute

Barnett, RD, Letter from Portsmouth to Bevis Marks JHSE *Transactions*, XX

Beattie, JM, *Policing and Punishment in London 1660–1750*

Benady, Mesod, The settlement of Jews in Gibraltar, 1704–1783, JHSE *Transactions*, XI

Benady, Tito, (editor) *Aaron Cardozo: life and letters*

Collins, Kenneth E, *Jewish Medical Students and Graduates in Scotland 1739–1862*

Cramer, J, *The Origins and Growth of the Town of Portsea to 1816*

Drinkwater, John, *A History of the Siege of Gibraltar*

Ellicot, JT and DM, *The History of Gibraltar's City Hall – An Ornament to the Almeida*

Endelman, Todd M, John King (formerly Jacob Rey), *Oxford Dictionary of National Biography*

Gaster, Rev Moses, *History of the Ancient Synagogue of the Spanish and Portuguese Jews, 1701–1901*

Goddard, Jonathan, *Journal of the Royal Society of Medicine (The Lancet)*, "A Seaman's Wager" (July 2003)

Historical Sketch and Laws of the Royal College of Physicians, Edinburgh

Hyamson, Albert M, *The Sephardim of England* (reprinted 1991)

Minute books and papers of the Bevis Marks Collection at the London Metropolitan Archives
Newpapers, *The Times* and *The Gazette*
Northup, Solomon, *Twelve Years a Slave* (1853)
Picciolotto, James, *Sketches of Anglo-Jewish History*
Rodger, NAM, *Naval Records for Genealogists* (HMSO 1988)
Roth, Cecil, The Amazing Clan of Buzaglo, JHSE *Transactions, XXIII*
Roth, Cecil, *Anglo-Jewish History* (1938)
Savory, William, of Berkshire, *Common Place Book* (1786)
Society of Genealogists, *The Jewish Museum Small Collection*
Strype, John, *A survey of the Cities of London and Westminster*
The Annual Register for 1794 (October)
The Bible, Genesis
The Spanish & Portuguese Jews' Congregation, London:
  Abstracts of the Ketubot or Marriage-Contracts of the Congregation from earliest times until 1837, Part II
  The Birth Register (1767–1881), Part V
  The Burial Register (1733–1918), Part VI
  The Circumcision Register (1715–1775), Part IV
Thomas. Ben and Wilson, Thomas, Editors, *CDE Fortnum and the collecting and study of applied arts and sculpture in Victorian England*
Yogev, Gedalia, *Diamonds and Coral: Anglo-Dutch Jews and eighteenth-century trade*